PHILOSOPHICAL EXPLORATIONS

JOSIAH THOMPSON, Assistant Professor of Philosophy at Haverford College, Pennsylvania, received his Ph.D. degree from Yale University, where he was for a time an instructor. Under the auspices of the *Undervisnings Ministerium* of the Danish government he spent fourteen months in Copenhagen studying the Kierkegaard manuscripts in preparation of *The Lonely Labyrinth*. He is the author of the recently published *Six Seconds In Dallas: A Micro-Study of the Kennedy Assassination*.

JOSIAH THOMPSON

The Lonely Labyrinth

Kierkegaard's Pseudonymous Works

FOREWORD BY

George Kimball Plochmann

CARBONDALE AND EDWARDSVILLE

Southern Illinois University Press

Feffer & Simons, Inc.

LONDON AND AMSTERDAM

Copyright © 1967 by Southern Illinois University Press

Library of Congress Catalog Card Number 67–10281

Printed in the United States of America

DESIGNED BY ANDOR BRAUN

This book is for

my mother and my father.

FOREWORD

ON COMING TO Kierkegaard, we are struck by the dialectical comprehensiveness and the subtlety of ideas put forth with the profuse generosity of a literary master. But so much of the personal is emplaced in his rolling sentences that some philosophers have suspected that Kierkegaard is not really one of their number, and is a literary artist instead. Any man endeavoring to save him as a star in the philosophical sky would have to defend a dialectic of personal reflection and of the utterly private, attempting to justify the old Dane's effort to communicate what is by definition incommunicable. What Professor Thompson has done is something rather different, and one will vainly search the pages of the present volume for a textbook account of a strict, carefully-structured system.

The distinction, however, between the literary and the philosophical may be taken as one between different types of order. The plausible sequence of events that is a plot and the rational sequence of propositions that is the argument of a treatise may have some likenesses, but the two are based upon fundamentally different materials and are purposed for different ends. If we find, then, that Kierkegaard used many stylistic devices of the orators and the poets, and moreover that he inserts many sequences that appear to be more plotlike than syllogistic, it becomes a very nice question whether Kierkegaard needs to be treated as a philosopher at all.

The style, of course, should pose no problem. Aristotle was not fooled into thinking that Empedocles was a poet, and the history of philosophy is indeed full of great surges of rhetoric in both prose and verse. But the other, the problem of order, poses a harder question. What hints does SK give us that he means to be taken seriously for his argument, his analysis, and not just for his outpourings of a distressed consciousness or for his edifying effect upon uncertain men?

Mr. Thompson has set out to exhibit certain lines of development in Kierkegaard's work that make the assumption that he is a therapist, not a technical philosopher, considerably easier to hold. If philosophy includes therapy, as many persons now assume, then of course Kierkegaard is a philosopher as well. But what Thompson has done especially well is to make clear an order in the succession of persons whom Kierkegaard used, in one way or another, as characters or types in the great reflective writings of his middle years. In all the rushing stream of Kierkegaard's ideas, we find over and over that hints of genuine disorder turn out to be false, that there *is* a succession whose explanation is reasonable. On the other hand, the first hypothesis of order that we come upon must often give way to a better and perhaps subtler explanation: the apparent succession often masks a more fundamental one. Mr. Thompson has tried to put his finger on what this latter succession is, and (if I may be permitted to reveal a little of this) it turns out to be based upon a thoroughgoing fusion between what are ordinarily called philosophical categories and psychological introspection. There is, in Kierkegaard, no ultimate difference between the two, and Kierkegaard's seemingly endless probing of his own psyche is not, for him, radically different from the suggesting of solutions to common esthetico-ethico-religious problems. In a subjective orientation such as Kierkegaard's there can be no diremption between the terms of true discourse and the eliciting of feelings which make this discourse true for the soul for whom these terms are subjective, unique. This point about SK has been well understood and documented in the past, but it is the special use that Mr. Thompson makes of it that appears to me, at least, to be so fruitful in his exposition of the works that begin with *Either/Or* and draw to a close with *Concluding Unscientific Postscript* and *Stages on Life's Way.*

This approach to Kierkegaard involves the assumption that in spite of the fact that there was a set of experiences through which Kierkegaard himself actually lived—the Deer Park, the public square, the houses of ill fame, Regine, all actual things open to geographical or historical study—in spite of this, one concludes from reading Kierkegaard's work that somehow the objective can be squeezed into the subjective. In some way, Regine seems more than ordinarily real to us when refracted through the lenses of SK's powerful, penetrating vision. That is, if one is able sympathetically to read Kierkegaard at all. The worry that many writers who discuss their own souls evince, that with analysis and especially self-analysis the immediacy of living experience is lost, did not seem to trouble Kierkegaard often, convinced as he was that reflection *realizes* the objective. Without this realization the young girl, the street, the daily hot bouillon would be evanescent, would be insubstantial, impermanent. These objects take up and hold their stations only when made to do so by a vivid act of the mind.

If Kierkegaard's overriding concern was the health of his soul, his ability to keep his consciousness from misleading him in the labyrinth of life's paths, then it would seem that "healthy" and "sick" are fundamental contraries in the dialectic not only of Kierkegaard and his own books, but of any worthwhile study of them. It is not, however, altogether easy to conclude just what these two words should mean. Certainly we might feel that a slowing down of his intense conscious activity would be an event that any psychotherapist of our day would applaud. But of course this is just the point. Being, for Kierkegaard, is something to be achieved, it is not conferred directly upon one, and in the act of realizing that life is, and what it is, the life itself takes on its unique lineaments. If mental health were to be gained at a cost of crippling or eradicating mind, then the pivot of the universe would lose its centrality and its fixity.

If, on the other hand, you were to say that Kierkegaard should apply himself to the sciences he neglected, even then the main power of consciousness would be dissipated. In Kierkegaard's

view consciousness grows by what it feeds on, that is, on consciousness itself. Hence concentration upon what is objectively
necessary or inductively derivable would be an othering of knowledge and would weaken if not destroy its very center. But if SK
had sought to divert himself from his famous seven desks (all of
which served as mirrors), applying himself Duchamp-like to games
of chess, then the whole purpose of knowledge would have failed,
for self-healing, self-creating could not be provided.

What Kierkegaard did was neither of these, but something
more interesting. He went to extraordinary lengths to diffuse his
consciousness among other characters, pseudonyms, and fractions
of characters. Had he been merely a novelist or dramatist, this
would again have scattered his self-knowledge in diverse places,
and it would have been hard for him to suggest a philosophy
speaking through mouthpieces connected merely by circumstances
of plot rather than by principle. The claims of story and illustra-
tion would, I think, have been too much for Kierkegaard and
his effort to preserve himself in others.

Resemblances and differences between Kierkegaard and other
philosophers who chose a dialogue form come to mind. Galileo,
for instance, frequently includes himself as an authority for the
phrasing or solving of problems, and it would be likely enough
for us to think of Sagredo or Salviati (who, as history tells us,
were flesh-and-blood men) as mere extensions of Galileo's own
personality. Cicero offers his speakers with hardly a disguise, and
Berkeley's Philonous is really a Greek name for an Irish aspirant
to clerical office, but there is a very different problem of impersonation in the dialogues by Hume; even the fixing of propor-
tionate dialectical responsibility between Philo and his companions
has been a matter of debate for generations.

All these instances are simple enough compared with the
vast question about Plato, for apart from the fact that we are
quite badly off for real corroborative evidence regarding many of
the men whom Plato names, there are plenty of anonymous par-
ticipants whose disguise is so heavy as to be impenetrable. We
can scarcely believe that to all characters Plato accorded the
same responsibility for his own views—one could not be a Socrates
and false judge of Socrates at the same time and receive equal

sanction from even the most broadminded of philosophers. On the other hand, there are complex relationships of opposition, similarity, absorption, subsumption, at work in all the dialogues and holding between individuals and between pairs and groups of men.

Something of this sort is in Kierkegaard, who sets up two differing types of relations between himself and the men whose names he invents with tongue in cheek. On the one hand, he has a branching between different works, so that SK first assumes the person of Victor Eremita, then of Johannes de Silentio, then of Constantin Constantius and so forth. These are patently different sorts of persons, shadowy and incomplete though they may be. But there is another kind of successive impersonation within a single work, a kind that reminds us of the old riddle about the three men with spots on their heads. This is an impersonation in which SK becomes for the length of a book Victor Eremita who in turn gives way to the aesthete A for half a book who in turn puts Johannes the Seducer in his place for a chapter. This is an extreme length for SK to go to in order that he may spread his consciousness, but it is a timesaver, so to speak, in the end, just as it is a timesaver for most of the good advice to be put into Virgil's mouth if Dante's questions in Hell and Purgatory are to be real questions.

But we notice that the names of these persons are invented, and have not only associations but general meanings; Vigilius Haufniensis is an example. Evidently the effort to hide his identity from the public by a dissembling was less important than his effort to focus that public's attention on certain important conceptual relations in the treatises. A man who is named "A" is clearly meant to convey something different from "The Watchman of Copenhagen." (Thompson does not believe that there must have been an overall, consistent plan when Kierkegaard set out to compose his pseudonymous works, though hundreds of germinal ideas for them have been found in earlier jottings; the question admits of no simple answer.) Not only that, but SK employs a number of words in a very emphatic way, giving them something of an independent, symbolical status: The Cloister, The Paradox, The Moment, etc. (Mr. Thompson himself will answer for The Labyrinth.) It is hardly clear just how these are to be stabilized in meaning. Certainly they play important parts in the teeming subjective life of Kierkegaard, but they are not at all invented persons and whether they could exist outside of their dialectical interconnections is another matter.

I have greatly enjoyed my own study of Mr. Thompson's book, which seems to me not only informative but also very sensitive, very perceptive, very human. For the most part SK's reputation has been in the hands of theologians, and certainly they have performed excellent service; but the present book is written from a different viewpoint, a perspective which I like to think that the Kierkegaard of 1843 would have vigorously approved.

George Kimball Plochmann

Carbondale, Illinois
April 12, 1966

PREFACE

IS THE PHILOSOPHER a "sick" man and his philosophy a "symptom" of his sickness? In one form or another this question haunts every page of the following study of Kierkegaard. For if any single thesis is to emerge from the study, it is that Kierkegaard was a profoundly sick man and that the character of his sickness established a privileged perspective for the understanding of his work. Again and again Kierkegaard commented in his journals on the intimate connection between his work as an author and his life as a man. It is no exaggeration, he told us, to think of his work as springing from the very "abscess" of his suffering as a man. His life was the frame and source of his work, and this life (he complained on his deathbed) was "a great, and to others unknown and incomprehensible suffering."

In the following pages I try to isolate this "suffering" through a close study of the contours and textures of Kierkegaard's life-world. From these contours and textures I claim to be able to read off the striations of concern which organized the major works of his middle period. Against the background of Kierkegaard's life-world, these works turn out to be, not abstruse theologico-philosophical treatises or mysterious aesthetic essays, but successive moves in a complicated dialectic of therapy.

It might be said that what follows is an "existential" study of the first "existentialist." This would be fatuous.

It might be said that what follows is a kind of case history.

This would be true, but lacking in one essential qualification: most case histories display no glint of self-recognition to the eye of the inquiring reader. So separated by the wall of illness, so lacking in any common world or experience, the reader and the patient remain utterly alien; health stands mute and incomprehending before sickness. Yet with respect to the Kierkegaardian case history all this changes. I must leave the final judgment up to the reader, but I would not hesitate to wager that there will prove to be few individuals either so happy or so lucky as to fail to discover some image of themselves reflected in the torments of this odd Dane.

It remains for me to express my warm thanks to all those institutions and individuals without whose generous assistance this study would not have been possible. To the American-Scandinavian Foundation, to the Garland Trust, to the State Department of the United States Government, and to the *Undervisnings Ministerium* of the Danish Government go my deep thanks for making financially possible a year's stay in Copenhagen. While there I had the good fortune to discuss Kierkegaard with such authorities as Dr. Phil. Gregor Malantschuk, Mag. Art. H. P. Rohde, and Pastor Niels Thulstrup, and I am sincerely grateful for the consideration they showed me. In Copenhagen I also had the opportunity of pursuing studies in Danish life and literature at *Dalgas Universitet,* whose *Rektor* and fellows spared no effort in facilitating my knowledge of Danish and of Kierkegaard's milieu. To all those at Bakkegaards Allé whose kindness meant so much to me and whose friendship I prize, I can only say: *"Mange, mange tak!"*

My thanks go also to Professors George Schrader and John Wild, and to Dr. Francis Ilg, all of whom, at a very early point in the development of the study, were kind enough to give me the benefit of their criticism and encouragement. My friend Carleton Dallery went over the manuscript with great thoroughness and suggested a number of important changes later incorporated in the final draft. His insightful critique is greatly appreciated.

No list of acknowledgments would be complete without a word concerning the efforts of Professors Robert S. Brumbaugh and George Kimball Plochmann. As my dissertation adviser at

Yale, Professor Brumbaugh set an example of scholarship and lucidity which I hope is reflected somewhere in this final result. During that year in Europe he kept in touch from as far away as the Greek island of Icaria, bringing the benefit of his Hellenic sunlight into the fog of northern Europe. For this, and for a list of kindnesses too numerous to name, I am most deeply grateful.

But a dissertation is not a book, and if this study has indeed made the transition, it is Professor Plochmann who must bear the credit. His ear for language, his insistence on economy of expression, his sensitivity to the issues involved: all these found a place in his accurate criticism. More than this, his patience and infectious good humor are virtues not common to the race of editors. He made the production of the book into an enlightening and happy experience, and for all this I thank him.

Finally there is my wife, Nancy. Unlike many wives, her contribution to this book was not perfunctory, but substantial. During our year in Copenhagen she was its sole critic, suggesting a word change here, a deletion there, telling me with as much tact as possible when a chapter was bad, and with more enthusiasm than required when it was good. Following our return to the United States she undertook the onerous job of checking and typing the footnotes and certain bibliographical entries—a task complicated by my miserable handwriting. For all these labors above and beyond the call of wifely duty she has my thanks, and also my hope that our next child will be easier brought to birth and firmer in feature and outline than the creature whose development these acknowledgments have chronicled.

Josiah Thompson

Haverford, Pennsylvania
January, 1966

CONTENTS

SHORT TITLES

Attack	*Attack Upon "Christendom."* Translated by Walter Lowrie. Princeton: Princeton University Press, 1946.
Christian Discourses	*Christian Discourses.* Translated by Walter Lowrie. Oxford: Oxford University Press, 1940.
Postscript	*Concluding Unscientific Postscript.* Translated by Walter Lowrie. Princeton: Princeton University Press, 1944.
Dread	*The Concept of Dread.* Translated by Walter Lowrie. Princeton: Princeton University Press, 1946.
Edifying Discourses, i, ii, iii, iv	*Edifying Discourses.* Translated by David F. and Lillian Marvin Swenson in four volumes. Minneapolis: Augsburg Publishing House, 1943–46.
E/O, i, ii	*Either/Or.* Translated by David F. Swenson, Lillian Marvin Swenson and Walter Lowrie in two volumes. Garden City: Anchor Books, 1959.
Trembling	*Fear and Trembling.* Translated by Walter Lowrie. Princeton: Princeton University Press, 1941.
Journals	*The Journals of Søren Kierkegaard.* Edited and Translated by A. Dru. Oxford: Oxford University Press, 1938.
Johannes Climacus	*Johannes Climacus.* Translated by Thomas H. Croxall. Stanford: Stanford University Press, 1958.

Love	*Works of Love.* Translated by Howard and Edna Hong. New York: Harper and Bros., 1962.
Fragments	*Philosophical Fragments.* Translated by David F. Swenson. Revised Edition. Princeton: Princeton University Press, 1962.
Repetition	*Repetition.* Translated by Walter Lowrie. Princeton: Princeton University Press, 1946.
Sickness	*The Sickness Unto Death.* Translated by Walter Lowrie. New York: Anchor Books, 1954.
Stages	*Stages on Life's Way.* Translated by Walter Lowrie. Princeton: Princeton University Press, 1945.
Gospel of Suffering	*The Gospel of Suffering.* Translated by David F. and Lillian Marvin Swenson. Minneapolis: Augsburg Publishing House, 1948.
Point of View	*The Point of View for My Work as an Author.* Translated by Walter Lowrie. New York: Harper Torchbooks, 1962.
x^5 A 132	*Søren Kierkegaards Papirer.* Second Edition. Edited by P. A. Heiberg, V. Kuhr, and E. Torsting. In 20 Volumes. København: Gyldendal, 1909–48; Volume x, Part 5, Section A, Item 132
Vaerker, vol. XIII, p. 183	*Søren Kierkegaards Samlede Vaerker.* First Edition. Edited by A. B. Drachmann, J. L. Heiberg, and H. O. Lange. In 14 Volumes. København: Gyldendal, 1901–1906; Volume XIII, page 183.
Breve og Akstykker	*Breve og Akstykker vedrørende Søren Kierkegaard.* Edited by Niels Thulstrup. København: Munksgaard, 1953–54.

All translations from untranslated Danish sources are my own. Unless otherwise noted, italicized phrases are so emphasized in the original text.

J. T.

The Lonely Labyrinth

KIERKEGAARD'S PSEUDONYMOUS WORKS

Every art and every philosophy may be seen as a healing and helping application in the service of growing, struggling life: they always presuppose suffering and sufferers.

FRIEDRICH NIETZSCHE, *Die fröhliche Wissenschaft,*
Number 370

Remember me to everyone, I was much attached to them all, and tell them that my life is a great, and to others unknown and incomprehensible suffering; it all looked like pride and vanity, but it was not . . . I had my thorn in the flesh . . . .

SØREN KIERKEGAARD, on his deathbed.

Part One

BEGINNINGS

By the early summer of 1835 Michael Pedersen Kierkegaard was becoming increasingly concerned about his youngest son. Although Søren had honored his father's wish by enrolling in the theological faculty of the university, and although he had passed his "Second Examination" in good time and was attending the required lectures in theology, nevertheless the old merchant was not pleased with the youth's progress. Having retired from active business nearly forty years before, Michael Kierkegaard had spent the intervening years carefully husbanding his sizable fortune and watching over his growing family, while at the same time pursuing an intense interest in matters theological. From later descriptions we know something of his voracious reading in the church literature of the time, and of the joy he took in engaging local clerics in dialectical conversations. We can imagine with what satisfaction he followed the theological career of his eldest son, Peter, who some six years before had received a doctorate from Göttingen, and we can imagine too the doubts he was even now coming to entertain concerning the development of young Søren. For by this summer of 1835 Søren was showing signs of increasing impatience under the restrictions imposed by a theological curriculum. "I am supposed to study for a theological degree," he wrote to P. W. Lund on June 1, 1835, "an occupation which does not interest me at all and so does not advance particularly quickly. I have always preferred a free and perhaps too, a somewhat indefinite study, to the table d'hote where one knows in advance the guests and the menu for each day of the week" (1 A 72). Already he had taken to spicing the rather plain fare of the theological table with liberal servings of Goethe and the German romantics, and he delighted in discussing these works with the young intelligentsia of Copenhagen. Only the December before he had tried his own hand at writing, and had produced for the *Flyvendepost* a witty but vapid piece entitled, "Also a Defense of Women's Superior Talents." The world of music, literature, and philosophy —the world of performances at the Royal Theatre and of discussions at the *Studenterforening*—was attracting Søren and drawing him away from the dour and pious atmosphere of the paternal home on the market square. The elder Kierkegaard could only see all this as highly unbecoming to a serious young man preparing for a post in the Danish State Church.

Perhaps then with an eye towards separating Søren both from his aesthetic companions and from the glitter of Copenhagen, in June of 1835 Michael Kierkegaard provided his son with ample means for a two month holiday in the country.

In late June Søren left Copenhagen and traveled north by coach the forty miles to the fishing village of Gilleleje at the northeastern tip of the island of Sjaelland. There he settled down at the local inn, which served him well as a base for almost daily excursions into the surrounding countryside. For a city youth of twenty-two this was a first encounter with nature—with the marshes, the pebbled beaches, the great forests of northern Sjaelland, and the quiet lakes. Sometimes he took a coach to visit the historical monuments in the vicinity—Gurre Castle and Esrom— or to journey south through Grib's Forest to Nødebo. But often he went by foot, striding over the gently rolling hills around Gilleleje or strolling along the beaches to the east and west. He took a two-day sailing trip to Kullen in Sweden, and on July 29 climbed to the top of the Gilbjerg, the highest point in the vicinity. Yet in his descriptions of these excursions—of driving through the shadows of Grib's Forest, or sitting by a still Northern lake, or listening to the gulls and the roll of the sea from the Gilbjerg—there is a curious remoteness. As one reads these journal entries (originally written down on odd scraps of paper as Søren jogged along in a coach or sat in his room at Gilleleje) one comes to feel that all these impressions occupy only the forestage of consciousness, and that behind them more personal concerns are being weighed, compared, and adjudicated. One comes to suspect that instead of being merely a healthful summer holiday, this sojourn in Gilleleje is proving to be a period of intense self-examination and reflection.

Such a suspicion soon finds its confirmation, for on August 1 Kierkegaard inscribes in his journal a long entry summing up the results of his reflections. It is a strange entry, nearly eight pages in the Danish edition, full of youthful enthusiasm and exaggeration, yet also intensely revealing as an early statement of Kierkegaard's intent as a writer and as a man.

What I really lack is to be clear about *what I am to do*, not what I am to know, except in so far as some understanding must go before every action. The thing is to understand myself, to see what God really wants *me* to do; it is a question of finding a truth which is true *for me*, of finding *the idea for which I can live and die*. What good would it do me to discover a socalled objective truth, to work through the philosophers' systems and then be able, if required, to review them all and point out the inconsistencies within each one;—what good would it do me to be able to develop a theory of the state and combine all the details into a single whole, and so construct a world in which I did not live, but only held up to the view of others;—what good would it do me to be able to explain the meaning of Christianity and many other particular phenomena, if all this had *no* deeper meaning *for me and for my life?* . . . What good would it do me if truth stood before me cold and naked, indifferent as to whether I recognized her or not, and producing in me a shudder of fear rather than a trusting devotion? I surely do not deny that I still recognize an *imperative of understanding* and that through it one can work upon men, *but it must be taken up into my life*, and that is what I now recognize as the most important thing. That is what my soul longs after, as the African desert thirsts for water . . . That was what I lacked in order *to lead a complete hu-*

man life and not merely one of the understanding, so that
I thereby should not come to base the development of my
thought—well, upon something that is called objective—
something that is in any case not my own, but upon something which grows together with the deepest roots of my
existence . . . (1 A 75).

Kierkegaard's intent is not to become a knowledgeable person, but
to become knowledgeable about himself, "to find a truth which is
true for me," to find that something "which grows together with
the deepest roots of my existence." He cares nothing for the philosophical systems with their theories of the state and their explanations of the meaning of religion. He rejects them, but we must
note, he rejects them *not* because they are "inconsistent" or "un-
true"—this would be to reject them on philosophical grounds.
Rather he rejects them on personal, existential grounds; he rejects
them because they are totally *irrelevant* to himself and to his situation. Eight years later he would sum up this irrelevance in the
following observation.

What the philosophers say about Reality is often as
disappointing as a sign you see in a shop window, which
reads: PRESSING DONE HERE. If you brought your clothes to
be pressed, you would be fooled; for only the sign is for sale.[1]

Yet in that summer of 1835 not only was Kierkegaard convinced of the irrelevance of much of speculative philosophy to
himself and to his situation, but in addition he suspected he knew
the cause of this irrelevance. For speculative philosophy spoke in
the language of universal propositions, and, masquerading as the
"I-am-I" of pure self-consciousness, it failed to attend to the very
considerable differences between individual human beings. In the
draft of a letter written on June 1, 1835, Kierkegaard remarks "how
bewildering is the contemplation of life when it shows itself in all
its richness, when we look over its astonishing variety of talents
and capacities," and continues by denigrating that "cold philosophy [that] will explain it all . . . , and not see it as an unending
pageant of life, its variegated play of color, and its innumerable
nuances" (1 A 72). It is this very "richness" of life—its detailed

textures and colors—which catches Kierkegaard's eye and makes him distrust the universal statements of speculative philosophy. In a marginal addition to the Gilleleje entry just now quoted, he emphasizes the individual, almost lyrical, quality of both philosophy and wit.

> A similar phenomenon is the mistaken view of understanding and its results; one speaks of the objective results and fails to remember that it is precisely the real philosopher who is in the highest degree subjective . . . In the same way one treats witticisms, seeing them not as the Minerva which necessarily springs from the author's whole individuality and surroundings, and therefore in one respect as something lyrical, but as flowers one can pluck and put to one's own use.[2]

It is the *differences* between authors and between people which make such a striking impression on Kierkegaard. As he will write three years later, "In this sense it is that the author's picture, his individuality, stamps itself on his work" (II A 720). Yet if it be these differences which give life its richness, it is also these differences which set limits to a universalizing philosophy, which, intending to speak to all men, ends by speaking to none.

Dealing in universal principles and thus inevitably failing to take into account the uniqueness of the individual, speculative philosophy finally is revealed as having no relevance to the concerns of the existing individual; in capsule form this is the recognition coming to birth in the young Kierkegaard's mind as he sits in his room at Gilleleje and takes stock of himself and his future. Yet if philosophy can only produce a very "cold and naked" truth, this does not prevent the individual from discovering a more hospitable truth of his own. Thus in a mood of high resolution, even buoyancy, Kierkegaard concludes the entry with the following words.

> So let the die be cast—I cross the Rubicon! This way surely leads me *to strife*; but I shall not give up . . . I shall hurry along the path I have discovered, greeting those whom I meet on the way, not looking back as did Lot's wife, but

remembering that it is a hill up which we have to struggle
(I A 75).

We may be permitted a wry smile in reading these words of
youthful enthusiasm. For how many of us have not made similar
resolves at the age of twenty-two, only to see them dissipate in
the fall of the years? Yet if we are to believe Kierkegaard's own
words in the matter, this resolve did not dissipate, but deepened to
form the life-stream of his authorship. "Magister Kierkegaard," he
writes in 1846, "is neither more nor less than what he gives himself
out to be: a self-thinker" (vii¹ B 88), and in the same year he
remarks, "I have never given myself out to be a man of science who
had something extraordinary to report . . . I have certainly not
given myself out to be a poet, who can give unusual enjoyment—
I am a 'poor individual human being' " (vii¹ B 86). It is this "poor
individual human being," this "self-thinker," who breathes in the
work of Kierkegaard and gives it its characteristic texture of urgency, power, and passion. Unlike some writers, this "self-thinker"
never managed to bring much distance between himself and his
works. "I became clear to myself through writing [i at producere]"
(ix A 213), he remarked; and at another place, "The production
is also my development, and little by little I have learned to understand myself in having grasped things correctly." [3] Writing became
for him almost a necessity of life. "How true are the words I
have so often used for myself," he writes in 1848, "that as
Scheherazade saved her life by telling stories, so I save my life, or
keep myself alive, by writing [i at producere]" (ix A 411). His
work was not something he did for amusement, or fame, or money.
It was rather something intimately connected with his own psychic
health, "I know also with God that this work of mine as an author
was the prompting of an irresistible inward impulse" (Point of
View, 7).

The fruits of the resolve announced for the first time at
Gilleleje, that is to find the "truth which is true for me," we find
expressed in the works themselves. They themselves, Kierkegaard
seems to be telling us, are in fact milestones "along the path I have
discovered," waymarkers along the bends and turnings of a personal quest. Moreover, if we turn to these works and to the jour-

nal entries which accompanied them, we can find evidence of a continuing effort on Kierkegaard's part to articulate that recognition which undergirded his resolve. Again and again in these works we find him emphasizing the heterogeneity of the existing individual. It is this heterogeneity, he reiterates, which reveals the necessity for a new kind of reflection, a reflection which will not ignore, but emphasize, the existing individual's uniqueness and historicity.

Six months after returning from Gilleleje to Copenhagen, in January 1836, Kierkegaard recorded some of his reflections on the difficulties of being an author. He observes how "it is quite often sad and depressing, when in life one would achieve something by one's words, and yet at the last sees that one has achieved nothing" (1 A 114). He ponders for a moment why it is that one's words often prove so ineffective, and concludes that it may be due to the uniqueness of the individual. "On the other hand," he continues, "it is something quite great that in this way every individual is always a world unto himself, has his holy-of-holies where no strange hand can force its way in." The conviction expressed here as to the uniqueness of the individual,[4] of him being a "world unto himself," of him always having what Kierkegaard will later call a "secret closet" (vii A 205) into which he may retire, this conviction comes to function almost as a postulate in Kierkegaard's later writings. In *The Sickness Unto Death* he remarks on the "angularity" of different selves, and denigrates that self which "for fear of men dare not be itself in its essential accidentality . . . by which in fine it is itself" (*Sickness*, 166). Yet perhaps the most explicit statement of this conviction is found in *Works of Love* where Kierkegaard not only emphasizes the uniqueness of the individual, but also points out how crucial the fact of this uniqueness is to his thought as a whole. After asserting that the "human superiority over the animals" resides precisely in the fact that "every individual is essentially different or unique" (*Love*, 217), he goes on to point out how without this uniqueness "the God-relationship would essentially be done away with." Moreover, not only the God-relationship, but also the concept of self-development as well as the category of "the single individual" [*den Enkelte*] would all be left without foundation were it not for the fact that each individ-

ual is "a world unto himself," and "essentially different or unique."
Even more importantly, if it were not for the fact of this uniqueness, Kierkegaard's call for a new "subjective" mode of reflection
would be without urgency or purpose.

> It is a fundamental confusion in recent philosophy to
> mistake the abstract consideration of a standpoint with
> existence, so that when a man has knowledge of this or that
> standpoint he supposes himself to exist in it; every existing
> individuality must precisely as existing be more or less one-
> sided. From the abstract point of view there is no decisive
> conflict between the standpoints, because abstraction pre-
> cisely removes that in which the decision inheres: *the exist-
> ing subject* (*Postscript*, 262).

It is precisely because an individual is "one-sided," because he can
never adopt a free-floating standpoint above existence, that he inevitably finds much of speculative philosophy to be irrelevant to
himself and to his situation. But is there another kind of reflection
which remains rooted in existence, and so stays relevant to the
concerns of the existing individual? In work after work Kierkegaard
calls for such a "subjective" or "existential" reflection, a reflection
which will coincide with the "path" he claimed in 1835 to have
discovered for himself.

Already in *Either/Or*, in the concluding remark that "only
the truth which edifies is the truth for you" (*E/O*, II, 356), we find
an echo of the Gilleleje entry with its appeal for "a truth which
is true for me." In a discourse published the following year (1844)
Kierkegaard articulates this appeal by distinguishing between two
kinds of truth. He writes,

> There is a truth whose greatness, whose sublimity, we
> are accustomed to extol by saying that it is an *objective* truth,
> that it is equally valid whether anyone accepts it or not;
> indifferent to the special circumstances of the individual.
> . . . There is another kind of truth which we might call
> concerned truths. . . . They are not indifferent to the par-
> ticular condition of the individual, whether he is young or
> old, happy or depressed; for this decides for them whether
> they may be truths for him (*Edifying Discourses*, III, 71).

This distinction between "concerned truth" and "objective truth" echoes once again the thoughts expressed in the Gilleleje entry. Yet it also looks forward to the much longer treatment in the *Postscript* of the distinction between "abstract" or "objective" thinking, and "concrete" or "subjective" thinking. Perhaps the following selection of passages from the *Postscript* may give a hint as to what Kierkegaard means by these terms.

The way of objective reflection makes the subject accidental, and thereby transforms existence into something indifferent, something vanishing. Away from the subject the objective way of reflection leads to the objective truth, and while the subject and his subjectivity becomes indifferent, the truth also becomes indifferent, and this indifference is precisely its objective validity; for all interest, like all decisiveness is rooted in subjectivity. The way of objective reflection leads to abstract thought, to mathematics, to historical knowledge of different kinds; and always it leads away from the subject. . . .

The subjective reflection turns its attention inwardly to the subject, and desires in this intensification of inwardness to realize the truth (*Postscript,* 173–75).

While objective thought is indifferent to the thinking subject and his existence, the subjective thinker is an existing individual essentially interested in his own thinking, existing as he does in his thought. This thinking has therefore a different type of reflection, namely the reflection of inwardness, of possession, whereby it belongs to the subject and to no other (*Postscript,* 67–68).

What is concrete thinking? It is thought where there is a thinker, and a definite particular something which is thought; where existence gives to the existing thinker thought, time, and place

(*Postscript,* 296; translation altered).

The person of an abstract thinker is irrelevant. An existential thinker must be pictured as essentially thinking, but so that in presenting his thought he sketches himself

(*Postscript,* 319).

These passages should indicate just how radical Kierkegaard means this distinction to be. He does not deny that there is an activity called "objective thinking" which performs a proper function in solving the problems of science, mathematics, and the historical disciplines. But he believes that in addition there is another activity, called "subjective" or "concrete" thinking, whose proper focus is the individual himself. Objective thinking points outward toward the world and its problems; subjective thinking points inward toward the individual. Objective thinking produces results which are universally valid; subjective thinking produces no results and is valid only for the individual thinker.[5] Objective thinking should function independently of the bias of time, place, and character imposed upon an existing individual—it should be free-floating, unfettered, wholly impersonal. Subjective thinking can never be free of this bias, since its very focus is the individual in all his uniqueness and historicity.

The "path" of the Gilleleje entry becomes now the subjective thinker's inward focused concentration on the problems and tensions of his existence. This concentration is not the detached contemplation of the speculative philosopher, but rather takes place in the ebb and flow of passion. "All existential problems," writes Kierkegaard, "are passionate problems. For when existence is penetrated with reflection it generates passion" (*Postscript*, 313). Moreover, it is precisely this *passion* which isolates the subjective thinker from his fellows and makes his path a solitary one. "Every man who has passion," remarks Kierkegaard, "is always to some degree solitary" (*Postscript*, 383). It is essentially this *passion* which makes of the individual "more or less one-sided," and which assures the incommensurability of the various "standpoints." Were it possible for a man to live without passion, then perhaps all thinking could remain "disinterested," "theoretical" in the Aristotelian sense.

> Abstract thought is disinterested, but for an existing individual, existence is the highest interest. An existing individual therefore has always a *telos*, and it is of this *telos* that Aristotle speaks when he says that theoretical thought differs from practical thought (*Postscript*, 278).

It is then the individual's interest in his own existence which establishes his heterogeneity, and at the same time establishes limits for theoretical reason. But how are we to interpret this interest, this passion? Is it a quest for meaning of a Heideggerian sort, or does it have a more obvious referent?

In answering this question we are helped by an etymological similarity between the Danish words for "passion" and "suffering." The infinitive "to suffer" is *at lide*. The noun for "suffering" is *lidelse*, while the noun for "passion" is *lidenskab*. In this way, then, the Danish words for "suffering" and "passion" have the same stem, and thus share a residual meaning. Kierkegaard himself is aware of this shared meaning, for he remarks in *Philosophical Fragments* how all emotion, all passion, is really a form of suffering.[6] Is it too much to suggest that this rather elementary etymological point is a crucial key for understanding Kierkegaard's portrait of the subjective thinker? For we have already seen how passion is at once the source of the subjective thinker's activity and of his radical heterogeneity. Now if we can see passion as Kierkegaard does as a *kind of suffering*, then the subjective thinker's activity takes on a new character. For as his identity as *sufferer* is revealed, his activity takes on the character of *therapy*. The "individual's interest in his own existence" becomes then an interest in his own *healthy* existence! The "truth" which the subjective thinker pursues is pursued not for its own sake but for its curative value. His project becomes then not a search for meaning, but a search for health.

To characterize the project of the subjective thinker in this way is, of course, only to specify with regard to Kierkegaard a later and more general suggestion of Nietzsche's that "in philosophizing it has hitherto not at all been a question of 'truth,' but of something else, namely health. . . ."[7] Yet when we consider the whole shape and texture of Kierkegaard's relation to his work, no other conclusion seems admissible. We recall now Kierkegaard's characterization of himself as neither a poet nor a man of science, but as a "self-thinker," a "poor individual human being." And we recall too his description of his work as "the prompting of an irresistible inward impulse," and of how, like Scheherazade, he kept himself alive by writing. Yet these few brief citations give no indication of

the extent to which Kierkegaard's literary production sprang from
the very abscess of his suffering as a man. In 1848 he writes in his
journal.

> How often has it not happened to me, what just now
> occurred? When I am sunken in the deepest suffering of
> melancholy, one thought or another becomes so knotted up
> for me that I cannot loose it, and then since it is related to
> my own existence, I suffer indescribably. And then when a
> little time has past, the abscess bursts—and inside lies the
> richest and most wonderful material for work, and just what
> I need at the moment. . . .
> I suffer as a human being can suffer, in indescribable
> melancholy, which always has to do with my thinking about
> my own existence—so it is just that which I need to use
>   (IX A 217).

This is not an isolated admission, for Kierkegaard's journal is re-
plete with similar confessions. "Only when I am producing do I
feel well," he writes in 1846, "Then I forget all of life's discom-
forts, all suffering, then I am in my thought and happy. If I let it
alone for a couple of days I immediately become ill, overwhelmed,
troubled, my head heavy and burdened" (VII A 222). The very
next year he goes on to admit that "hitherto, I have defended myself against my melancholy by intellectual work, which keeps it
away . . ." (VIII A 250), while a few years later, in summing up
his authorship, he offered this characterization: "Understanding
myself to be fundamentally different from others, also with a thorn
in the flesh, I became an author in great inner suffering" (x^4
A 560). This theme of inner suffering as the source and energy
behind Kierkegaard's authorship runs as a *leitmotiv* through the
journal entries from their beginning in 1834 to their end in 1855.[8]
In 1849 he goes so far as to speak of his suffering as "the condition
for my intellectual activity," and concludes the entry by observing
enigmatically that "the significance of my life corresponds absolutely to my suffering" (x^2 A 92). It is then no importation of a
later viewpoint to point out how, in confronting Kierkegaard's
authorship and its exemplification of "subjective thinking," we
confront an authorship which takes suffering as both its frame and

its presupposition. Surely from the perspective we have gained we must find it difficult to disagree with Camus' judgment that above all things "Kierkegaard wants to be cured." [9]

The "path" of the Gilleleje entry has become now the lonely way of the "subjective thinker," a way where no landmarks can be laid down in advance, where no "results" are intersubjectively valid, and where the thinker has only his passion as companion, and only the changing patterns and problems of his existence as a landscape. Yet we must not lose sight of the fact that it is Kierkegaard's characteristic life-suffering which lies at the base of his passion, and that it is this passion which establishes the unique geography of his quest. If we are to understand this quest, we must come to understand the passion which directs it, and to understand this passion we must appreciate the suffering out of which it grew. Thus inexorably we are drawn back to Kierkegaard's life as the genesis and frame of his work. If we are to understand that work we must somehow penetrate to the center of that "to others unknown and incomprehensible suffering" which was his life. More concretely, we must make ourselves familiar with that curious melancholy under which Kierkegaard strained, that melancholy which was the source of both his passion and his suffering. If at the end of this study we have gained some understanding of the lonely passion which guided Kierkegaard's authorship, we will have accomplished our central purpose. But to gain such an understanding we must first become familiar with Kierkegaard's existence, with the shadows and the empty places which give to his life such an air of austere poignancy. Here then is where we must begin —with an examination in depth of Kierkegaard's life and world.

The possibility of such an examination is, of course, contingent upon the existence of a large enough body of autobiographical material (apart from the works themselves) to permit us to gain an accurate picture of Kierkegaard's existence. Here we find ourselves remarkably fortunate. For in the eight to ten thousand pages of the *Papirer* we have a source of autobiographical material virtually unparalleled in world literature. Here, in addition to the voluminous diaries and journals which Kierkegaard kept, are preserved first drafts of some of his later manuscripts, as well as remarks he appended to the works of others. Lest anyone fear that

these papers lack immediacy or candor, we should note Kierkegaard's resolve in 1837 that in these papers he would "let my
thoughts step out with the umbilical cord of their first mood," and
that in them he would "expectorate" himself "as though in a letter
to a close friend" (II A 118). These *Papirer* form the basis of a
body of autobiographical material which makes it possible for us
to penetrate very close to the center of Kierkegaard's existence.

In the following chapter we will begin our study with a comprehensive reading of this and other biographical material available
to us. In the reminiscences of Kierkegaard's friends and acquaint-
ances, in his letters to associates, and most of all in the notes and
journal entries preserved in the *Papirer*, in all of these Kierkegaard,
the man, stands clearly before us. Through this material we get a
generally unclouded picture of Kierkegaard's life-world—a picture
of the tensions, fears, hopes, and concerns which lay behind his
authorship. This is not to say that there still do not remain mysteries in Kierkegaard's life. Any individual has his secret closets;
Kierkegaard more than most. Yet the mysteries in Kierkegaard's
life, mysteries which have prompted so much effort on the part of
Danish scholars, are mysteries of detail. Was Kierkegaard led astray
in May or June of 1837? Did the "earthquake" he refers to occur
in 1835 or 1838? They are not mysteries concerning the main constants of his experience, not mysteries concerning his basic awareness of the world and of himself in time. These constants are
accessible to us, and it is upon them that our study will focus. The
intent of the next chapter will be to illuminate some fundamental
landmarks of the Kierkegaardian life-world, the hope being that in
coming to understand them, we come close to understanding
Kierkegaard himself.

In succeeding chapters we shall examine certain of Kierkegaard's works, and there our intent will be slightly different. Armed
with the knowledge gained from our investigation of the autobiographical material, we shall attempt to see how these works are
linked together as different moments in Kierkegaard's lifelong
project of subjective thought. For if, as we maintain, these works
are all efforts on Kierkegaard's part to find not *truth* but health, if
they are *indeed* various moves in a dialectic of therapy, then they
should be greatly illuminated by our knowledge of Kierkegaard,

the man. Having taken the measure of that "to others unknown and incomprehensible suffering" which was his life, we will be in a better position to spell out the logic of attempted cure. It is in this qualified sense, then, that we heed Nietzsche's suggestion in contending that at least Kierkegaard's art and philosophy may best be seen as a "healing and helping application in the service of growing, struggling life."

2

KIERKEGAARD'S WORLD

1. A *"Still Life"*

Writing in 1858 in the *Nordisk Universitets Tidskrift*, Rasmus Nielsen had this to say about Kierkegaard, his deceased friend.

> It belongs to the peculiarity in Kierkegaard's nature, that from the beginning he is so one with himself, so inwardly finished. He was not a young one who with the years became old; not a jolly one, who since became serious; not an aesthete who later became religious; no, he was originally everything he was in a peculiar doubling: in his youth old, in his jest serious, in his pain happy, in his strictness mild, in his bitterness sad. Kierkegaard is to such a degree an *apriori* nature, that he almost lacks the perfectible.[1]

As we read Kierkegaard's diaries and letters, as we follow him from youth through adulthood to death, we cannot help but concur in Nielsen's judgment of his friend. For in these notes and letters we do not gain an impression of a man whose ideas are constantly in flux, whose opinions change, and who is affected by the movement of the world around him. No, just the opposite. We feel the rightness of Nielsen's observation of Kierkegaard's "apriori" nature, of the way in which everything seems laid out in advance for him. Here is not flexibility, but rather a curious rigidity. The Danish critic, Frithiof Brandt, has pointed out how Kierkegaard's judgments on associates never changed, how they were "as though cut in stone"; [2] and other writers have called attention to how little change there is in Kierkegaard's basic ideas.[3] In future chapters we will have ample opportunity to see how Kierkegaard's authorship itself does not take up different themes in sequence, but keeps returning to the same theme; how in a curious way he seems not to be writing *different* books at all, but only rewriting the *same* book in different ways. Development, growth, change, flexibility: all these words seem peculiarly inappropriate to Kierkegaard. With respect to him everything seems to be so strangely *the same*.

Of course, the arena of Kierkegaard's life itself did in fact remain *the same*. He lived his whole life in Copenhagen, leaving its environs on only five occasions—once on a pilgrimage to the ancestral home in Jutland, and four times on brief visits to Berlin. No matter how unhappy Kierkegaard became he never remotely considered leaving his Copenhagen. His environment remained ever the same: the same streets, the same shops, the same climate, the same people, and even the same meals day after day.[4] In his diaries we do not learn of encounters with new places and new people; rather we meet always the same places and the same people. His carriage drives bring him always to the same familiar haunts: to the Deer Park, or Fredensborg, or Røjel's Inn at Nyholte.[5] And in these pages we keep meeting the same familiar faces. Here we meet Mynster, his father's priest; Martensen, his university tutor; his two companions from student days, Emil Boisen and Hans Brøchner; his faithful servant, Anders; and finally, here too we meet all his many relatives among the Lunds and the Kierkegaards. It seems as though all of Kierkegaard's lasting personal relationships were established in his early youth, never really to be changed or added to. They are *there* in the background; just as are his bookseller, his tobacconist, and his doctor. They seem sometimes as permanent as the streets Kierkegaard knew so well, as permanent as the Frue Kirke he passed on his daily walks.

Moreover, if we look at the likenesses of Kierkegaard which have come down to us, this sameness seems to have characterized his person. Here we have him in 1838 (his 25th year): [6] umbrella under arm, right hand gesticulating, his body slightly tipped backward—as if to increase the distance between himself and the

speaker. And here too we have the characteristic profile: the withdrawn lips—pursed as if in refusal, the eager eyes, the top hat
tipped back to where it meets the curve of the shoulder. But if now
we look at a later likeness,[7] his appearance seems so unchanged.
Here he sits absorbed in work perhaps in the late 1840's or early
50's: the shoulders may be more bent, the body frame thinner, a
few more wrinkles under the eyes and the brow more prominent—
but all these changes seem so inconsequential. For all the old an-
gularities of body movement and position, the eager (often shin-
ing) eyes, the curve of head-neck-shoulder: all these constants seem
to appear and reappear unchanged in all our likenesses of Kierkegaard. Not only his world, but his figure itself, it would seem, en-
dured virtually untouched by time and change.

The "apriori," "finished" character of Kierkegaard's world
means that the picture of his lived experience to be presented in
succeeding pages will not be a "motion picture" (as it were), but
rather a "still life." [8] It will not show change and growth—the
coming-to-be and passing-away of different types of experience—
but rather will illustrate the endurance of a rigid, almost paralyzed,
order of experience through several decades. Since, then, our essay
will describe the chief features of an enduring mental landscape,
rather than chart a course of development, it might be well at
the outset to lay out certain reference points.

II. Reference Points: The Two Poles

In 1836 Kierkegaard noted in his journal his belief that "the
square is the parody of the circle; all life, all thinking, etc. is a
circle, while life's petrifaction goes precisely into the forms of
crystallization . . . The angular is the inclination to remain static
—to die" (I A 313–14). Thirteen years later, in 1849, he wrote in
his journal that he himself was "a unity of age and youth, the
severity of winter and the mildness of summer" (x^1 A 374). It may
seem that these two entries, separated as they are by a span of
13 years, are virtually unrelated. Yet for the person who has followed Kierkegaard through the intervening years, these two entries
will seem not unrelated, but rather very close indeed. For in a real
sense they define the two orders of experience, the two poles, between which Kierkgaard's existence is stretched.

On the one hand is the pole of the square and of winter, the pole of angularity, fragmentation, irregularity, disorder; the pole of discontinuity. On the other hand is the pole of the circle and of summer, the pole of wholeness, integration, order; the pole of continuity. In later sections of this chapter we will see in detail how Kierkegaard's experience is tensed between these poles. But it might now prove enlightening to turn to the works themselves, where, by anticipating later chapters, we can verify the rather startling observation that all of Kierkegaard's value categories line up along the axis of continuity/discontinuity.

"Continuity," he observes in *The Concept of Dread*, "is salvation's first manifestation," [9] and later, in the *Postscript*, he goes on to remark that "the eternal is the factor of continuity" (*Postscript*, 277). The ideal in these works is the ideal of wholeness, integration. For it is the attainment of personal integration which is the object of the cultivation of that "inwardness" which Kierkegaard recommends in work after work.[10] And it is in that moment of integration, whether it be called the "ethical act," "repetition," or "faith," that (for Kierkegaard) personal fulfillment is to be found. Yet of course if continuity, wholeness or integration define the locus of value in Kierkegaard's work, then the opposite terms will describe the locus of disvalue. Hence throughout his work we find fear directed always toward the loss of continuity. "I can imagine nothing more excruciating," he writes in *Either/Or*, "than an intriguing mind which has lost the thread of its own continuity" (*E/O*, I, 304). It is the threat of losing this "thread of continuity" which haunts Kierkegaard, and finds expression in his description of the psychological states of "dread" and "despair." These states constitute the pole of disvalue which ever threatens the agonized leap toward wholeness, the grasping of continuity in the moment of "repetition" or "faith."

Yet perhaps this polar distinction in Kierkegaard's work may best be seen by examining some of the metaphors he employs. The metaphors of disvalue always seem to betoken the failure of an attempt to assert continuity. "Speculation's success in comprehending," he writes in *The Sickness Unto Death*, "is just this, of sewing without knotting the end fast" (*Sickness*, 224), and in another connection he asks, "For how does it come about that a

man's life becomes so spiritless that it is as if Christianity could
not be brought into relation to it, as when a jackscrew . . . cannot
be employed because there is no solid ground but only moss and
bog?" (*Sickness*, 232). While in *The Point of View* he remarks,
"Require the navigator to sail without ballast—he collapses. Let
the race, let each individual, make the experiment of doing without
the unconditioned—it is a whirlpool and remains such . . . Even
the greatest events and the most laborious lives are whirlpools, or
they are like sewing without knotting the thread" (*Point of View*,
157–58). In each of these metaphors the threat of disvalue is in
the form of chaos, disorder, lack of continuity. The thread is not
made fast and hence no continuity is asserted—the sewing opera-
tion which seeks to bind together fails in its purpose. Since the
particles of earth do not adhere closely, the ground is unstable and
"the lifting jack" of Christianity will not work. Without the unconditioned, individuals and races are overwhelmed by the chaos,
and disappear in the whirlpool. As for metaphors of value, what
could be more illustrative than the metaphor of "the leap" [11]
which enables the individual to assert a continuity over his life,
just as the same leap enables the mountaineer to assert a continuity
over space? And what is the failure of the leap but the endless fall
which the mountaineer fears worse than death itself? This brings
us to Kierkegaard's metaphor of being "suspended over 70,000
fathoms," [12] which he employs again and again to characterize the
precarious nature of the life of faith. The curious thing about this
metaphor is that the water seems to have been transmuted into
void, since 5 fathoms are just as threatening to the non-swimmer
as are 70,000. The water has become void, and so to be suspended
over 70,000 fathoms is a dizzying experience. It must be sustained
by the continuity of "the leap" which never terminates, which
never leaves the religious believer in a position of safety.

From this resemblance of metaphor we can read off the asso-
ciation at a very primitive level of Kierkegaard's mind of continuity
with value, and of discontinuity with disvalue. But as we noted
above, the pole of continuity (that is of the circle) is also asso
ciated with summer—with the natural rhythms, the trees swaying
in the Deer Park, the warm air, the sound of voices—in short with
life itself. While on the other hand, the pole of discontinuity (that

is of the square) is associated with winter—with the cessation of rhythms, the death of the leaves, the cold atmosphere, silence—in short with death. Hence, in *Stages on Life's Way* we find Kierkegaard describing with such tenderness the natural beauty of Grib's Forest in the evening light (*Stages*, 34), and in *Either/Or* painting such an idyllic picture of a summer Sunday when the sun shines into his room "bright and beautiful," when "the air is so warm," and when from a neighboring garden he can "clearly hear the lark pour forth its song" (*E/O*, 1, 41). Likewise, we should not be surprised in finding that Kierkegaard's most beautiful work is a discourse entitled, "The Lilies of the Field and the Birds of the Air"—a paean to the simplicity and vitality of natural life. While on the other hand, it seems only natural that in *Repetition* the despairing Constantine Constantius should exhibit such an affinity for the imagery of the mountains—for an imagery involving the "anguish of the abyss," "fissures," "caverns," and the "piercing shriek" of the wind—when he comes to describe how an individual self "strays at random amongst its own possibilities" (*Repetition*, 44). In a similar way, it should not surprise us that in *Either/Or* the aesthete will use images of death and stillness to describe his despair—that he will complain that his soul "is like the Dead Sea, over which no bird can fly; when it has flown midway, then it sinks down to death and destruction" (*E/O*, 1, 36). All these images only articulate in different ways a polarity we by now have come to recognize.

Life and death, continuity and discontinuity, the square and the circle: these are the polar opposites, the two orders of experience, between which Kierkegaard's world is stretched. Yet if we examine this world, we soon discover how much one pole dominates over the other. For Kierkegaard's experience is not divided equally between continuity and discontinuity. Rather his mental landscape is a wintry one, a Scandinavian one, sensing only on its periphery the promise of summer. It is upon this promise that we now shall turn our gaze.

III. *Moments of Continuity*

On June 10, 1836, Kierkegaard made the following entry in his journal.

A wandering musician played the minuet from *Don Juan* on a sort of flute (I could not see what it was as he was in the other courtyard) and the apothecary pounded his medicines and the girl in the courtyard scoured the steps and the stableboy groomed his horse, knocking the currycomb against the stone, and from another part of town came the sound of the shrimpman's voice, and they noticed nothing nor the flute-player perhaps, and I felt so good (1 A 169).

The mood expressed here is an uncommon one for Kierkegaard. Nowhere else in all his journals and letters do we find him giving vent to such a feeling of pastoral contentment. It seems probable that like his pseudonym, Constantine Constantius, Kierkegaard never knew real contentment for more than a few hours' time.[13] Yet what is most illuminating about this entry is the precise form in which Kierkegaard's contentment appears. Through the repetitive use of the conjunction (so reminiscent of Hemingway) we feel the continuity of the scene—we feel how the apothecary *and* the cleaning girl *and* the stableboy *and* the shrimpman *and* the flute player form parts of a continuous whole which *includes* Kierkegaard. There is a unity and a closeness here. Kierkegaard, we might say in a revealing common idiom, seems to feel "at one with the world." All the various parts form a whole in which he is included. It is a moment of simple joy over the inclusion—"and I felt so good."

If we can understand quite readily the joy Kierkegaard feels in this moment, there are other moments of greater intensity not so familiar to most of us. In January 1837 he asks, in an almost expectant tone,

> There yet may be given something that is so blissful that it does not permit itself to be expressed in words— otherwise, why are men to whom something great has been revealed: dumb?
> On the highest stage the sands run all together . . .
> (1 A 327).

"On the highest stage the sands run all together." What a mysterious utterance! It strikes us almost as a prevision of an experience Kierkegaard will have later that year, and which he will report in these words.

> Sometimes there occurs a phenomenon, which although occurring in the realm of spirit might be compared to a kind of vegetative, digestive slumber—to a comfortable feeling of convalescence. Consciousness here appears as a moon, overshadowing the stage from proscenium to background; one slumbers on in the whole . . . , in the Oriental ondreaming in the infinite, where it soon becomes, as if all were a fiction,—and one gets the same mood as from a grandiose poem: the whole world's existence, God's existence, my existence, is poetry, wherein all the multiplicity, the frightful irregularities of life, the things which are indigestible for human thought, are smoothed out in a foglike, dreaming kind of existence . . . (II A 125).

The moment where all multiplicity, all irregularity, everything "indigestible" to human thought, is smoothed out in an experience of existence as poetry: this is the moment of pure continuity. As far as we know, it will recur in slightly different forms three more times during his lifetime.

The following year Kierkegaard reports a similar experience with great punctuality.

> 10:30 A.M. 19 May 1838
>
> There is an *indescribable* joy which glows through us as unaccountably as the Apostle's outburst is unexpected: "Rejoice, and again I say Rejoice."—Not a joy over this or that, but the soul's full outcry "with tongue and mouth, from the depth of the heart": "I rejoice over my joy, of, in, at, by, on, through, and with my joy"—a heavenly refrain, as it were, cuts short our other song; a joy which cools and refreshes like a breeze, a gust of the tradewind which blows from the Groves of Mamre to the eternal habitations (II A 228).

The intensity of this joy makes it *indescribable*, yet it is suggested by a metaphor of continuity—the tradewind that caresses Kierkegaard, and, leading all the way to the eternal habitations, refreshes

him with a new-found joy in existence and in the world around
him.

Exactly 14 months later, on July 20, 1839, Kierkegaard reports a further experience more closely duplicating the earlier
moment which saw existence transformed into poetry.

> Just as in nervous cases there are moments when the
> nerves of the eye become so microscopically sharpened that
> the person can see the air; so too in respect to spiritual mat-
> ters there occur ecstatic moments when the whole of exis-
> tence is seen so poetically, so distended and transparent for
> contemplation, that even the most insignificant part of the
> "bad infinity's" mass products seems at the least allegorically
> to be the most profound truth, indeed seems only to have
> reality in so far as it is an allegory . . .[14]

As parts of an allegory the "bad infinity's" mass products seem
less foreign, less distant. Moreover, it is perhaps not insignificant
that Kierkegaard's closest analogy to this ecstatic state is a nervous
condition where the air, usually transparent and void, becomes
visible—that is, transmuted into a thicker medium. It is as if the
victory of the eyes over the void of air and the separations produced by it, is echoed by a similar victory of the mind over the
separate "meanings" of things through their transfiguration into
allegory.

In Kierkegaard's final known experience of ecstasy the victory
is not so much over the void which separates things, but rather (as
in his 1838 experience) it is over the void which separates him
from the world. He reports in 1848.

> NB   NB   19 April
> My whole being is changed. My hiddenness and self-
> isolation are broken—I must speak.
> Great God Give Grace! (vii[1] A 640).

Again and again in the years between 1839 and 1848 Kierkegaard
remarks on the suffering caused him by his melancholy [Tungsind]
and his self-isolation [Indesluttethed]. He reports how "From my
earliest childhood there sat an arrow of sorrow in my heart" (viii[1]
A 205), how he has been a "more or less defective casibus" who

only problematically "belongs under the concept 'human being' . . ." (II A 162). His melancholy and self-isolation have made him "completely heterogeneous with mankind in general" (VIII¹ A 177). Now, for a moment, this self-isolation is broken, and as he subsequently remarks, "life comes closer to me, or I come closer to myself." [15]

These then are the sunlit shafts of continuity that fill Kierkegaard's existence from time to time. For a moment the world becomes not an alien landscape, not a shattered surface whose fragments defy understanding, but rather a home and resting place. For one joyous moment the pieces fall together; the world reveals her meaning as allegory.

Yet always following in the wake of these ecstatic moments comes the recognition of their momentary character. Already at the close of the first entry comes the recognition, "Oh so sadly, I wake up again and just so sadly begin to see the unhappy relativity in everything, the un-ending question about what I am, etc." (II A 225). And only a few days after telling us that his "hiddenness and self-isolation are broken," he will sadly admit, "No, no, my self-isolation cannot be broken, at least not now" (VIII¹ A 645). The background to these moments is always the world as it usually is with its vapid bustle. Kierkegaard paints this background most vividly in describing an earlier experience which was of a slightly different order. He had climbed to the top of the Gilbjerg near Gilleleje, and there, lulled by the pounding of the surf, he remembered the deceased members of his family. "The few that are dear to me came forth from their graves," he writes, "I felt myself so content in their midst, I rested in their embrace, and it was as if I were out of the body, and, in a higher ether, was wafted to and fro with them" (1 A 68). But the moment of elegy did not last, "And the hoarse screech of the gulls reminded me that I stood alone, and all vanished before my eyes, and I turned back with a heart filled with sadness to mix myself in the swarm of the world without yet forgetting this blissful moment." This experience at the age of 22 strikes us as such a paradigm of the later Kierkegaard. The experience of communion which cannot last, but which must be carried in memory as a counterpoint to the confusion and disorder of the world. How often will we not find Kierkegaard in a

similar situation—awakened by the raucous present to stare dis-
turbed and querulous at what he calls here "the swarm of the
world!"

Perhaps now it might prove enlightening to look at Kierkegaard's perception of this "swarm"; that is, at his perception of a
world populated by the annoying "little things" of everyday life.

IV. The "Little Things"

"It is those little things which embitter life so," writes
Kierkegaard in 1837, "I can gladly push on against a storm until
the blood is ready to burst out of me, but the wind that blows a
bit of dust into my eye can make me so angry that I stamp my feet.
Those little things—just as a person would carry out a great work
. . . —and then a fly settles on his nose" (1 A 335). Kierkegaard's
irritation with the innumerable annoyances and incongruities of
life was of long-standing duration. A close friend, Hans Brøchner,
recalls how at a much later time Kierkegaard took great pains in
arguing for the thesis that experience makes one not wise but mad,
and how he would "adduce his proofs with much piquancy, by
pointing to all the innumerable contradictions in concrete experience." [16] Moreover, even as late as 1847 Kierkegaard confesses in
his journal "how unsuited I am to practical affairs," and goes on
to complain how he "suffers so indescribably under the confusion,
inaccuracy, and nonsense which is the secret of practical life" (VIII[1]
A 246). All the minor annoyances which a man of affairs would
accept with an indifferent shrug, Kierkegaard finds quite unbearable. Often times his physical surroundings would disturb him,
and he sometimes changed apartments in Copenhagen to avoid a
minor annoyance. In 1850 he moved from the corner of Rosenborg-
gade and Tornebuskgade because of an unpleasant smell in the
tanner's yard, and the following year he moved from 38 Nørregade
because of a reflection of sunlight from across the street, and the
barks of a dog on the floor above.[17]

All these "little things" may seem to us to be so trivial, but
for Kierkegaard they have a more sinister aspect. Hans Brøchner
relates how Kierkegaard always blew out a candle at some distance,
due to a conviction that "the smoke of a candle was dangerous to
inhale and might injure his chest," [18] and Kierkegaard's copyist,

Israel Levin, tells how deathly afraid of fire his employer was. He reports how a half-extinguished taper would give Kierkegaard a paroxysm of fright which could only be quieted by quenching the offending taper in a bucket of water. Even then, Levin continues, "it was a quarter of an hour before he really became calm, so that his shaking ceased and the sweat no more appeared on his brow." [19]

To us these rather odd phobias may appear as the idiosyncracies of a neurasthenic temperament. But we should not let their oddness blind us to the significance they have for an understanding of Kierkegaard's life-world. For they are not isolated anxieties but are indices of a more primitive anxiety before existence itself. Kierkegaard writes in 1839,

> The whole of existence makes me anxious, from the smallest fly to the mystery of the Incarnation; everything is unintelligible to me, most of all myself; the whole of existence is infected for me (II A 420).

It is in this sense that all of existence has a sinister aspect for Kierkegaard. Even the existence of a fly becomes a source of anxiety, since it, like all the other little things, is one of the "bad infinity's mass products"—a representative of an alien order. In a later work Kierkegaard will use these words to describe his awareness of existence as "infected" and foreign.

> I loathe existence, it is without savor, lacking salt and sense . . . One sticks one's finger into the soil to tell by the smell in what land one is: I stick my finger into existence —it smells of nothing. Where am I? Who am I? How came I here? What is this thing called the world? What does this word mean? Who is it that has lured me into the thing, and now leaves me there? Who am I? How did I come into the world? Why was I not consulted? (*Repetition*, 114).

This is perhaps one of the first descriptions in European literature of what Camus later called "that divorce between man and his life, the actor and his setting, [which] is properly the feeling of absurdity." [20] Moreover, it is precisely this awareness of divorce, of estrangement, which informs the very core of Kierkegaard's experience of the world. Anticipating the seminal experience of a later generation of writers, Kierkegaard too confronts a world which is "irreducibly strange and dense." [21] And it is precisely this strangeness of the world which supports both Kierkegaard's annoyances and his phobias. The little things are annoying and the phobias real only because they reveal their source in a world which is alien, recalcitrant to man's questions, and mute to his questions —a world which "smells of nothing."

This fundamental alienation of self and world is a primitive in Kierkegaard's experience. Although it is refracted in every element of that experience, it perhaps shows itself most clearly in what his biographer describes as a characteristic "agoraphobia." [22]

Turning to the *Papirer* we can find examples of such agoraphobia. Writing under the autobiographical pseudonym Johannes Climacus,[23] Kierkegaard relates in the *Papirer* how as a child he was "interested in filled space," how he "could not get it sufficiently tightly around him" (IV B 1). He describes how he would look out the drawing room window at a mound of grass and imagine that it were "a great forest which had all the denseness and darkness that this grass had." But suddenly his perception would shift and "now instead of that filled space his mind took in the empty space. He gazed again but took in nothing except the enormous extension."

This is an odd little story yet it provides an invaluable clue for understanding Kierkegaard's characteristic sense of space. What seemed to disturb him about space was its void, its "enormous extension," the fact that he could not "get it sufficiently tightly around him." In another book he will describe walking down a street in Christianshavn where "one can hear one's own footfall," and where "one feels so deserted and imprisoned in the quietness which isolates, where one is surrounded by non-conductors" (*Stages*, 259). For Kierkegaard, space does not join things in the perceptual field, but rather isolates them both from each other and from the perceiver. Space is a nonconductor, a nothingness which introduces separation. But in a world so infected by the void, so smelling of nothing, it is not the unity of things which is most evident, but rather it is the isolated details which stand out. And therefore in looking out over a scene in Frederiksborg, Kierkegaard's attention is not caught by the totality of the scene but rather by isolated details. "When in this way I stand and look out over the old Røyen estate," he writes in 1839, "and the wood in its immensity thickens in the background and makes it dark and secret in the thicket which is made even more striking by the single isolated trunks overgrown only with a crown of leaves" (II A 238). How warmly his eyes caress the "filled space" of the thicket, and how sharply his memory is etched by "the single isolated trunks overgrown only with a crown of leaves" standing out against the blackness of the wood. It is always the void between things which catches Kierkegaard's eye, and which breaks up the totality of a scene into isolated fragments. And perhaps it was the awareness of this void which made it virtually impossible for Kierkegaard to walk a straight line, which made him zig-zag up a street pushing his walking companion at one moment into the gutter and at the next into the window wells of the adjacent houses.[24] Finding only discontinuity in the world around him, it is not surprising that Kierkegaard's very movements exhibited a similar discontinuity.

The fact that Kierkegaard perceived the world around him as infected, and that he suffered such annoyance at the hands of the little things, is not then unrelated to the fact that he perceived space as a void and nonconductor. Both spring from a fundamental alienation, an ineradicable fissure sundering self from world. Likewise, the joy he felt in the aforementioned moments of ecstasy is not unrelated to the lack of joy which characterized so much of his experience. But we can expand the pattern still further. For holding in mind what we have learned of Kierkegaard's primitive awareness of the world and of space, we can see how he adopted certain strategies to keep this world at a distance. We can see how he endeavoured to evade the "swarm of the world" both by retiring into the artificially arranged life of the 19th century gentleman, and by immersing himself in the "renewing bath" of the world of fairy tales.

v. Servants and Fairy Tales

We remember Kierkegaard's complaint of how he suffered under the confusion and hurly-burly of practical life. Hence, we should not be surprised in finding that his personal life was characterized by a high degree of precision and order. His servants arranged all the necessities of his life with the greatest exactitude. His meals were nearly always the same: hot soup—tremendously strong, fish and melon, with a grass of fine sherry, followed by strong coffee, cream, and sugar from a bowl refilled daily. When he went out his faithful Anders would air the room and relight the stove, so that upon returning his master would always find the room temperature the correct 57°F.[25] When he moved to a new apartment, he would drive off in the morning, returning that night to find that Anders had put everything in order, even to the precise arrangement of his books. According to Han Brøchner, when Kierkegaard visited Berlin "everything in his room was arranged so as to conduce to the right mood for his work: the lighting, the communication between the rooms, the arrangement of the furniture—everything to a definite plan." [26] By inserting this matrix of artificial order between himself and the world, Kierkegaard could evade both its disorder and its annoyance. If the world did not provide an order, at least he could construct one.

And too if the world did not provide an order, there were ways one could escape into another order and another world. For example, there was the world of fairy tales and magic.

Kierkegaard's love of fairy tales and the joy he took in enchanting others is well-known. He owned many books of fairy tales—the auction catalogue of his library lists 64 volumes [27]—and the reading of these always gave him great enjoyment. "Why does the soul rest itself," he asks in 1837, "and find such strength in reading fairy tales? When I am tired of everything and 'filled with the days,' a fairy tale is always the renewing bath that is so beneficial to me" (II A 207). These tales of magic and adventure continued to fascinate him in later life, as witness this entry from 1845.

> Curiously, this evening I went out by Vesterport, it was dark; in one of the narrow alleys I passed by a couple of boys. I hardly noticed them, had already passed them when I heard one say to the other: "then they came to an old fortune teller . . ." In the summer the same thing happened to me one evening at dusk out by Peblingsøen; there were

two little girls and the one said: "then a long way off she saw an old castle . . ." I do not believe that even the greatest poet could produce such an effect as those thrilling memories of fairy stories: of "the old castle a long way off," and the "then" or "they went on a long way *until*," etc. (VI A 125).

The source of this fascination is not hard to find. For the magic world of the fairy tale was not flawed with the same facticity as the world in which he lived. In the world of the "once upon a time" and the "then" and the "until" things happened only within the ordered structure of magic, and the "thereness" of things was shadowed in enchantment; in this world things lost their drabness and appeared more brilliant, more significant, more magical than in the world of the everyday. No wonder then that Kierkegaard found refreshment here, and no wonder too that he took such joy in contriving enchantment for others.

His niece, Henriette Lund, tells of the bother he went to in order to provide an enchanted evening for a young cousin and herself. Upon their arrival at Kierkegaard's apartment the two girls were presented with corsages of lily of the valley together with carefully-chosen individual gifts. Then Anders announced that a coach was waiting. " 'Then we must go,' cried Uncle Søren, 'Where to?' But that nobody discovered until we arrived at the different stopping places, all prearranged, where some of the sights were pointed out to us . . ." [28] Returning to the apartment, the two girls played children's games with their host until the evening meal was served. "It consisted of open sandwiches, a cake of marzipan with a specially magnificent flower-bedecked covering, and champagne. Uncle Søren was our attentive and indefatigible host, and Anders an equally kind waiter."

There is something touching in this story of the writer of *Either/Or* and the *Postscript* going to great pains to provide two young girls with an enchanted evening they would never forget. Equally touching is the following anecdote reported by Troels-Lund.

He [Kierkegaard] was an unseen witness to a conversation between two poorhouse inmates. The one said, 'It's the devil that one never is happy.' The other, 'Nonsense! What's happiness?' The first, 'It is as if an angel dropped down from heaven and gave me a "blue one."' ' This last SK could not resist. He took a five dollar note (a 'blue one') from his purse, unexpectedly stepped up, presented it with a deep bow and disappeared without saying a word.[29]

We can imagine how Kierkegaard chuckled over this, how he enjoyed so much bringing a touch of magic into an all-too-factual world.

Finding the world a strange and threatening landscape, Kierkegaard retired from it. Endowed with a considerable fortune, he withdrew behind servants into the ordered and comfortable serenity of the 19th century drawing room. Within this cocoon he could work, letting his imagination play at will among its creations. Here too he could imaginatively install himself in the tinsel world of the fairy tale—letting his fancy freely roam in the larger-than-life milieu of "the castle a long way off." And here too on a winter afternoon he could create an enchanted world to delight his young niece. In all these different ways Kierkegaard was able to evade contact with the world of actuality. Yet after all this has been pointed out, there remains to be mentioned the one truly fundamental mode in which Kierkegaard chose to relate himself to the world. This is the mode of observation.

VI. *Observation*

Even if the world at large was alien, even if it was "unintelligible" and "infected," this did not mean that it could not be utilized. For if one kept one's eyes open, if one did not become too closely involved in it, but viewed it with the slightly quizzical gaze of the scientist inspecting a new specimen, if one did all this, then the world could become a rich source of anecdotes, psychological aperçus, and suggestive ideas. It need only be observed.

And so again and again we have before us the picture of Kierkegaard, the observer; "the spy," as he was wont to call himself, who used his daily outings to provide rich materials for his books.[30] Here we have him in 1840, rolling in his coach through Jutland. He notices a peasant girl leaning from a window and considers addressing her in these words.

Greetings! Thou village beauty . . . , do not take fright, I shall not disturb thy calm. Oh but look straight at me, that I may not forget thee (III A 17).

And four years later we have him sitting in Josty's Konditori watching a pair of lovers wend their way through Frederiksberg Gardens, eagerly following their movements and imagining their thoughts of one another.[31] In these same gardens he customarily took his walks with Hans Brøchner, and Brøchner remembers how Kierkegaard would always stop for a moment at the entrance. "He would inhale the scent of the flowers for a few moments, and then take away the memory of this 'moment' with him." [32] We learn too from Brøchner how rich a source of material were Kierkegaard's walks in the streets of Copenhagen. He once explained to Brøchner "how one can make psychological studies by putting oneself *en rapport* to passersby." [33] And as he explained this theory he was at the same time putting it into practice. "There was no-one," Brøchner tells us, "on whom his glance did not make an obvious impression."

Yet we often feel that it is not really other people and scenes which Kierkegaard is watching, but rather that he is observing their entrance and exit on the field of his own consciousness, and that it is really this consciousness which is the focus of attention. He mentions in 1837, for example, how he loves to ride in the coach, "lingering in beautiful places only to feel languor" (II A 637). It is not the place itself which is the focus of attention, but rather the mood which it stimulates. Like Johannes in *Either/ Or*, Kierkegaard often seems to be "collecting moods," seems to be "watching over himself" (*E/O*, I, 379–80), almost as a scientist might oversee a curious new experiment. As we watch Kierkegaard moving through his familiar Copenhagen, experimenting with unusual situations, holding in memory the momentary scent of a flower, we feel how accurately his own experience was described by Sartre in writing of Baudelaire, "He was the man who never forgot himself. He watched himself see; he watched in order to see himself watch; it was his own consciousness . . . that he contemplated. He only saw things through this consciousness; they were paler, smaller, and less touching as though seen through an eyeglass." [34] For Kierkegaard too "never forgot himself," complain-

ing in 1836, "Death and hell, I can abstract from everything but
not from myself; I cannot once forget myself even when I am
asleep" (1 A 162). And Kierkegaard too seemed to experience
things "as though seen through an eyeglass," as witness this long
description of his life written in 1848.

> So I fared forth into life—initiated into all possible
> enjoyments, yet never really enjoying, but rather . . . labor-
> ing to produce the impression that I enjoyed. . . . That is
> to say, I was constrained to be and was an observer. By such
> a life, as an observer and as spirit, I was quite extraordinarily
> enriched by experiences, got to see quite near at hand that
> aggregation of pleasures, passions, dispositions, feelings, etc.
> My imagination and reflection constantly had material
> enough to operate with, and time enough, free from all
> bustle, to be idle. For long periods I have been employed
> with nothing but the performance of reflective or dialectical
> exercises with an adjunct of fantasy, trying out my mind as
> one tunes an instrument—but I was not really living . . .
> in the proper sense of the word I had not lived, except in
> the character of spirit; a man I had never been, and child
> or youth even less
>
> (*Point of View*, 79–80; translation altered).

As observer, Kierkegaard still maintained a contact with the
world around him. But this contact was muted, grey, lacking in
intensity and color. Viewed always through the medium of a
consciousness watching itself, the world became for Kierkegaard
almost as a distant scene viewed through an eyeglass. So involved
in reflection and imagination—in following the bends and turnings of his own consciousness—he feels as if he "had not lived."
This theme of Kierkegaard's *hyperconsciousness*, of there being as
he says "something ghostly about me," we shall follow in the
next section.

VII. *"Something Ghostly About Me"*

Meier Goldschmidt recalls from the summer of 1837 a walk
he took with Kierkegaard. They had been visiting the Rørdams in
Frederiksberg and were now making their way back to the city
center, engrossed in talk of literary matters. "There was a long

pause," he tells us, "and then all at once he [Kierkegaard] gave a little jump and tapped himself on the leg with his Spanish walking stick." As Goldschmidt recalls, there was something odd about this seemingly spontaneous gesture.

> There was something sprightly about it, but it was altogether different from the sprightliness one sees elsewhere in the world. The movement was peculiar and almost painful to me. I know well enough that I stand in danger of remembering that scene with the admixture of a later time's knowledge, but I am certain that there appeared to me something painful about it, approximately in this way: It was as if this learned, slender man wanted to bring himself into the joy of life, but either could not or must not.[35]

How vividly this little incident pictures the Kierkegaard we know from the journals, his pathetic attempt at spontaneity only succeeds in making his companion uncomfortable!

Again and again Kierkegaard complains of his lack of immediacy. "I have never had any immediacy," he admits in 1848, "and therefore, in the ordinary human sense of the word, I have never lived. I began at once with reflection; it is not as though in later years I had amassed a little reflection, but I am reflection from first to last." [36] Even in childhood, it would seem, Kierkegaard lacked immediacy. "I never knew the joy of being a child," he complains in 1849, "I was always, always outside myself" (x^1 A 8). This feeling of being always *outside*, watching the changes of mood and scene which occur *inside* consciousness, did not abate even during the period of Kierkegaard's engagement. For he will tell us of how he debated again and again the question of whether he should be engaged, of whether he should marry, while all the time his fiancée was sitting on the couch beside him! (x^5 A 150.4). He was, he tells us, "a lover with an artificial leg" who could not take a single step without reflection.[37] He was "strung a whole tone higher than other men," and never "had to do with the particular, but always with a principle and an idea" (x^1 A 476). As he tells us, "At the best, most people think which girl they ought to marry; I had to think about marriage itself—and so in everything" (x^1 A 476).

Kierkegaard's hyperconsciousness expressed itself not only

in the questioning of general principles but also in the construction
of a series of masks which he employed to shield his real thoughts
and feelings from the world-at-large. In his social relations Kierkegaard always seemed to be playing a role.

> I am a Janus bifrons; with the one face I laugh, with
> the other I weep (II A 662).

> Everyone takes his revenge on the world. Mine consists
> in bearing my care and sorrow shut deep within me, while
> my laughter entertains the crowd (II A 649).

> As I said, it is frightful to think on that life I have
> led in the hidden center of my soul, naturally never a word
> revealed to anyone . . . and that I was able to clothe that
> life with such an outwardly lively and cheerful existence
> . . . (IX A 411).

Kierkegaard was always aware of what he called "the costume of
my deceit," [38] that is, of the mask he interposed between himself
and the world. Hence, when Professor Sibbern writes that he never
knew Kierkegaard to be melancholy,[39] we are to take this to mean
that "the costume" never was a melancholy one. There are always
two Kierkegaards: the smiling aesthete who every evening appears at the *Kongelige Theater* for exactly ten minutes, and the
serious author who turns his back on the footlights and the excited
patter of his friends to return to the empty house at #2 Nytorv.[40]
And what of the life behind the masks lived out in the empty
rooms and corridors of the house on the square? It is not coincidence that both Kierkegaard and his copyist, Levin, describe it
in much the same way. Levin recalls that "it was as if he lived in
a spirit-world [*Aandeverden*]," [41] and in a later self-description
Kierkegaard repeats Levin's phrase.

> There is . . . something ghostly [*Geisteragtigt*] about
> me, which accounts for the fact that noone can put up with
> me who must see me in everyday intercourse and so have a
> real relation to me. Of course in the light *surtout* in which
> I commonly show myself it is different. But at home it will
> be observed that essentially I live in a spirit-world [*Aande-
> verden*] (x² A 3).

In reading these passages we come to feel that Kierkegaard, like his creation Johannes the Seducer, lived in "a world of gauze, lighter, more ethereal, qualitatively different from the actual world" (*E/O*, I, 302). Encased in his reflection, stimulated by a prodigious imagination,[42] it seems at times that Kierkegaard too almost "dwindles away . . . vanishes from reality." At times his physical weakness becomes an embarrassment to the power of his mind. "As a sick man longs to cast off his bandages," he writes in 1845, "so does my healthy spirit long to cast off the body's languor (that sweatstained sultry poultice which is the body and its languor) . . . as a steamship whose machinery is too powerful for its structure: so suffer I" (VI A 103). In reading such entries we feel how accurately Kierkegaard described himself when he wrote of Johannes, "He was not unequal to the pressure of reality; he was not too strong; but this strength was really a sickness" (*E/O*, I, 302). The strength of his consciousness had become a sickness—how accurately this describes the Kierkegaard we have come to know!

Recognizing this strength for the sickness it really is, Kierkegaard struggles under its onslaught. "While I can win every argument," he complains in 1837, "I have a ghost of my own fantasy on my back which I cannot argue away" (II A 607). Often times it seems as if the very power of his consciousness will only serve to quicken the pace with which it tears itself apart. In these entries from his middle years Kierkegaard seems to sense the approach of a disintegrating madness.

> The one thought succeeds the other; just as it is thought and I will write it down, there is a new one—hold it, grasp it—Madness—Insanity! (I A 336).

> Sometimes there is such a tumult in my head, that it feels as though the roof has been lifted off my cranium, then it seems as though the hobgoblins had heaved up a mountain and now are holding a ball therein—God forbid it! (II A 702).

> At particular moments my consciousness is far too roomy . . . ; while at other times it can contract itself together around a single thought. It is now so large that it

hangs loose about me, and several of us could manage with it (II A 549).

My doubt is terrible—nothing can withstand me—it is a cursed hunger; every argument . . . I can gobble up—I run with a speed of 10,000 miles per second through every obstacle (III A 103).

In entries such as these we see Kierkegaard tortured by the power of his own consciousness, and dimly aware of the madness this power threatens. It is the very strength of consciousness which has become a sickness, and which, by shrinking life to the field of vision of an eyeglass, has killed immediacy. "Most people complain that the world is so prosaic," Kierkegaard laments in 1840, "I complain that life is not like a novel where one has hardhearted fathers to battle, maidens' bowers to storm, and convent walls to scale. I have only the pale, bloodless, hard-lived, midnight shapes to struggle with, to which I myself give life and existence" (III A 218). He longs for a world more resistant, more actual, a world less flawed by the volatilizing pressure of consciousness. Most of all, he longs for a world of real *duration*.

VIII. *Temporality*

A ready access to Kierkegaardian temporality may be found in the celebrated "problem of vocation" which no less a critic than Denis de Rougemont feels is the central problem of Kierkegaard's life.[43]

This problem always had a peculiar obstinacy for Kierkegaard. We remember his ponderings at Gilleleje—"what I really lack is to be clear about *what I am to do*." Later on, it recurs as the central problem around which cluster his worries concerning his engagement to Regine. Even later, it takes the form of a quandary in Kierkegaard's mind over whether to retire to a country parsonage or stay on in Copenhagen as an author. If the vocational problem is ever solved by him, it is solved only in his last years when he comes to see himself as the "needed corrective" (x⁴ A 596) who launches an attack upon Christendom in the name of Christianity.

But what concerns us is not the obvious fact that Kierkegaard had difficulty making up his mind about what he should do in life. Rather, we are concerned with the experience of *time* out of which this questioning grew.

This may be seen if we note an early attempt on Kierkegaard's part to solve the vocational problem. In an early journal entry (10 Sept. 1839) he offers the following diagram and commentary.

> Foreboding lies not in the direction of the eye, towards existence (and its future), but in the reflection of vision towards the past, so that by gazing upon that which lies behind (in another sense that which lies ahead) the eye develops a disposition for seeing what lies ahead (in another sense what lies behind).
>
> C ←——————— A ————————→ B
>
> If A is the present time, the time in which we live, and B the future, then it is not by standing at A and turning toward B that I see B; for if I face that way I see nothing; but if C is the past, then it is by turning toward C that I see B
>
> (ii A 558).

If the individual, by intently peering into his past, could discern there his future (his future, that is, as it *should* be), then of course the vocational problem would be solved. But is it this easy? Only four years later, Kierkegaard rejects his early attempt at solution with another entry in his journal.

> It is perfectly true, what philosophy says, that life must be understood backwards. But thereby one forgets the other proposition, that it must be lived forwards. And if one thinks through this proposition it becomes more and more evident that life can never be rightfully understood in time, precisely because at no instant can I find the necessary resting place to understand it—backwards (iv A 164).

The individual cannot come to understand his life by looking backward into the past. For he himself is in time and never reaches a point at which his life is complete. Since life must be "lived forwards," the individual can never forge a union of past and future through understanding.

But note what this means. It means that in asking the question "What am I to do?" Kierkegaard is speaking from a situation in which the temporal continuum is fractured. Paralleling his experience of space as a discontinuous medium, is this experience of time as a continuum fissured on either side of the present moment. His life has been broken, so to speak, in the middle and he looks down on the pieces.

Looking in one direction, he peers toward the darkening horizon of his future. It is so empty of content, so unknown, that he cannot make contact with it. "So it is," he writes in a letter in 1838, "that some people act consistently, while I first manage to find the consistency afterwards. The future I know nothing of; I haven't been able to 'board' the future or even to catch hold of it with the boarding hooks. It is like when a spider, hurling itself down from a fixed point in the continuity of its own production, sees before itself only empty space in which it is not possible to get a foothold." [44] Toward the future there is no continuity, only the black void into which the individual must hurl himself. Facing in this direction Kierkegaard is "alone in the company of the most terrible *possibilities*, which transform even the most frightful *actuality* into a refreshment and relief" (*Point of View*, 70).

Looking in the other direction, he peers down the long corridor of his past, there to discern only the fading image of a child at play. He writes in 1837,

> Sometimes it happens to me that just as I have gone to bed and am about to fall asleep, a cock crows at midnight; it is so unnerving how it can occupy one's imagination. I remember just last night how vividly my childhood memories of Frederiksborg came back to me, where the crowing of the cock announced a new happy day, how I had everything again: the slightly cool morning air, the dew on the grass which prevented me from tumbling about as one would have liked (II A 205).

And the following year at the scene of his childhood memories, in an entry we should recall from an earlier section, he remarks,

> When in this way I stand and look out over the old Røyen estate deep into the Hestehaven . . . —so it seems

that I see myself so vividly as a little boy running around in my green jacket and grey trousers—but sadly I have become older, I cannot *recapture myself*. It is with one's perception of childhood as with one's perception of a beautiful country-side when one rides backwards; one first becomes aware of the beauty in that instant, in the same Now, as it begins to disappear and the single thing that I still have from that happy time is the ability to weep as a child (II A 238).

The image of the child is there, but it seems so hazy, so distant, that the thread of continuity joining it to the present appears all but severed. He can't go home again; he can't recapture himself. As he will write so sadly in the margin of the first entry, "It was not a morning crow, but a *midnight crow*" (II A 206). The only thing he carries from that happy time is "the ability to *weep as a child*."

Looking both forward and backward Kierkegaard can feel only that the continuity of his life has been ruptured on either side of the present moment. He looks back to a past which is no longer, and forward to a future which is not yet. Removed from both, he occupies a moment which is, as it were, wrenched out of time. This moment—isolated, discontinuous, lonely—is the moment of the "dreadful still life" which lies at the very heart of Kierkegaard's existence.

"And when one has lived a half-score years in that dreadful still life," Kierkegaard writes, "so miserable and thin a life, that only so much cream has risen to its top as can be swallowed in a single moment without appearing gluttonous. The beat of that life is too slow for me to march to" (III A 225). In this still life time seems to have slowed, even stopped. Living in this discontinuous moment, Kierkegaard feels himself removed from time itself. In such entries as the following he bears witness to a life which has become frozen, petrified.

At the present time I live like a piece in chess of which the opponent says: that piece cannot be moved—as an idle onlooker, for my time is not yet come (II A 435).

It is frightful the way I have to purchase every day, every hour—and the price is so variable (II A 495).

As the captive animal goes around the cage once each day for the sake of the exercise, or measures the length of the chain; so I measure the length of each day by turning to the thought of death—for the sake of the exercise and to hold out in life.[45]

In these entries we are brought very close to the center of Kierkegaard's existence—an existence which we feel has "run out of time." Kierkegaard speaks at the age of 25 of how he should like to write for a reader "who like me is dead" (II A 690), and during his engagement he remarks that Regine was "as young as a child," while he was "as old as a very old man" (x^5 A 150.7). We recall how, lacking all immediacy, he "never knew the joy of being a child," and we recall too his complaint that "in the ordinary human sense of the word, I have never lived." How true these earlier statements seem to us now. For in an odd way Kierkegaard's experience *does* seem to be the experience of a dead man; it *does* seem to be the experience of a man about whom there was always "something ghostly." Existing in a discontinuous moment, he lacks a sense of personal *duration*. His life-thread snapped in the middle, he exists in a moment which has exploded to fill all time, and in so doing has become atemporal. For him time has slowed and stopped; it has backed up and become stagnant, just as a stream backs up and becomes stagnant behind a dam.

I feel so dead and joyless, my soul is so empty and void that I cannot conceive what could satisfy it (III A 54).

My head is as empty and dead as a theater after the performance is over (III A 224).

It seems as though I were a galley slave, linked together with death; every time life stirs itself, the chain rattles and death withers everything—*and that happens every minute* (II A 647).

I am so tired that it seems to me I should require an eternity to rest in; so troubled that it seems I should require an eternity to forget my sorrow; I wish that I could sleep so long that I would wake up an old man, so as again to lie down and sleep into eternity (IV A 221).

With the cessation of time there has come too the congealing of the life-flow, the onset of winter and of death. The world has become "*idem per idem*" [46]—stale, flat, and inexpressibly weary. It has become the world of the square and of discontinuity—the world of crystalline forms, death, and petrifaction. The frost of a Scandinavian winter has entered the soul presaging its death. "All the flowers of my heart," writes Kierkegaard, "turn to ice flowers" (II A 641).

IX. The Lonely Labyrinth

Franz Welding, one of Kierkegaard's childhood schoolmates, remembers him in these words.

> He went his own way, almost self-isolated . . . For us others, who knew and lived a more genuine boy's life, SK was a stranger [*en Fremmed*] and an object of pity . . . SK lived his schooltime in silence and, so it seemed, without joy . . . and thereby he became even more strange [*end mere Fremmed*] and without connection with the rest of us.[47]

We may disagree about whether Kierkegaard is a pitiable figure, but it seems difficult indeed to disagree with Welding's judgement that "SK was a stranger." For Kierkegaard himself remarked in 1848 that "I feel myself to be a stranger [*fremmed*] among my contemporaries," [48] and all our research thus far only serves to reenforce this judgement. Like Quidam of the *Stages*, Kierkegaard seems always "a lost wayfarer" who "has come into a strange land where the people talk a different language and have other customs" (*Stages*, 290).

Yet surely it is no exaggeration to point out that in this "lost wayfarer" most of us will recognize aspects of ourselves. For Kierkegaard's estrangement is not the estrangement of the psychotic who seems ever to inhabit a universe beyond our ken. On the contrary, his estrangement, his "sickness" if you will, is familiar to us. His world—though sharpened, attenuated, more intense—seems nevertheless to be our world. His sufferings—though more lacerating and more openly revealed—seem our sufferings. In Kierkegaard's sickness we detect resonances of the universally human. Why?

Is it not because we recognize behind Kierkegaard's sickness and his attempts at cure the very struggles of *human consciousness with itself?* Is it not because we recognize in his struggles echoes of our own?

Buried at the heart of Kierkegaard's struggle toward health lies hidden a subtle truth concerning the dialectic of consciousness with itself. His struggle is not an idiosyncratic one, nor is his sickness a peculiarity for the shelf of psychopathology. His struggle and his sickness have rather a universal basis, springing up as they do from the mere fact of being conscious. Kierkegaard's struggle is with no less an adversary than consciousness itself, for it is finally consciousness which supplies both the source of his estrangement as well as the pressure to overcome it. His awareness of the world as alien and "infected" is only one specification of that more general distinction between self and world which is necessary to consciousness. For what is the state of "being conscious" if it is not this distinction between subject and object, self and world? And what finally supports this distinction other than the mere awareness of it? Thus the estrangement Kierkegaard feels is only an intensification of one term of the dialectic of consciousness—of that fissure between self and world which consciousness requires.

Nor is the other term of the dialectic absent from the Kierkegaardian landscape. For hovering always in the background of the distinction between self and world is a pressure toward reconciliation, an "insistence upon familiarity." [49] It is precisely this pressure which motivated Kierkegaard's turn away from an "infected" world and informed his exploration of the world he found within. Here in the interior world of consciousness the alien did not intrude. Here he could roam at will among his ideas and memories. They were *his*, totally *his*, and were not tainted by the outside and the "other." Here behind the many masks, exploring the bends and turnings of his own psyche, Kierkegaard felt he could remain—alone and happy.

We should not underestimate the price Kierkegaard paid in yielding to this pressure. For it was precisely by retiring into the hermetic world of consciousness, that he made his exit from time into the wintry world described in the last section. By so retiring he assured the death of the tenses, that fatal splaying of the present moment. Superimposed upon the vital experience of the moment came consciousness of that experience. Watching always only "in order to see himself watch," the outline of the present moment of experience blurred. It dissolved under the gaze of a presence from beyond which never joined with that moment. Consciousness was not the present, nor the past (only remembered *in* consciousness), nor the future (only awaited *in* consciousness). It was always beyond: watching, remembering, waiting. Beyond the tenses it was also removed from time itself. Under its stare Kierkegaard's sense of personal duration withered and died. He came to feel "as a chessman must when the opponent says: that piece cannot be moved."

The void of space which Kierkegaard turned away from in the world now returned to haunt him in a doubly agonizing way. For he had become somehow "too strong" for the pressure of reality, and this strength only served to exacerbate his sickness. His consciousness itself became "far too roomy," and he had only to do with its "pale, bloodless, hard-lived midnight shapes." The void had become a part of consciousness itself, and with its entrance had come the threat of a disintegrating madness. Yet even greater than the abyss which had opened around the periphery of consciousness in the threat of madness, was the abyss which had opened at its core. For Kierkegaard came to feel at the very heart of his existence a deadening—a growing paralysis which had to do with his total inability ever to really *be* in any given moment. Always conscious, he could never join with the present moment. There was an emptiness, a void, at the very center of his existence which made him feel "as empty and dead as a theater after the performance is over." He was inured in the world of the square. Here the texture of life was "simply nothing, a mood, a single color . . . always the same, an *idem per idem*. No variety, always a rehash!" (*E/O*, I, 28–29). By retiring within Kierkegaard had only assured the entrance of the void into his own heart where it would turn all its flowers to ice flowers.

Existence in this wintry world would not have been so agonizing for Kierkegaard were it not for his awareness that consciousness could be vanquished. In those few brief moments of continuity the total deficiency of the present moment had been overcome; at one with the world, he had felt no longer a stranger. The memory of these moments was to pursue Kierkegaard throughout his life. "The terrible thing about the total spiritual incapacity from which I suffer," he wrote in 1840, "is precisely that it is coupled with a consuming longing, with a spiritual passion" (III A 56). Beyond the horizon of his wintry world, Kierkegaard senses the promise of summer.

Hast thou gone on ahead, thou my *longing*, dost thou beckon to me transformed from another world? (II A 347).

Faith is the anticipation of the eternal which holds the factors together, the cleavages of existence . . . (VII¹ A 139).

Poetically speaking, immediacy is what one wants to return to (one wants childhood back again, etc.), but Christianly speaking, immediacy is lost and shall not be *wished* back again, but shall be attained once more (VIII¹ A 643).

Presentiment is the homesickness of earthly life for something higher, for the *perception* which man must have had in Paradise (II A 191).

Father in Heaven! As a father sends his child out into the world, so has Thou placed an individual here on the earth; he is separated from Thee as by a world (VII¹ A 136).

The world of the square only stands *between* Kierkegaard and the world of the circle. We are separated from Thee, O God, "as by a world"; immediacy *is* to be attained once more; presentiment is the homesickness of earthly life for the *perception* of Paradise: with such statements Kierkegaard points to the transfigured world lying beyond winter which beckons to him in the distance. Once he had felt its closeness, only to see it vanish. But no matter, he will break through to it again; he will discover it once more. Out of this nostalgia begins an authorship which is at base a kind of personal quest, a voyage of rediscovery. "Faith," "repetition," "the ethical act": What are these but different names for the same moment of discovery?—that moment when the walls of consciousness are sundered, and a sense of fulfillment, of continuity, breaks through.

The vision of Kierkegaard we take with us is then a poignant one. He is a stranger, "a lost wayfarer," who "has come into a strange land where the people talk a different language and have other customs." Installed in this world he nostalgically longs for the other world which lies always just over the horizon. There is poignancy in this vision of Kierkegaard wandering the lonely labyrinth of the self, tormented by a void both without and within, trying to rediscover the path which leads out of the labyrinth, the opening which leads outwards from the world of the square to the world of the circle beyond. In succeeding chapters we shall view some of these attempts at exit.

3

PREPARATIONS

1. *Forward or Backward?*

Scattered here and there through the twenty volumes of
Papirer we find prayers composed by Kierkegaard for his own use.
Written with a candor and immediacy lacking in the more literary
entries, they are often intensely revealing. Consider the following
example written on August 16, 1839.

> Father in Heaven! Avert Thy countenance from me no
> longer, let it once again shine upon me so that I may walk
> in Thy path, and not lose myself farther and farther from
> Thee, where Thy voice can no longer reach me. Oh, let
> Thy voice sound for me, be heard by me, even though it
> come upon me with terror on the wrong path, where I live
> isolated and alone, as though sick and besmirched, far from
> communion with Thee and mankind . . . Thou, the good
> shepherd, let me hear Thy gentle voice, let me know it, let
> me follow it (II A 538).

Sounding through the lines of this prayer we detect the voice of
the Kierkegaard we have come to know in the last chapter. Here
once again is the "lost wayfarer" wandering the labyrinthine ways
of the self. Out of the depth of his lostness he prays for deliverance, to be shown the way back.

The word "back" is not idly used here. For often during
these years it seemed to Kierkegaard as if the way out of the

labyrinth in some curious way did lie *back*. It was as if he had left the world of the circle *behind* him, and that his task now was to retrace his steps. In 1839, for example, he likens his own life-situation to the lost state of a traveler who must find his way back along the way he has come. "So it is as one experiences when going for a walk," he writes, "that when one has reached the destination and once again must go *back* the same way, the whole country appears quite different, and how much more so in the world of the spirit where no exterior landmarks are set outside oneself, and where the whole thing depends upon the working out of one's thoughts" (II A 515). This theme of lostness and return is a familiar one in the journal entries of the late 1830's. In 1836 Kierkegaard observes that "one has to go back along the same road where previously one went forward" (I A 174), and the following year he points out,

> One must run back along the same road one has come, just as magic first ceases when the musical piece (the Elf-King piece) . . . is played back exactly in the reverse direction (II A 65).

All these entries reveal Kierkegaard aware of his lostness and looking back over his shoulder toward a salvation to be found by somehow retracing his steps.

What Kierkegaard saw when he looked back over his shoulder, of course, is not difficult to discover. It is the image of a child at play. It is that "little boy running around in green jacket and grey trousers" who awoke early on a summer morning to "the crowing of a cock [which] announced a new happy day." It is to this remembrance of childhood in all its immediacy that the "road back" leads. "Thus in deep sadness," Kierkegaard remarks in 1839, "the mind often turns back to the reality of childhood, threadbare though it be, and dead to the world wraps itself in it as in a shroud" (II A 174).

Yet as we saw in the last chapter, in the very moment when the innocence and freshness of childhood stands out in all its vividness, in that same moment Kierkegaard realizes the impossibility of ever returning to it. As he tells us so unequivocally in the entry mentioned above, "I cannot *recapture myself* . . . the single thing that I have from that happy time is the ability to *weep as a child.*" And Kierkegaard also recognized quickly enough that Christian salvation is not just another name for the immediacy of childhood, "Poetically speaking, immediacy is what one wants to return to (one wants childhood back again, etc.), but Christianly speaking, immediacy is lost and shall not be *wished* back again, but shall be attained once more." This desire to escape from the labyrinth by retracing one's steps backward to the immediacy of childhood is for Kierkegaard no more than a *wish*—a *wish*, which in the very moment of its utterance, he recognizes to be an impossibility.

But if the way backward turns out to be no more than a wishful remembrance, there may yet be another way—another escape from the deadly still life of consciousness. We recall Kierkegaard's resolve in 1835 "to hurry along the path I have discovered," to discover that "which grows together with the deepest roots of my life," the idea "for which I can live and die." Here at least is a resolve to move in another direction, to set off (dare we say forwards?) on a quest which would culminate in the discovery of a new kind of truth—a "truth which is true for me." But where does this path lie? Along what way can this truth be found? And when found, what shape will it take? In those years in the late 1830's before Kierkegaard's serious authorship began he was asking himself these questions and probing towards an answer. He finally found it in the notion of the "life-view" (*Livs-Anskuelse*).

II. *Livs-Anskuelse*

In any story of Kierkegaard's intellectual development, one of the most interesting parts will always be his fascination with the world of magic and fairy tales. We pointed out in the last chapter how at his death 64 volumes of folk tales and sagas were found in his library, and noted too the relaxation he never ceased to find in the "renewing bath" of fairy tales. It was not only diversion, however, which Kierkegaard drew from his reading of folk literature and tales of magic, for in a very real sense his whole outlook on life as a young man was sewn from its fabric. It is no exaggeration to say that, at the beginning of his authorship, he held what is essentially a "magical" view of life.

We can see certain glints of this view in the famous Gilleleje entry cited so often in the preceding pages. Recall now the language in which Kierkegaard formulates his life-project, "it is a question of *finding* a truth which is true for me; of *finding* the idea for which I can live and die" [italics mine]. The idea of *finding* this curious "truth" seems vaguely reminiscent of those folk tales in which the hero must *find* the magic talisman—the key which opens the secret door or the phrase which solves the terrible riddle. This impression is strengthened by Kierkegaard's admission (at another point in the same entry) of his admiration for "those great men who have *found* the precious stone for the sake of which they sell all, even their lives" [italics mine]. In an entry written just three days earlier, he remarks,

> Lucky is the man [who] . . . has *found* what the great philosopher—who by his calculations was able to destroy the enemy's engines of war—desired but did not find: that Archimedean point from which he could lift the whole world, the point which for that reason must lie outside the world, outside the limitations of time and space.
>
> (1 A 68; italics mine)

It is not insignificant that at just this time Kierkegaard begins speaking of life as a "riddle"—as a puzzle whose solution can be found. "Life has interested me most in virtue of reason and freedom," he writes in a letter dated June 1, 1835, "and to elucidate and solve the riddle of life [*Livets Gaade*] has always been my desire" (1 A 72). Nor was this view of life as a "riddle" [*Gaade*] only a passing fancy, for in a journal entry written a year and a half later he will use the same phrase in remarking, "I want to go into a madhouse and see whether the profoundity of madness will not solve the riddle of life [*Livets Gaade*] for me" (1 A 333). Still another aspect of this magical life-outlook is illustrated by a journal entry of a few years later. In quoting Herodotus he notes,

> When one has one thought, but an infinite one, then one can be borne through the whole of life, light and flying, like the hyperborean Abaris, who, borne by an arrow, traveled round the whole world (IV A 21).

The picture of the youthful Kierkegaard painted by these passages is a characteristic one. He seems to stand before life as before a magic door whose key is missing. Life is a "riddle" whose solution can be found. There is a "precious stone," a magic talisman which gives one the peace of mind to risk everything. There is a standpoint, an "Archimedean point," outside the bounds of time and space, from which position the individual can metaphorically "lift the whole world." Behind all these statements lies the presumption that something can be *found* which will transform life. Fundamentally, this a *magical* view, a view woven out of the fabric of those stories in which the hero *finds* the mysterious key, the enchanted elixir which cures the sickness, the magic word whose discovery removes all difficulties. It is against the background of this *magical* view that Kierkegaard develops the crucial notion of the "life-view" [*Livs-Anskuelse*].

In Danish the term *Livs-Anskuelse* has the fairly straightforward meaning of an "outlook on life," a "philosophy of life," a "life-view." When later in *Either/Or* Kierkegaard chooses to define the term as "a conception of life's significance and purpose" (E/O, I, 184), it is this more ordinary meaning he has in mind. But this brief definition gives no indication of how Kierkegaard's use of the term finds its genesis in the *magical* view sketched above. It is the "life-view" which becomes the final name for the mysterious and transforming "something" described above.

The notion of the "life-view" plays an important role in Kierkegaard's first published work, a minor essay in literary criticism entitled, *From the Papers of One Still Living*. Published on September 7, 1838, it is a sustained assault on Hans Christian Andersen as a novelist. Yet for our purposes, its main interest lies in the way Kierkegaard attacked Andersen. For Kierkegaard's chief complaint is that Andersen lacked a "life-view," and that thereby his work was without either depth or purpose. In a long passage Kierkegaard gives a persuasive explanation of what he means.

> A life-view [*Livs-Anskuelse*] is more than an essence or a sum of propositions, held fast in its abstract impersonality; it is more than experience, which as such is always atomic; it is, to wit, the transubstantiation of experience, it is a con-

quest over all empirical standpoints, an unshakable certainty in oneself . . . If we are now asked how such a life-view can be acquired, then we reply that for him who does not let his life be frittered away, but so far as possible seeks to trace all its particular manifestations back again to a source in himself, to such a man there must come the moment in which a curious light spreads out over life. This does not in the least demand that one has understood all the possible details in life (to whose successive understanding, however, one has the key). Yet may I reiterate that there *does* come this moment when, as Daub remarks, life is understood backwards through the idea.[1]

Kierkegaard's mention here of "the moment in which a curious light spreads out over life" will not escape our attention. This once again is the "moment of continuity," that nodule instant when consciousness is transformed, and the individual feels himself reconciled with both the world and time.

A few years later, in reviewing the work of another author, Kierkegaard once again employs the notion of the life-view as a critical tool. After outlining the life-view of the author he is considering, he remarks,

Every life-view knows the way out, and can easily be identified by which way out it knows. The poet knows fantasy's way out . . . , the religious person knows the religious way out. The life-view is the way out. . . .[2]

How fitting the notion here expressed of the life-view as a "way out" is to our metaphor of the labyrinth, finding a life-view now becomes identified with finding one's way from the world of the square to the world of the circle. In the moment when the life-view is attained, in this moment a light breaks over existence, signalling one's entrance into a transfigured world.

Although these passages illustrate in what ways Kierkegaard interprets the life-view as an agent of transformation, they do not directly indicate the truly *magical* identity of this curious notion. This identification, however, is made in a journal entry from the year 1839.

There is a life-view which is acquired through tears; but which is stronger than iron, like the shirt: "wenn sie ihn unter Thränen spinnt, mit Thränen bleicht, ein Hemde draus unter Thränen näht, schützt mich dis [sic] besser als alles Eisen, es ist undurchdringlich." But this life-view protects only he who himself has forged it, not like that shirt—anyone.

    cfr. magyarische Sagen v. Graf Mailath, p. 152, n.

    (II A 449).

The reference at the end is to one of the volumes of folk tales which Kierkegaard owned,[3] and it is revealing that he should speak of the life-view against such a background. For truly such a notion of a life-view which "protects" does find its rightful home in the world of magic. Such a life-view is only the last in a series of names for the "infinite idea" which bears one through the whole of life light and flying, for the solution to "life's riddle," for the "truth which is true for me." All of these notions, predicated on the possibility of a radical transformation of life, are sewn from a fabric of folk tale and magic. But if the fabric out of which these notions are sewn is a magical one, the needle itself is not. For we have seen that this marvelous life-view must be forged by the individual who will use it, and an earlier passage has indicated that this forging is essentially an intellectual activity: a "tracing" of all life's "particular manifestations back to a source in oneself." It was perhaps the intellectual side of the quest which Kierkegaard had in mind when he remarked in his journal.

    I have too good a head not to feel the labor of knowledge and too bad a head not to feel its blessedness.—And the knowledge which leads to blessedness, and the blessedness which leads to the knowledge of the truth have hitherto both been to me a secret (III A 44).

How accurately this last passage summarizes Kierkegaard's whole view of life as a young man. He desires knowledge, not because knowledge in itself is desirable, but because it leads to blessedness. This blessedness however is a "secret"; life is a "riddle"; the "truth which is true for me" must still be found. And so Kierkegaard stands before the "unfound door" (to quote Thomas Wolfe),[4] seeking a key, a magic talisman, a "solution" to "life's riddle," a unique life-view which protects.

Note now the pattern which is being set up by this discussion. Like Plato in his image of the cave, Kierkegaard seems to have in mind a structure of two radically distinct conscious worlds linked by an intellectual-spiritual activity. Within the cave are those who have found no life-view. For them no truth can be found, since they are even unaware of the existence of such a truth. But for those who care to risk it, Kierkegaard seems to be saying, there is a "way out." Through a process of self-exploration one can, so to speak, "locate" oneself within existence. By probing one's own life-view one comes to see it in relation to other views, and in this way one is enabled to find that quite singular life-view which transfigures consciousness. Bathed in the "curious light" of this view, all of existence seems changed; one has an "unshakeable certainty in oneself"; one has the "key" to all the innumerable details of life. Existence has become poetry.

This then is Kierkegaard's notion of the life-view—a strange amalgam of intellect and magic. It becomes for Kierkegaard the way out to the world of the circle which always beckoned in the distance, and in this role it shares an identity with the "truth which is true for me." The search for this truth and the search for the life-view which "protects" are indeed the same search; the search for that renewal of consciousness which Kierkegaard knew in those scattered moments of bliss. But now we might ask, how was this search carried on? How did Kierkegaard actually go about finding the unique life-view which would be a "way out?" To find the answer to this question we must turn once again to the *Papirer*.

III. *"Practice Behind the Scenes"*

During the years which separate the Gilleleje entry from the beginning of Kierkegaard's serious authorship (say from 1835 to 1842), his mind was not empty nor his pen idle. On the contrary, he was using these years to fill his notebooks with what he called, in 1837, a kind of "practice behind the scenes." "Practice of this sort, behind the scenes," he wrote, "is no doubt necessary for every person who is not so gifted that his development is in a sense public" (II A 118).

The material from these years fills over 900 pages in the

present Danish edition, and essentially, it is of two distinct types. There are, first of all, autobiographical reflections and lyrical effusions of the type we surveyed in the last chapter. These form perhaps one third of the total, leaving the bulk of the material to be made up of what Danish critics call *Studier* [5]—that is, "studies" which trace out an idea or question in any number of fields. It is in these studies that Kierkegaard makes his first probing steps toward finding that life-view which would be a "way out" for him, and it is upon them that our examination will now focus.

The studies which Kierkegaard undertook during this period are of great variety. At this time, he was nominally a student of theology, and hence we have a number of exercises in biblical exegesis as well as discussions of comparative religion.[6] Yet the greater part of these studies lie in the aesthetic sphere, there are studies of figures in European folk literature such as the Master-Thief,[7] Don Juan,[8] Faust,[9] and Ahasuerus; [10] there are studies of the differences between such aesthetic categories as "irony" [11] and "humor"; [12] finally, there are even studies of plays Kierkegaard saw at the Royal Theater.[13] As one reads these studies, however, it becomes increasingly evident that a certain pattern runs through all of them. Under the jumble of ideas, aphorisms, and reflections one senses the presence of a single motivating purpose.

In an entry for January 2, 1838, Kierkegaard imagines a person with a rather unusual life-outlook. The details of this outlook are not important, but what is important is a parenthetical comment Kierkegaard makes in regard to it. He remarks, ". . . and it is only that it contains a life-view which makes it interesting . . ." (II A 683). This may seem like an insignificant comment, but it is crucial to an understanding of these studies. For what gives them their unity is the fact that they are all attempts by Kierkegaard to isolate different life-views as preparatory to finding that singular life-view discussed in the last section. In them we see Kierkegaard knocking on different doors, inspecting different consciousnesses—different life-views, or better, different "life-worlds" [14]—in hopes of finding that one which "protects." This is made apparent in a great number of ways.

One would have thought that a theological student would have been more interested in the niceties of theological argument, than in comparisons of Christianity with other views. But this is not the case with Kierkegaard. In a remark pregnant for the future, he compares Christianity with philosophy, "Philosophy's idea is Mediation—Christianity's, the Paradox." [15] He compares Christianity with Paganism.

> [In the myth] that everyone arriving at Elysium must drink of Lethe, the Pagan world set aside a coming existence for the present one; the Christian view teaches that man shall be held responsible for every unjustifiable word, which among other things is to be understood to presuppose the total presence of the past.[16]

He even compares "religion" (and here he means Christianity) with the life-views represented by Don Juan, Faust, and Ahasuerus.

> The three great ideas (Don Juan, Faust, and the Eternal Jew) represent, so to speak, life outside religion in its threefold direction . . . (ı A 151).

In contrasting Christianity against this wide field, it is evident that Kierkegaard is not interested in Christianity as a body of dogma, but rather in what he calls "the Christian life-view." [17] It is the Christian life as lived from within, as a viable life-option for himself, which interests Kierkegaard, and not a framework of propositions.

This same interest in *life-view* can be found in other studies from this period. As we mentioned before, Kierkegaard often compared the aesthetic categories "irony" and "humor." But note now that they are compared not as aesthetic categories but as alternative life-views. "Humor," he writes, "is also the joy which has won a victory over the world" (ıı A 672), and "the Humorist like the wild animal always walks alone" (ıı A 694). Irony is "aristocratic," while "humor is reconciled with the whole of existence" (ııı B 20). It should be evident from these brief remarks that Kierkegaard is not thinking of irony and humor as different literary rubrics, but rather as each exemplifying a definite way of confronting the world. The so-called "three great ideas" mentioned above likewise are not unusual folk-literature curiosities, but each represents a definite life-view. Don Juan is the immediate life—the pure sensualist; Faust personifies the life of doubt, and Ahasuerus the life of despair.[18] As such it is the life-view they represent, or rather as Kierkegaard pointed out above, the fact that they do represent a life-view, which makes them objects of interest.

These studies become for Kierkegaard the laboratory in which a great number of different life-views are sorted and analyzed. During these years he often comes to resemble a collector of rare specimens in the natural sciences. Now he journeys into literature to bring back a fine specimen of one of the standard species. Now he makes a short excursion to the Bible to acquire a particular variety of the religious genus. Now he treks into the never-never land of his own imagination to bring back a truly unique specimen. And like any collector his activity has two main parts. First, he must isolate the specimen. Second, he must order it in a schema with other specimens.

To isolate different life-views Kierkegaard uses the device of contrast. As we saw above, Christianity is contrasted with philosophy, Paganism with "the three great ideas." Moreover, Faust is isolated by contrasting his life-view with that of Don Juan,[19] and both views are contrasted with the despair of Ahasuerus.[20] Further afield, the Christian view is contrasted with the Greek Weltanschauung on a number of different points,[21] and as we saw, both humor and irony are illuminated by being contrasted with each other. In this way, by using one life-view as a foil to the other Kierkegaard succeeds in isolating the outstanding features of each. This technique will serve him well in later years.

Nor is contrast the only technique employed by Kierkegaard in isolating and investigating different life-views. Israel Levin speaks of the ease with which Kierkegaard could "poeticize himself into any existence," [22] and the Papirer abounds in examples of the use to which Kierkegaard put this imaginative facility.

In 1835 he had been reading about a hero in folk literature called "the Master-Thief." Simply the mention of the name was sufficient to set off his prodigious imagination. He begins creating imaginary situations involving the Master-Thief (1 A 15–18): He is loved by a virtuous girl who would reform him, but is too afraid of his violent moods to say anything. He loses his father at an early age, leaves home, and then many years later cheers his old mother with a visit. Kierkegaard goes on to imaginatively insinuate himself into the consciousness of the Master-Thief. He imagines an occasion when the robber band is celebrating a successful raid. Their leader wanders off by himself. "For the Master-Thief," Kierkegaard writes, "the long depression manifests itself, a definitely melancholic trait, an isolation [*Indesluttethed*] in himself, a dark intuition of the life-circumstances, an inner discontent" (1 A 18).

Again and again during this period we watch Kierkegaard worm his way into the consciousness of another. Once he imagines a man who had no recollection of childhood, who yet in teaching children "comes to discover the meaning of childhood, and reproduces a childhood of his own" (11 A 683). He goes on to imagine what this man might think of, and even supposes how a certain melody might affect him. In reading this entry we are astonished by the extent to which Kierkegaard has become his imaginary creation. He has so successfully created the whole life-world of his character that it often seems he has assumed his very identity. In this way, we often gain the impression that Kierkegaard is "trying on" different life-views, much as an actor might "try on" different costumes. By imaginatively installing himself in this or that life-view, Kierkegaard comes to see clearly what it involves—comes to understand what it must feel like to live this life-view from *within*.

Kierkegaard is interested not only in isolating different life-views, but also in seeing how they are dynamically related, and he makes several attempts to schematize them. Don Juan, Faust, and Ahasuerus are all seen as being not only *different* from the religious life-view, but as also *preparatory* to it. The complete entry takes this form.

> The three great ideas (Don Juan, Faust, and the Eternal Jew) represent, so to speak, life outside religion in its three-fold direction, and only as these ideas are merged in the individual and become mediate, only then does the moral and the religious appear; this is my view of these three ideas in relation to my dogmatic standpoint (1 A 151).

And the "three great ideas" themselves seem to be internally related to each other. Kierkegaard remarks at one point that "it is interesting that Faust (whom I perhaps more rightly put in a third standpoint than in the more immediate one) includes in himself both Don Juan and the Eternal Jew (Despair)" (1 C 58). This particular schema was perhaps only tentative,[23] but it indicates Kierkegaard's interest in finding what relations obtain between alternative life-views. This interest is best exemplified by a long entry from 1837. Entitled "Something about the Page in Figaro; Papageno in The Magic Flute, and Don Juan," it outlines the same development which is later charted in the first volume of Either/Or. The first paragraph accurately summarizes the entry.

> For the first time I shall see this evening The Magic Flute which has appeared to me as necessarily having significance with respect to Don Juan, and to fill in a state between him and the Page in Figaro. Namely, I believe that Mozart in these three stages has consummately presented a love-development in its immediate standpoint (1 C 125).

Here we find one of the first uses of the term "stage" [Stadium] by Kierkegaard, and it is perhaps significant that in talking of the deficiencies and contradictions which arise in Don Juan's life-view, he remarks, "Through that contradiction appears the importance of the married life." Since the very next entry is an unusual one entitled, "Something on Life's Four Stages," it is likely that the schematism of "stages on life's way" was already becoming clear to Kierkegaard as he sorted and ordered the various life-views which interested him.

It is upon this crucial point of interest that the analogy breaks down between the natural scientist collecting his specimens and Kierkegaard collecting his life-views. For the natural scientist's study is disinterested, while Kierkegaard's is interested. All specimens have an equal right to the attention of the natural scientist, while Kierkegaard is attentive only to those which promise an exit from the labyrinth, a cure for his sickness. Kierkegaard's researches are hence limited by his interest, while the natural scientist's enjoy an unrestricted field. But there is an even more important difference between the two. For while the natural scientist always stands outside his researches, in a very curious way Kierkegaard himself becomes the focus of his researches. The motivating force behind Kierkegaard's work is always an interest in his own existence, and we have seen how this interest becomes finally an interest in his own *healthy* existence. Hence, we should not be surprised in finding that Kierkegaard's own existence has become a part of the field of investigation. For therapy requires diagnosis, and diagnosis requires a thorough examination of the patient. In a later work Kierkegaard will observe that "the individual has a multiplicity of shadows, all of which resemble and for the moment have an equal claim to be accounted himself" (*Repetition*, 43). It should come as no surprise to us, then, that in these studies Kierkegaard has exhibited several of these "shadows."

There is certainly more than a shadow of Kierkegaard in the figure of the Master-Thief, that lonely misanthrope who felt such "an isolation [*Indesluttethed*] in himself, a dark intuition of the life-circumstances, an inner discontent." For often in the future Kierkegaard will use this same word—*Indesluttethed*—to describe his own mental state.[24] Then too there is the haunting figure of the schoolteacher who came to recognize the significance of childhood only through his teaching of children. How often have we heard Kierkegaard complain similarly about his lack of a proper childhood, he, who at this very time, was teaching Latin at the *Borgerdydskole!* [25] Yet the remarkable dual focus of Kierkegaard's search—the way it looks both outward at a definite life-view, and inward at Kierkegaard himself—is best seen if we look at some of the studies he carried out in detail—Don Juan, Faust, and Ahasuerus, for example.

Kierkegaard remarks in 1839, "In a way I can say of Don Juan what Donna Elvira says to him: 'Thou murderer of my happiness . . .' For in truth this is the play which has so diabolically grasped me that I can never more forget it; this is the piece that drove me, like Elvira, out of the still night of the cloister" (II A 491). He does not have merely a scholarly interest in Don Juan, but the character—and the opera which bore its name—have touched him deeply. As one Danish critic suggests, Don Juan, as the incarnation of immediacy and the sensual, may be identified in Kierkegaard's mind with both the immediacy of childhood for which he longs, and with his youthful infatuation for Regine.[26] Kierkegaard stands fascinated before Don Juan, viewing in him a region of his own psyche which had atrophied at birth. In trying as he does to place the life-view of Don Juan in relation to other views, he tries to locate himself vis à vis Don Juan. Has he advanced beyond Don Juan's stage, or will he never reach it? What is the source of Don Juan's immediate health? In trying to understand Don Juan, Kierkegaard also is trying to understand himself.

Faust is a more ambiguous figure. On the one hand Kierkegaard did see in Faust the suggestion of a possible way out for himself. In his journal for the year 1837, for example, he speaks in two adjoining entries of Faust's desire "to know evil . . . , to feel all the floodgates of sin opening within his own heart" (II A 605), and of his own desire "to give myself to Satan so that he might show me every abomination, every sin in its most frightful form" (II A 603). This romantic facet of the Faust figure, the idea (as Kierkegaard will note in another entry) of "coming to know the world through sin," [27] did indeed attract him. Yet there was another side of Faust which meant something else to Kierkegaard. He stood for a factor of hesitation, a thoroughgoing doubt, which Kierkegaard knew in his own person. Already in 1835 he is using Faust as a screen for talking about himself. In a letter to P. W. Lund he describes his inability to commit himself to a definite lifework, and identifies this with "the Faustean element which to a greater or lesser degree asserts itself in every intellectual development" (I A 72). And two years later he remarks to an imagined friend, "I told you the other day about an idea for a Faust, now for the first time I feel *it was myself* I was describing" (I A 333). The reason Kierkegaard studied the figure of Faust so intensely was that he recognized so much of himself in the legendary doctor. If he could understand Faust, if he could locate him in the scheme of possible life-views, then perhaps he could come to some understanding of his own situation.

The figure of Ahasuerus probably stands closer to the center of Kierkegaard's mental landscape than all the others. This pitiful figure doomed by Christ to spend eternity wandering an alien world is the perfect exemplar of that frozen, timeless world Kierkegaard knew so well. In 1835 he described Ahasuerus in words from Hoffmann's *Meister Floh* as, "the Eternal Jew who wandered through the gay tumult of the world without joy, without hope, without pain, in dull indifference, which is the *caput mortuum of* despair, as though through a dreary and disconsolate desert" (1 C 60). How closely this description of Ahasuerus' sufferings parallels Kierkegaard's own. For Kierkegaard himself complained, in words reminiscent of Ahasuerus, that his life too was "a retreat through desolate and devastated provinces . . . a retreat as slow as a bad year, long as an eternity monotonously broken by the sound of the complaint: these days please me not" (II A 420). In Ahasuerus, Kierkegaard had found a fellow sufferer, a fellow creature who had full acquaintance with that "dreadful still life" of which he speaks. In coming to understand Ahasuerus he could come to understand himself; in understanding Ahasuerus' situation, he could perhaps come to understand his own. And with luck, this understanding might give a clue to the direction in which salvation lay.

These studies are then both colored and limited by the interest which Kierkegaard brought to them. A driving urgency to find an exit from the labyrinth, a surcease from suffering, gives to all of them a kind of unity. In them Kierkegaard is carrying out the search we postulated in the last section, a search the outstanding characteristics of which should by now be apparent.

It is a search with a double focus.

On the one hand, it looks outward to the various life-views which crossed Kierkegaard's path. In focusing his attention on these views Kierkegaard seeks to isolate and thereby comprehend each specimen that catches his fancy. By contrasting one life-view with another he hopes to define more clearly the characteristics of each, and by imaginatively installing himself in one or another view he hopes to trace its fullest implications for the person who holds it. Yet in addition to simply isolating the several views, Kierkegaard also desires to see how they are related. For perhaps the quite singular view he seeks may only be reached by passing through other views, and hence only by tracing the relations between views can he be led to it. On this obvious level then, the search is an outward-directed canvassing of alternative life-views. But as we saw, it also has another level and another focus.

For in exploring some of these life-views Kierkegaard is also exploring the "multiplicity of shadows" which constitutes his own person. He is fascinated by the Master-Thief, Don Juan, Ahasuerus, and Faust not principally because they constitute ways out for him, but rather because they are all, in different ways, shadows of himself. By understanding them, by seeing where they stand in respect to each other and in relation to still other life-views, he hopes to come to understand himself—this "understanding" being equivalent to a comprehension of that "to others unknown and incomprehensible suffering" which is his life. By determining which of these "shadows" has more of a claim "to be accounted himself," Kierkegaard hoped to comprehend both his own identity and the character of his sickness. For it is only through such knowledge that he will be able to know in what direction cure lies. The doctor must diagnose before he prescribes, and when doctor and patient share the same identity this only means that self-diagnosis must precede self-cure. In this way the search takes on an inward focus as the healer and patient, searcher and searched, become one.

IV. *Deflections*

By the late 1830's the outlines of Kierkegaard's quest were visible. In the dual conviction that there were alternative life-views and that an individual could move between them, the vague notion of the "path" he mentioned in 1835 had taken on form and content. In examining different life-views as he came upon them in literature, in daily life, and in his own imagination, in sketching their outlines and tracing their relations with one another, in all these ways Kierkegaard endeavoured to explore and map that unknown country which lay between him and his ideal. By examining exemplars of conscious states which approximated his own he sought to come to a clearer understanding of the character of his suffering and of the direction in which health lay. All this had been accomplished by the late 1830's.

It was at just this time when the outlines of his quest were becoming clear, that Kierkegaard was to be deflected from it by two events. The first was the death of his father on August 9, 1838, and the second was his engagement to Regine Olsen in September 1840.

Old Michael Pedersen Kierkegaard had always wanted his youngest son to take a theological degree. But as we noted in Chapter 1, young Søren found the fare of the theological table a bit plain and had allowed his interests a freer play. The result was that when "old Kierkegaard" [28] died at 82, Kierkegaard was in no position to take the theological examination. Although while his father was alive, Kierkegaard had been able to put him off with excuses, his death put the matter in a different light. "So long as Father lived," Kierkegaard told Hans Brøchner, "I was able to defend my thesis that I ought not to take it [i.e. the theological examination]. But when he was dead, I had to take over his part in the debate as well as my own, and then I could no longer hold out, but had to decide to read for the examination." [29] Kierkegaard managed to hold out until the late summer of 1839, at which time he decided to put away his quest, and read unremittingly for the examination. He takes leave of his thoughts with these words in his journal.

> I must give up you too my *lucida intervalia*, and you my thoughts who sit imprisoned in my head, I can no longer allow you to walk abroad in the cool of the evening, but do no lose courage, learn to know each other better, associate with one another, and now and then I can still creep in and take a look at you—*au revoir!*
>
> SK
> formerly Dr. *Ecstaticus* (II A 576).

Kierkegaard's thoughts, and with them his quest, were put away for ten months, during which time his journal is silent. It resumes on July 4, 1840—the day after he passed the examination.

Two weeks later, Kierkegaard took the mail-stage to Kalundborg to begin a pilgrimage to the family home at Saeding, on the Jutland heath. His mood during this journey seems to match the lonely heath he visited. Outside Holstebro he comes upon a carefree vagabond lying in the heather (III A 67). They walk together for several miles stopping at Non Mill for a cool drink from the stream. Kierkegaard remembers the vagabond stretched out, drinking the cool water, and this sticks in his mind as a symbol of the simple, happy life which is denied him. As he nears Saeding his thoughts become more solemn. He speculates how strange it would be if he were to fall ill and be buried in Saeding churchyard (III A 73). And while in Saeding he relates a peasant story about a man who once lived in a nearby house, and who, in a time of plague outlived all his neighbors and had to bury them. "He dug deep trenches in the sod," Kierkegaard observes, "and buried the corpses in long rows" (III A 75). In the background of these entries in his travel diary one senses a growing weariness, the ebb and flow of an all too familiar *Weltschmerz*. It was during this journey that he wrote in his diary,

> The terrible thing about the total spiritual incapacity from which I suffer is precisely that it is coupled with a consuming longing, with a spiritual passion. And yet it is so formless, that I do not even know what it is I lack
>
> (III A 56).

The journey itself has become a kind of sufferer's progress. "Just as one is accustomed to say *nulla dies sine linea*," Kierkegaard writes, "so I can say of this journey *nulla dies sine lacryma*" (III A 77).

He stayed with his aunt in a poor peasant's cottage for several days, but soon this tired him and he started back to Copenhagen. He arrived in the city on August 7, 1840, and once again took up the free life of a man of letters which he had put aside the year before. All was unchanged—all that is, with one notable exception—for in early September he became engaged to Regine, daughter of State Councillor Olsen. Once again the quest was put aside for more pressing concerns.

Kierkegaard had known Regine slightly for several years. They met first at a party at the Rørdams in Frederiksberg, and Kierkegaard had been quite enchanted by this nymph of fourteen. But for several years he paid her few attentions, and it was only after he returned from Jutland in the late summer of 1840 that he began to court her in earnest. He acted quickly, and by September 10 he had proposed, she had accepted, and Councillor Olsen had put his blessing upon the match. Regine was seventeen, and Kierkegaard twenty-seven.

On the very next day, Kierkegaard admits in retrospect, "I saw that I had made a blunder" (x⁵ A 149.5), and although more than a year would pass before the engagement was broken, it was already over for him. Like the young man in *Repetition*, "At bottom he was through with the whole relationship. At the very moment of beginning he took such a tremendous stride that he had leapt clear over the whole of life." [30]

What could have motivated Kierkegaard to carry out this whirlwind courtship which ended so quickly and so disastrously for both parties? Why did a man who usually took such pains over the smallest decision rush headlong into this very serious relationship?

It seems likely that P. A. Heiberg described Kierkegaard's act correctly when he called it "an attempt at flight out of the prison of melancholy, a result of the urge towards freedom, of the desire to release himself, to break the chains of melancholy." [31] We saw how during his Jutland journey the "chains of melancholy" were tightening for Kierkegaard—how the outlines of that "dreadful still life" were settling inexorably around him. It seems likely, then, that on his return to Copenhagen he permitted himself one final, violent spasm to break these chains, to explode the shape of his winter world before it trapped him forever. Eight years later he characterized his experience with Regine in these words.

> Oh, how hard it is to be as old as eternity makes one when one is still a man, above all a man, and when the whole of existence speaks to one in the language of youth. There was a young girl I loved, how charming she was, and so young (how blissful it must be to be so young), so attractive and engaging: Oh dreadful sorrow, I was an eternity too old for her (ix A 108).

Regine stood for the youth which Kierkegaard never had, for the immediacy he could never achieve. In becoming engaged to her he sought to break through to this life. It was only through her, he tells us, that he was given "a yardstick for how happy a human being can be" (ix A 130). With her he hoped to become like other human beings who could laugh and love without their laughter and their love being turned to dust by that all-seeing demon of reflection.[32] "On those days—few and far between—when I was really humanly happy," Kierkegaard writes, "I always longed for her indescribably" (ix A 67). In trying to love Regine, Kierkegaard was launching what another critic has called "a powerful frontal attack towards life, a bearing up of the original strength of the erotic, immediate and irresistible." [33] In this girl of seventeen he thought he had found the Ariadne who would lead him out of the labyrinth, who would bring him immediately to that far-off land toward which his intellectual labors were only pointing. Like the Quidam of *Stages on Life's Way* he hoped to find in her health a cure for his sickness.[34]

But of course this was an illusion, a "blunder" as he calls it. Regine was no Ariadne, but only a pretty girl of seventeen. He was "an eternity too old for her"; "she could not break through the silence of my melancholy" (VIII[1] A 641); "there was an infinite distance between her and me" (IX A 451). Slowly Kierkegaard realized that just as salvation could not be won by returning to childhood, just so little could it be won by rushing precipitously into a second childhood of romantic love. No, if it came, it would have to come at the end of the long "path" he had discovered and along which his quest lay. And so as the engagement year advanced, Kierkegaard felt a growing inclination to return to the quest from which he had been deflected by this erotic aberration. Retelling the story of his engagement three years later in *Stages on Life's Way*, he lets the fictitious Quidam remark,

> Before I was engaged to her my life was like a painful inquisition of myself, then I was interrupted and summoned out to the most dreadful decisions; and when I am through with that, if ever I am, then I can begin again with myself where I left off.[35]

And again a few pages later in a similar vein.

> I have no time to think about myself, and yet my inward life is of a sort to give me enough to think about . . . . If only I get through this year of mourning when I have to mourn for her . . . , then I can throw myself into these conflicts, and then surely the thing will succeed.[36]

Realizing that Regine could not guide him, that her youth was utterly beyond him, in the fall of 1841 Kierkegaard returned to his original quest. On October 11 the final break was made, and two weeks later he took ship for Berlin. Part of the manuscript of *Either/Or* he carried in his suitcase.

v. *Pseudonyms*

As Kierkegaard walked up the gangplank of a Swedish steamer on that morning in late October, he carried along much more of his future authorship than the few scattered parts of *Either/Or* which lay in his suitcase.[37] Both the fundamental insight upon which this authorship would be based, as well as its general form were now clear to him.

The fundamental insight was, of course, focused in the conception of the life-view. In Kierkegaard's conviction that there were alternative life-views, and that one could move freely between them, was concentrated, if not the core of his later authorship, then at least a fundamental theme. Just as in the *Papirer* we have seen Kierkegaard exploring a multitude of different life-views, so in the works of the early 1840's we see this exploration renewed on a more thorough and systematic scale. Instead of the few lines or pages in which a life-view was discussed in the *Papirer*, now a whole book or several books are devoted to the same purpose. Instead of Ahasuerus, we now have the despairing aesthete in his various guises, and instead of Faust we have Constantine Constantius, Johannes de Silentio, and Frater Taciturnus. But the intent is the same: to discover that single life-view which will offer an escape from the labyrinth. As we shall see, it is not until later, when this search has run itself to exhaustion, that the notion of the life-view recedes in importance, as Kierkegaard turns to other concerns. Yet even in these later works—in *Stages on Life's Way* or *Concluding Unscientific Postscript* for example—even in these works the notion of the life-view still continues to play a major role. For Kierkegaard never abandoned, I suppose, the hope that he could find the life-view which would offer him release, and it is upon this notion (call it a "conviction" or a "hope") that much of his later authorship is based. As we have seen, this notion was already part of the intellectual baggage he carried to Berlin.

Yet in addition, he also took with him a fairly clear conception of the *form* his later authorship would take. By "form" I mean simply the *literary form* in which much of his work appeared—that is, the obvious fact that he chose to write under pseudonyms.

Already in 1835 Kierkegaard had found a prototype for the

pseudonyms in the work of Schleiermacher. As a review of Friedrich Schlegel's novel, *Lucinde*, Schleiermacher had written a series of letters from fictitious persons, each expressing a definite point of view. After reading these letters, Kierkegaard wrote in his journal.

> It ought to serve as a model for a review, and in addition as an example of how such a review can become in the highest degree creative. For starting from the book itself, he constructs many personalities, and through these, he elucidates both the work under review and also their individuality. Instead therefore of being a review stating various points of view, we get a group of personalities each representing one of these different standpoints. Each is a complete entity, so that we are enabled to get a glimpse into the personality of each person, and yet through their many judgements, each being only relatively true, to arrive at our own conclusion. In this way it is a true work of art (1 C 69).

For Schleiermacher this idea was only a passing fancy—an interesting way to write a book review. But for Kierkegaard it became the very natural literary form of a whole authorship. Why? The answer is of course found in Kierkegaard's intent as a writer; in the idea of pseudonymity he had found a literary form which fitted his intention.

Given Kierkegaard's intent of exploring different life-views, what better vehicle could be chosen than that of a pseudonymous authorship? Certainly the standard philosophical essay would be of no use to him; it was simply designed for another purpose. The novel was a possibility. But only the novel written in the first person [38] would permit the full exploration of consciousness which Kierkegaard desired. Yet if he chose this form, he could only deal with one life-view at a time, and would be unable to employ his favorite device of contrast. No, the best literary form would be "dramatic," but we should note, not "dramatic" in such a way as to emphasize the surfaces of things: acts, events, social consequences, etc.; rather, it would dramatically emphasize the *interiors* of conscious life. Thus Kierkegaard would not write plays (although he did start one in 1838),[39] but would create a group of pseudonymous authors, who, in essays, diaries, and letters would reveal the shadows and highlights of their interior life. These pseudonyms one critic has called "Søren Kierkegaard's marionette theatre." [40] Each of them, Kierkegaard tells us in his explanation of the pseudonyms at the end of the *Postscript*, is "a poetically actual individuality" who has "his definite life-view expressed in audible lines." [41] As he relates in an early draft of this same explanation, ". . . the speaker's voice comes from me, but it is not my voice, the writing hand is mine, but it is not my handwriting" (VII[1] B 75). In these pseudonyms, Kierkegaard found the perfect literary vehicle for his search. By fully utilizing that unusual imaginative facility of which Israel Levin speaks, he could create whole conscious worlds, each of which was ascribed to a different pseudonym. Then, by ruses of various sorts, he would manage to combine the work of different pseudonyms in the same book—in this way, illuminating each view by contrasting it with the other. There is then no deep secret concerning Kierkegaard's use of pseudonyms. It was simply the literary form which best suited his purpose.

Equipped thus with the notion of the life-view and the idea of pseudonymity, on October 25, 1841, Kierkegaard left for Berlin. He arrived in the German capital a few days later and immediately took up residence in a small hotel. At first things did not go well; he speaks in a letter to Emil Boisen of suffering under "a tremendous productivity-obstruction." [42] His worries about Regine (and about the enforced isolation which his break with her entailed) tormented him, and made it difficult for him to work. But soon this torment became itself the source of a new-found creative energy. The "obstruction" cleared, and he wrote to Boisen on December 14. "I write as though it were a life-and-death struggle. Already I have written enough to fill fourteen closely printed sheets . . ." [43] For the next four and a half years this "life-and-death struggle" was kept up without a single pause. *Either/Or* (1843), *Repetition* (1843), *Fear and Trembling* (1843), *Philosophical Fragments* (1844), *The Concept of Dread* (1844), *Stages on Life's Way* (1845), *Concluding Unscientific Postscript* (1846): these are the pseudonymous works which streamed out in a virtually uninterrupted flow during the years immediately following Kierkegaard's break with Regine. As Alexander Dru has pointed out, during these years Kierkegaard worked like "a clerk in his office without a single break. The works published under pseudonyms during these years form a complete whole within his work." [44] We will now turn our attention to this whole, examining it from the perspective gained through the biographical researches of this and the preceding chapter. Viewed from this perspective, it is our hope that this central segment of Kierkegaard's authorship will exhibit at once a unity and a texture which up to now has gone unnoticed.

We begin with *Either/Or*

Part Two

4

EITHER/OR

Either/Or was published on February 20, 1843, in a two-volume edition of some 838 closely printed pages. Its huge bulk explains in part the response it received. The contemporary critics were simply overwhelmed. The book was too big both in conception and in size to be readily assimilated, and thus they contented themselves by quoting a few passages here and there and by speculating on the identity of the author.[1] The dean of the local literary set, J. L. Heiberg, admits his annoyance at its great length, and then grudgingly expresses admiration for the "deep meaning" contained in certain sections.[2] Yet one is never told just what this "deep meaning" is, and one leaves Heiberg's review feeling that he too never managed to penetrate the book. It was planned on too great a scale for the Copenhagen of 1843. Published in Paris or Berlin it might have gained the appreciation and understanding it deserved. But in Copenhagen it could only be read with a faint sense of awe, with the awareness (as Heiberg put it) of its being the work of "a rare and highly gifted mind,"[3] yet without any clear understanding of what this mind was doing.

But we should not be too hard on the critics of Kierkegaard's day, for *Either/Or* is indeed a highly unusual—even mystifying—work. Its very format is enough to bewilder the casual reader.

It carries no author's name on the title page, but claims to be edited by "Victor Eremita," who relates in the preface how he had found various parts of the manuscript hidden in an old desk. By comparing the handwriting of the papers, Victor comes to the conclusion that they are the work of two persons: a civil magistrate named William (whom Victor designates "B"), and a nameless "young friend" of the magistrate (whom Victor designates "A"). The papers of Judge William consist first of two long letters ("treatises" one might call them) addressed to "A" on the subject of marriage and ethics. In these letters Judge William diagnoses A's aesthetic view of life as "despair," and prescribes as treatment his own ethical life-view. These two long letters are followed in turn by a sermon written (so Judge William tells us) by an obscure Jutland priest. Together, this sermon and the two letters make up the second volume of *Either/Or*, leaving the first volume to be made up of the scattered papers of A. These cover a wide range. There are a number of aphorisms and lyrical outbursts grouped under the rubric "Diapsalmata"—a Greek word meaning "refrain." There are several essays in literary criticism as well as speeches written for a private club of aesthetes. Last but not least, there is the famous "Diary of the Seducer" which A claims to have stolen from a friend named Johannes. A is thus the author of the first, the "either" volume, while Judge William is the author of the second, the "or" volume.

In light of this bewildering array of different authors and literary forms, it is no wonder that the critics of Kierkegaard's Copenhagen were more astonished than comprehending. He had confronted them with a mystifying work and had provided no ready key for its understanding.

The critics of Kierkegaard's day were not privy to that mass of autobiographical material surveyed in our preceding chapters. Most of them were unaware even of its author's name, and, if they knew his name, they had no inkling of the odd melancholy which lay behind his sardonic smile. Yet above all it is this melancholy, this suffering, which constitutes at once the source and frame of *Either/Or*. It is our familiarity with this suffering which makes it possible for us to locate the work within the logic of sickness and cure. It is this familiarity which permits us to see the "either" as an essay in diagnosis and the "or" as a prescription for cure.

1. *Despair*

The term "despair" [*Fortvivlelse*], and the sickness to which it refers, lies at the very heart of *Either/Or*. It is not only the sickness with which the aesthete A is afflicted (and hence the chief exhibit of Volume I), but it is also the focus of Judge William's attempts at cure in Volume II. Our understanding of *Either/Or* will hinge upon our understanding of it.

Much later Kierkegaard will devote a whole volume to despair, calling it "the sickness unto death."

> The concept of the sickness unto death must be understood, however, in a peculiar sense. Literally it means a sickness the end and outcome of which is death. . . . In this sense despair cannot be called the sickness unto death. . . . On the contrary, the torment of despair is precisely this, not to be able to die. . . . It is in this last sense that despair is the sickness unto death, this agonizing contradiction, this sickness in the self, everlastingly to die, and yet not to die, to die the death. . . . This is the hot incitement, or the cold fire in despair, the gnawing canker whose movement is constantly inward, deeper and deeper in impotent self-consumption (*Sickness*, 150–51).

Surely this description of despair must remind us of Kierkegaard's characterization of his own mental state in the *Papirer*. For here is that same world-weariness, that same longing for death and its release, which we noted earlier in his journal. Dare we suggest that despair is only another name for that "dreadful still life," that it is this agonizing death in life which constitutes the "either" Kierkegaard so desperately seeks to escape? If we turn to the first section, entitled "Diapsalmata," we can perhaps see the correctness of such a suggestion.

In this section we are introduced to A, and in his aphorisms and lyrical effusions we get an accurate picture of the sickness from which he suffers. Since 28 of the first 29 diapsalmata were drawn from Kierkegaard's own journal,[4] there seems little doubt who was the original victim of this disease. Yet it may prove enlightening to trace similarities in the symptoms of the two victims.

Many of the lyrical outbursts contained in this section complain of a gradual slowdown and stoppage in A's sense of lived
time. One of the following citations should already be familiar
to us.

> Time flows, life is a stream, people say, and so on. I do
> not notice it. Time stands still, and I with it. All the plans
> I make fly right back upon myself; when I would spit, I even
> spit into my own face (E/O, 1, 25).

> Life has become a bitter drink to me, and yet I must
> take it like medicine, slowly, drip by drip . . . (E/O, 1, 25).

> I feel the way a chessman must, when the opponent
> says of it: that piece cannot be moved.[5]

Once again we are brought near to a mental landscape where
time, growth, and change are all strangely absent. Time has
stopped and we are left with "simply nothing, a mood, a single
color" (E/O, 1, 28).

In place of vitality and movement we encounter a characteristic paralysis of emotion and purpose. An all-embracing indolence,
a crushing boredom, seems to have taken hold of A.

> I do not care for anything. I do not care to ride, for
> the exercise is too violent. I do not care to walk, walking is
> too strenuous. I do not care to lie down, for I should either
> have to remain lying, and I do not care to do that, or I should
> have to get up again, and I do not care to do that either.
> Summa summarum: I do not care at all.[6]

> How terrible tedium is—terribly tedious. . . . I lie
> stretched out inactive; the only thing I see is emptiness. I
> do not even suffer pain. The vulture constantly devoured
> Prometheus' liver; the poison constantly dripped down on
> Loki; that was at least an interruption even though a monot-
> onous one (E/O, 1, 36).

He lies immersed in this great "emptiness" which muffles the
sounds of the outside world and leaves him alone with a consciousness that never changes. Images of castles, sieges, and en-
chainment appear over and over again in this section. "I live these

days like one besieged," A remarks, "I say of my sorrow what the Englishman says of his house: my sorrow is my castle." [7] He relates that he is "bound in a chain of dark imaginings, of unquiet dreams, of restless thoughts, of dread presentiments, of inexplicable anxieties" (*E/O*, 1, 33). He sits far-removed from the world, upon the peak of a mountain lost in the clouds.

> Carking care is my feudal castle. It is built like an eagle's nest upon the peak of a mountain lost in the clouds. No one can take it by storm. From this abode I dart down into the world of reality to seize my prey; but I do not remain down there, I bear my quarry aloft to my stronghold. My booty is a picture I weave into the tapestries of my palace. There I live as one dead. I immerse everything I have experienced in a baptism of forgetfulness unto an eternal remembrance. Everything temporal and contingent is forgotten and erased. Then I sit like an old man, grey-haired and thoughtful, and explain picture after picture in a voice as soft as a whisper; and at my side a child sits and listens although he remembers everything before I tell it
> (*E/O*, 1, 41).

Isolated within the castle of his thoughts, A sits like an old man telling and retelling stories to a child who "remembers everything before I tell it." What better image could be found for that "dreadful still life" of which Kierkegaard speaks?

But the similarity of symptoms can be traced even further. For just as Kierkegaard looked back at childhood as at a time of fresh immediacy which had passed forever, so A can ask, "And is it not so with all the mingled colors of childhood? The hues that life once had gradually become too strong, too harsh, for our dim eyes" (*E/O*, 1, 23). And just as the moments of continuity broke into Kierkegaard's world like rays of winter sunlight, so do similar rays of warmth penetrate A's despair. In an adaption of an earlier cited *Papirer* entry, he writes,

> Music finds its way where the rays of the sun cannot penetrate. My room is dark and dismal, a high wall almost excludes the light of day. The sounds must come from a neighboring yard; it is probably some wandering musician

. . . —the apothecary pounds his mortar, the kitchen maid
scours her kettle, the groom curries the horse, and strikes the
comb against the flagstones; these tones appeal to me alone,
they beckon only me. Oh! Accept my thanks, whoever you
are! My soul is so rich, so sound, so joy-intoxicated.[8]

Here in A's boredom and isolation, in his longing for a childhood
whose colors are "too harsh for our dim eyes," in his joy in a
melody which penetrates even into a room "dark and dismal": in
all these diverse symptoms of his despair we detect the all-too-
familiar outlines of Kierkegaard's "dreadful still life." It was this
"either," now known by the name despair, which Kierkegaard so
desperately sought to escape.

II. A Hall of Mirrors

Coming first, the section entitled "Diapsalmata" gives us a
vivid (if a bit impressionistic) description of A's despairing life-
world. In succeeding sections A makes various forays out of this
life-world by discussing a number of literary figures from Marie
Beaumarchais to Job. Yet the extraordinary thing about all these
discussions is that they invariably turn back upon A himself. The
figures discussed seem not so much to be independent characters
with a life of their own, as to be only reflections of A himself. This
can be seen most clearly in the little essay, "Shadowgraphs."

This essay takes the form of a speech to be delivered to the
society of the Symparanekromenoi—the "fellowship of buried
lives." [9] This group is made up of despairing aesthetes who like A,
"live aphorismenoi and segregati, like aphorisms in life, without
community of men, without sharing their joys and their griefs"
(E/O, I, 218). At occasional meetings each one of the members
reads a paper on a literary theme of his own choosing, and A has
chosen to discourse on the theme, "reflective grief." Note how this
theme is described.

> Retiring thus within, it finds at last an enclosure, an
> innermost recess, where it hopes it can remain; and now be-
> gins its monotonous movement. Back and forth it swings
> like a pendulum, and cannot come to rest. . . . Like the
> monotonous sound of water dripping from the roof, like the

monotonous whir of a spinning-wheel, like a monotonous sound of a man walking with measured tread back and forth on the floor above, so this movement of reflective grief, gives to it a certain sense of numb relief (*E/O*, 1, 168–69).

One feels that what A is describing might just as well be called "despair" as "reflective grief." In the images of water dripping, a turning spinning-wheel, a man walking back and forth: in these images of cycles which repeat and repeat, but never advance, one has the objective correlate for the slowdown and stoppage in lived time so characteristic of despair. And in the image of retirement into "an innermost recess" is once again reflected the trapped and isolated quality of the life of despair. All this can be seen even more clearly if we look at some of the examples of "reflective grief" offered by A. He describes Antigone in these words.

> She does not belong to the world she lives in; even though she appears flourishing, her real life is concealed. Although she is living, she is in another sense dead.
>
> (*E/O*, 1, 155)

And here is Marie Beaumarchais.

> Now she is lost to the world, lost to her environment, immured alive. With sadness she closes the last aperture. . . . The things going on nearest her—the sound of music, the noisy conversation—sound so far away that it is as if she sat in a little room by herself far from the entire world
>
> (*E/O*, 1, 182).

Finally, here is Donna Elvira.

> She is young, and yet her life's supply is exhausted, but it does not follow that she dies. In this respect she is every day anxious for the morrow. . . . So she lives on. . . . As she considers over and over again, she seizes every way out, and yet she finds none (*E/O*, 1, 200).

All these characters seem to have little independence of their own. They are all victims of the strange isolation which afflicts A himself. They all seem trapped within themselves, trying every way out and yet finding none.

The very next essay by A is a little piece entitled, "The Unhappiest Man." With a glance backward to the *Papirer* studies of
Ahasuerus, and forward to the definition of despair as the "sickness
unto death," the unhappiest man is described as that pathetic
creature who could never die—who could never slip down into the
grave and there find peace. Note how in A's description of this
unfortunate creature he seems once again to be describing himself.

> Alone, he has the whole world over against him as the
> *alter* with which he finds himself in conflict. . . . He cannot
> become old, for he has never been young; he cannot become
> young, for he is already old. In one sense of the word he
> cannot die, for he has not really lived; in another sense he
> cannot live for he is already dead (*E/O*, I, 224).

Virtually everywhere we look in *Either/Or*, Volume I, we find only
reflections of A's despair. The list could be greatly extended. Mar-
garet from *Faust*; Niobe; Emmeline (the heroine of Scribe's play,
The First Love); Job: all of these figures discussed by A are described in terms which might better be applied to himself. One
feels that A is walking down a long hall of mirrors which, with
maddening regularity, reflect back at him always the same image—
himself!

The persistent self-reflection becomes explicit in A's preface
to the "Diary of the Seducer." In this preface A tells us that he
stole the diary from a friend named Johannes, whom he then proceeds to describe. But already in the beginning preface by Victor
Eremita we have been told that A is lying, that Johannes is
a creature of his own imagination, and that hence his description
of Johannes is really a self-description. Holding all this in mind,
note how A describes the Johannes who is really himself.

> As he has led others astray, so he ends, I think, by go-
> ing astray himself. . . . I can imagine nothing more excru-
> ciating than an intriguing mind which has lost the thread of
> its continuity and now turns its whole acumen against it-
> self. . . . It is in vain that he has many exits from his fox-
> hole; at the moment his anxious soul believes that it already
> sees daylight breaking through, it turns out to be a new en-
> trance, and like a startled deer pursued by despair, he con-

stantly seeks a way out, and finds only a way in, through
which he goes back into himself. . . . Conscience exists for
him only as a higher degree of consciousness, which expresses
itself in a disquietude that does not, in a more profound
sense, accuse him, but which keeps him awake, and gives
him no rest in his barren activity (*E/O*, 1, 304–305).

This passage has been quoted at length because it gives perhaps
the most vivid picture found anywhere in Kierkegaard's work of
that "gnawing canker whose movement is constantly inward"
which is *despair*. Note how the despairing individual seems to have
become hermetically sealed in the labyrinth of his own consciousness. For him consciousness has become a "gauze curtain" (*E/O*,
1, 302), a crystalline canopy which lets through only the faintest of
echoes from the outside world, yet constantly reflects back the
image of self. This is the Kantian predicament become nightmare.
The hapless victim of despair seeks a way out, and "finds only a
way in, through which he goes back into himself." Aimlessly he
wanders, left alone with a consciousness which "keeps him awake,
and gives him no rest in his barren activity."

It is this hermetic quality of despair which Kierkegaard has
dramatized for us in these essays. It is one thing to tell us that
consciousness becomes an isolating envelope for the despairing individual; it is another thing to show us dramatically how this isolation becomes palpable for the victim of despair. It is this latter
drama—a "showing" rather than a "telling"—which is carried out
in these essays. In each of them we follow A as he inspects diverse
literary figures. Yet soon we awake to the realization that wherever
A looks he sees only himself—that all these figures are only reflections from different directions of his own despair. In following
A as he wanders among these images we learn how impossible it
is for the victim of despair ever to see beyond the labyrinth of
consciousness—how for such a person the world in all its richness
shrinks to the deadly monotony of a hall of mirrors.

At the final limit of despair the individual loses his way in
the tangle of his own consciousness. But now we might ask, how
does an individual come to despair? By what stages does he lose
his way? Why does he permit himself to be led astray? In answering these questions, Kierkegaard brings his discussion of despair

full circle. For it is consciousness, he will tell us, that is at once the tangled terminus of despair and also the source of the movement which culminates in despair. It is in trying to cope with the fact of consciousness that the individual is led into the labyrinth of despair.

III. *"The Immediate Stages of the Erotic"*

"So it appears," Judge William remarks in *Either/Or*, Volume II, "that every aesthetic view of life is despair, and that everyone who lives aesthetically is in despair whether he knows it or not" (*E/O*, II, 197). Despair seems to follow as the necessary consequence of embracing a particular life-view. But what is this "aesthetic" life-view? Once again Judge William proves helpful. "Every man," he observes, "feels the need of forming a life-view, a conception of life's significance and purpose. The man who lives aesthetically does that too, and the universal expression which has been heard from age to age, and in all stages is this: one must enjoy life" (*E/O*, II, 184). Despair then follows as a consequence of rendering absolute the principle of enjoyment. But why, might we ask, does a person choose to live aesthetically? Why does a person choose to organize his life around the principle of enjoyment? It is in answering these questions that Kierkegaard completes the circle of description we have pointed out earlier. To find his answers we must turn first to the opening essay of *Either/Or*.

In this essay Kierkegaard offers a description of the stages culminating in the fullblown aesthetic life. These he calls the "immediate stages of the erotic," and they might be briefly indicated by the terms "dreaming," "seeking," and "desiring" (*E/O*, I, 79). The first stage is exemplified by the Page in *Figaro*. Desire is here not yet qualified as desire per se. It "is present only as a presentiment about itself, is without movement, without disquiet, only gently clarified by an unclarified inner emotion" (*E/O*, I, 75). The first stage evolves into a more qualified one midway between dreaming and explicit desiring. This second stage, exemplified by Papageno in *The Magic Flute* manifests itself in a yearning, a seeking after a yet unspecified object. These two earlier stages culminate finally in explicit desiring, symbolized by Mozart's Don Juan. Finding its object, desire now becomes determinate. It is this stage of *desiring*, of *enjoying* life, which is the essence of the aesthetic life. What must be noted here is that the aesthetic life is not a bare immediacy, not a "first" from which a person begins. For it has come about through a process of evolution; the aesthetically-determined person has already passed through the states of "dreaming" and "seeking" before reaching the state of explicit "desiring." Let us scrutinize this movement. "Dreaming," "seeking," "desiring"—certainly first and foremost these terms seem to describe varying degrees of consciousness. In dreaming a person is neither conscious nor unconscious; he floats between the two states. In the second stage the dreaming becomes more clearly specified; the person *seeks* an unidentified "something." Finally, in desire, the person becomes fully conscious, focusing his yearning on a definite object in the world. Might not these three stages be seen as transitional states in the movement from unconsciousness to consciousness?

We mentioned earlier that the plan for "The Immediate Stages of the Erotic" is sketched in a *Papirer* entry for 1837. Note how Kierkegaard there describes the first stage.

> The Page in *Figaro* is the first standpoint in the development; it is the indefinite awakening desire in an unconscious [*bevidstløs*] conflict with the surroundings. . . . Just as becoming is a polemic so also is life itself; at the first standpoint not conscious [*bevidst*] but a continual approximation to consciousness [*Bevidsthed*]. In a way it identifies itself with the world (the child's "me"), but just because it is life, a development, precisely therefore is there an approximation to the definite conscious [*bevidste*] desire
>
> (1 C 125).

The first stage, then, corresponds to that early period in infancy when the child has not yet made the distinction between the world and himself. He dreams, floating in the between-world of semi-consciousness. Later on Kierkegaard describes this state in *Either/Or* as at once "painful" and "sweet," "sad yet fascinating" (E/O, 1, 74). "The sensuous awakens," he writes, "not yet to movement, but to a hushed tranquillity; not to joy and gladness, but to a deep melancholy. Desire is not yet awake, it is only a gloomy foreboding. . . . The desire is quiet desire, the longing quiet longing, the ecstasy quiet ecstasy, wherein the object of desire is dawning" (*Idem*). Desire here is quiet desire; lacking an object it is not yet qualified as desire. It is "infinitely deep" (*Idem*), and yet characterized only by a nascent perturbation, a faint awareness of disequilibrium. In this state the child *dreams*, but his dreams have no object; he dreams of nothing.

Little over a year later Kierkegaard will devote a whole volume [10] to the description which he will now call "dread" [*Angest*]. "Dread," Kierkegaard tells us, "is a qualification of the dreaming spirit. . . . When awake the difference between my self and my other is posited; sleeping it is suspended; dreaming it is a nothing vaguely hinted at" (*Dread*, 38). In dread, spirit is dreaming in man, and this dreaming state (as we noted in *Either/Or*) is both painful and sweet. "Dread," Kierkegaard continues, "is a sympathetic antipathy, an antipathetic sympathy. . . . If we observe children, we find this dread more definitely indicated as a seeking after adventure, a thirst for the prodigious, the mysterious" (*Idem*). And finally (again as we noted in *Either/Or*), in this state one dreams, but one dreams of nothing.

> In this state there is peace and rest, but at the same time there is something else, which is not dissension and strife, for there is nothing to strive with. What is it then? Nothing. But what effect does nothing have? It feeds dread.[11]

The vague apprehension of dread rests in the very bosom of the dawning consciousness. It is this apprehension which provides the energy for the ascent to consciousness. In the dreaming state man is aware of a vague lack, an emptiness. He feels as if the tiniest of cracks has opened in the pure substance of his being; a nothingness has intruded and with its entrance there arises the possibility of movement. In his dream he feels he is no longer whole; the long breaths of the deep sleep become shorter, more fitful; consciousness stirs. With the first vague hints of a "homesickness for himself" [12] he turns outward to the world to recover the closure which was his, and is now unaccountably lost. Perhaps this world whose outlines are even now emerging from the mists of dream may offer up to him that primaeval unity he seeks. The vague yearning of the dream becomes a thirst for adventure, a quest for discovery.

> The longing breaks away from the earth and starts out wandering; the flower gets wings and flits inconstant and unwearied here and there. Desire is directed toward the object, it is also moved within itself, the heart beats soundly and joyously, the objects swiftly vanish and reappear; but still before every disappearance is a present enjoyment, a moment of contact, short but sweet, evanescent as the gleam of a glowworm, inconstant and fleeting as the touch of a butterfly. . . . Only momentarily is a deeper desire suspected, but this suspicion is forgotten. In Papageno the desire aims at discoveries (*E/O*, 1, 79).

In each isolated moment of discovery the dreamer-become-seeker experiences a "moment of contact"—a brief, poignant taste of the original unity that was his. For a moment he savors it; but then in a flash it is gone. Yet no matter, he can find another object, another scintillation of enjoyment to replace the present one. And so he skips from moment to moment, from sparkle to sparkle, with hardly a glance towards the deeper desire which lingers in the background.

In the next stage—the stage of outright desiring exemplified by Don Juan—this deeper desire becomes more pressing. For Don Juan is inspired by dread.

> There is a dread in him, but this dread is his energy. It is not a subjectively reflected dread, but is a substantial dread. Don Juan's life is not despair; but it is the whole power of sensuousness which is born in dread, and Don Juan himself is this dread, but the dread is precisely the daemonic joy of life (*E/O*, 1, 128–29).

With the energy of dread behind him Don Juan concentrates all his power into the sensuous. And how is this power concentrated? It is concentrated by desiring absolutely the particular, "Desire has its absolute object in the particular. It desires the particular absolutely" (*E/O*, 1, 83). The desire which was only nascent in the first two stages now awakens. "This impulse with which desire awakens," Kierkegaard observes, "this trembling, separates desire and its object, and affords desire an object" (E/O, I, 78). In that same instant when the primordial lack becomes palpable in the pang of desire, the object of desire is born. By grasping a particular object in the world and possessing it fully, Don Juan would attempt to recover that primitive wholeness which once was his. By desiring this object absolutely, by possessing it in a moment of intense sensation, he would possess himself. He would be fully by joining with this other, and would thus overcome the discontinuity of dread. That tiniest of cracks which had awakened him from the dreamless sleep would be annealed in the fiery moment of sensation when consciousness closes around itself. In this brief moment of possession the primitive closure would be recovered—man would become again flesh pure.

We should remember that Don Juan is just this—he is "flesh incarnate" (E/O, I, 87), he is the representative of "desire as principle" (E/O, I, 83); he is pure desire with the admixture of no foreign element. As such he stands as the ideal of the aesthetic life. Like Don Juan the aesthete too would concentrate his life and his yearning in a desire for a particular object in the world. He too seeks the healing fire of sensation. He too wishes to concentrate his life in this fiery instant and so "make the instant of enjoyment a little eternity" (E/O, II, 22). The figure of Don Juan, exemplifying as it does the last of the immediate stages of the erotic, stands as the representative of the aesthetic life under its ideal aspect. He represents the ideal of the aesthete's project; he is the aesthete as he would desperately like to be. Yet as we now shall see, he also represents the aesthete as he can never be.

IV. The Failure of Aesthetic Concentration

If the aesthete could really be Don Juan, then he would have solved the problem of dread at the aesthetic level. Yet he cannot be Don Juan, for Don Juan is only a legendary figure, an ideal which like all ideals must stand outside of life. The dread of Don Juan is "substantial" but is not "subjectively reflected." Kierkegaard means by this that Don Juan is in a substantial state of dread, but that he is unconscious of it. Moreover, he is uncon-

scious of it because, in a deeper sense, he is unconscious of anything. "To be a seducer," Kierkegaard remarks, "requires a certain
amount of reflection and consciousness. . . . This consciousness is
lacking in Don Juan" (*E/O*, I, 97). Don Juan is unconscious; as
we saw he is "flesh incarnate," the mere symbol for "desire as
principle." And as wholly flesh, as utterly unconscious in a way a
human being can never be, his project of desire "is absolutely
sound, victorious, triumphant, irresistible, and daemonic" (*E/O*,
I, 83).

Yet for an aesthete—that is, for a flesh and blood, existing
individual—such a project of absolute desiring inevitably meets
shipwreck on the fact of consciousness. The project of the aesthete
is one of concentration—of the focusing of the yearning of dread
onto a particular object, and the collapsing of an individual's life
into a moment of intense sensation. Yet the fact that an existing
individual can never become purely flesh, the fact that he is conscious, entails that he can never focus his yearning on a particular
object nor concentrate his life in a moment. He always evades such
constriction. His yearning seeks beyond any object in the world,
and his life overflows the instant.

For this reason the aesthete always finds himself beyond any
momentary pleasure. "Occasionally you plunge into pleasure,"
Judge William admonishes his young friend, "and every instant
you are devoting yourself to it you make the discovery in your
consciousness that it is vanity. So you are constantly beyond yourself, that is, in despair." [13] Even in the most acute pleasure the
aesthete finds himself "standing out." He finds it more and more
difficult to find gratification in pleasure. The pleasures must become more and more intense, and finally, even the most intense
pleasures fail to satisfy. This is the tale of Nero whom Kierkegaard
describes in *Either/Or*.

> An instant will arrive when the splendor of the throne,
> his might and power, will pale, and for this he has not the
> courage. Then he grasps after pleasure; all the world's clever-
> ness must devise for him new pleasures, for only in the in-
> stant of pleasure does he find repose, and when that is past
> he gasps with faintness. The spirit constantly desires to break
> through, but it cannot alter the metamorphosis, it is con-

stantly disappointed, and he would offer it the satiety of
pleasure. The spirit within him gathers like a dark cloud, its
wrath broods over his soul, and it becomes an anguishing
dread which ceases not even in the moment of pleasure
(E/O, I, 190).

No matter what delicacy is offered it, consciousness is never satisfied. It looks always beyond.

And looking always beyond, consciousness soon becomes
bored. The problem of boredom hence comes to loom large in the
aesthete's thoughts. In an essay entitled, "The Rotation Method,"
A offers a number of schemes to outwit boredom. "Boredom," he
says, "depends on the nothingness which pervades reality; it is a
dizziness like that produced by looking down into a yawning
chasm, and this dizziness is infinite. Everyone who feels bored
cries out for a change" (E/O, I, 287). Traveling outwits boredom
for awhile, but soon the variety of new sights and sensations pales,
and the traveler once again cries out for a change. Other methods
may be tried. One might limit the field of consciousness by attempting to blank out both memory and hope. One might try
arbitrarily reading the last chapter of a book first, or going only to
the third act of a play.[14] By thus limiting the number of sensations
present in memory and by increasing the variety of sensation, the
aesthete hopes to have always something new to amuse him, and
so to introduce change and vitality into his life. Yet we feel that
even the greatest variety of sensations will prove unequal to the
task of staving off the gathering nothingness of boredom. A deadness, a coldness, has crept into the aesthete's life on either side of
the present moment, and we feel that even his most frantic efforts
to remove it will prove unsuccessful.

v. The Retreat from the World

He also has other problems. For in reaching out to the earthly
to silence his dread, he has become dependent upon it. "You
know," Judge William warns his young friend, "that the instant
is not in anyone's power" (E/O, II, 103). For the gratification of
his desire, the aesthete is dependent on the world, and the world
is not always amenable to his wishes. We see this particularly
clearly in "The Diary of the Seducer" at the point where Johannes

waits two hours in the wind and rain just to meet a young girl on the street. "Today she doesn't come," he complains, "just when I was so eager to see her. Her greeting creates a mood in me" (*E/O*, I, 391). Throughout his seduction of Cordelia we are aware of how dependent he is on the external, of how contingent is the whole project. Even as the seduction draws to a conclusion, he is aware of the contingency of the final result. "How much I have gathered into the one moment which now draws nigh," he exclaims, awaiting the carriage which will take him to Cordelia, "Damnation— if I should fail!" (*E/O*, I, 439).

Finding his dependence on the world to be a source of frustration, the aesthete moves to adopt a new strategy of enjoyment. Instead of enjoying the world immediately he will enjoy his enjoyment of the world. He interposes his consciousness as a screen of enjoyment between himself and the world. "You are hovering above yourself," Judge William cautions his young friend, "and what you behold beneath you is a multiplicity of moods and situations" (*E/O*, II, 203). The aesthete comes to enjoy the world only as it is reflected in the moods and sentiments which appear on the screen of consciousness. He thus moves back one step from the world. Johannes the Seducer looks down on himself and remarks, "I scarcely recognize myself. My mind is like a turbulent sea, swept by the storms of passion. Let your dashing waves hurl their foam against the sky. Serene I sit like the king of the cliff" (*E/O*, I, 320). Six days later he remarks in a similar vein, "I shall now keep very quiet, for this condition, this vague, indefinite, but still strong disquiet, has a sweetness of its own" (*E/O*, I, 321). In such remarks we can see Johannes savoring his moods: he has become a connoisseur of moods. He has moved to his "eagle's nest" (*E/O*, I, 41), to a position where he can survey both the world and himself in it. He has moved behind the curtain into "a world of gauze, lighter, more ethereal, qualitatively different from the actual world" (*E/O*, I, 302).

Such a strategy of enjoyment, of course, proves unsuccessful. Judge William remarks,

> So here we have a view of life which teaches one to enjoy life but expresses it thus: "Enjoy yourself, in enjoyment it is yourself you must enjoy." So the difference is that he

enjoys reflectively, not immediately. To that extent even this Epicureanism is dependent upon a condition over which it has no control (*E/O*, II, 28).

The various moods of the aesthete are not posited by him, but simply appear. They are stimulated by the world and hence infected with its contingency. Still another move must be made if the aesthete would gain independence from the world. This is the move of "recollection."

"You are able to make yourself an old man," Judge William reminds his young friend, "in order to imbibe in slow draughts through recollection what you have experienced" (*E/O*, II, 28). Instead of turning to the world for enjoyment, the aesthete turns to the illusory world of his recollections. And we should note that there is a difference between "memory" and "recollection."

> Memory is immediacy and comes immediately to one's aid, whereas recollection comes only by reflection . . . To recollect and to forget are not opposites . . . To bring back to oneself the past by enchantment is not so difficult as to remove from oneself by enchantment the object nearest to one for the sake of recollecting it.[15]

Recollection thus involves not only the bringing close of the past in an enchanted form, but also the setting at a distance of the present circumstances. "Recollection is ideality" (*Stages*, 28). It involves both the ideal "bracketing" of the present and ideal reformulation of the past. The person who successfully recollects reconstitutes his world as dream. Having moved to his enchanted castle the aesthete now immerses everything he has experienced "in a baptism of forgetfulness unto an eternal remembrance." He lives "as one dead." In his dream of recollection "everything temporal and contingent is forgotten and erased." [16] In this way he puts at a distance the deadness of the present by submerging his existence in the poetic. He poeticizes both his present circumstances and his past to such an extent that he escapes the world entirely.

In his final movement of recollection the aesthete comes full circle. He began by attempting to forge an immediate unity with the world through a momentary intensity of sensation. Finding

the world recalcitrant, he retires to a dream world where immediate sensations are muted, where he is stimulated only by the
fantastic shapes of his imagination. His venture into the world
has ended in a retreat from the world of the most radical sort. To
use Kierkegaard's words, he comes to "thus dwindle away, aye,
almost vanish from reality" (E/O, i, 302). He dwindles away,
farther and farther, until the world itself dissolves in the final extremity of despair, "Like a startled deer, pursued by despair, he
seeks a way out, and finds only a way in, through which he goes
back into himself."

vi. *The Retreat From Time*

Breaking with the world, the aesthete retires into himself in
a never-ending, inward-turning spiral of reflective recollection. The
bond between self and world, asserted first in the intensity of sensation, is now dissipated in his retirement from the world. What
we have not mentioned heretofore is that the aesthete undergoes
a similar retirement with respect to time.

From previous sections it should be evident that the aesthete's project of desire presupposes on his part a rather extraordinary relationship to time. In the first place, we should note, the
focus of the aesthete's yearning would seem to lie in the past. In
the moment when his desire is satisfied he feels a vague tremor of
his primordial past. For an instant he gains a brief glimpse of a
wholeness which once was his and is no more. It has slipped from
him, the moment has fled, but no matter—he will attain it once
more. Thus, as moment follows moment the aesthete seems always to be looking back over his shoulder. "Like the Spanish
knight of the doleful countenance," the Judge tells A, "you are
fighting for a vanished time" (E/O, ii, 143). This "vanished time"
is populated with those unique "firsts" which so haunt the aesthete's consciousness. The first kiss, the first smile, the first sensation of falling in love: these all enjoy a privileged status for him.[17]
The first kiss, even the Seducer admits, "is qualitatively different
from all others" (E/O, i, 412). Any "first" functions as the ideal
towards which all succeeding repetitions aspire. And as ideal it
is finally seen to be incommensurate with its repetitions. As material for recollection it evades duplication.

Note, however, what an extraordinary relationship to time the aesthete now must maintain: The locus of his desire lies in the *past* yet he wills it as a *future* possibility. Situated thus with respect to time he suffers the contradiction of nostalgia.

In making his nostalgia a life-project, in pursuing innumerable repetitions of "the first," the aesthete's intention is coincident with the actual accomplishments of the legendary Don Juan. Being unconscious, Don Juan was unaware of his own seductions: he did not *plan* them or even *will* them, but was simply carried forward on the wave of sensuality. Each new seduction (even the 1,003rd) could be for him "the first," "He constantly finishes and constantly begins again from the beginning, for his life is the sum of repellent moments which have no coherence" (*E/O*, I, 95). Each moment of desire is radically severed from all past moments; with each new woman Don Juan sheds the skin of his past and begins life over. But for the aesthete such a sloughing-off of the past is impossible. The aesthete has a memory, and no matter how many times he recommends forgetfulness as an aesthetic strategem, we recognize that there is a profound sense in which he cannot forget. Moreover, the aesthete, unlike Don Juan, can anticipate the future, and no matter how many times he recommends ignoring the future, we recognize that he is virtually foredoomed to grasp it in advance. His very desire caused him both to remember the past and to anticipate the future. It is not instinctive but intentional—penetrated with consciousness—and being conscious it is inevitably tainted with time. It is always desire of a *past* experience; yet he wills it as *future*. It is at this point that the temporal oscillation described in the essay, "The Unhappy Man," sets in.

The essay begins with the following description.

> The unhappy person is one who has his ideal, the content of his life, the fullness of his consciousness, the essence of his being, in some manner outside himself. He is always absent, never present to himself. But it is evident that it is possible to be absent from one's self either in the past or in the future (*E/O*, I, 220).

The tenses beyond the present define that territory in which consciousness can become lost to itself; it can absent itself either in

recollections of the past or in expectations of the future. The aesthete, however, does not live either in recollection or expectation.
Not simply a man of hope or of memory, he is a desperate amalgam
of the two.

> When the man of hope would have a future which can
> have no reality for him, or the man of memory would re-
> member a past which has had no reality, then we have the
> essentially unhappy individual (*E/O*, I, 221–22).

Such an "unhappy individual" is the aesthete, who, in the deepest
recess of his mind, recognizes that the future he seeks is illusory,[18]
and that the past he tells himself he remembers is only the product of an idealizing "recollection." His predicament is revealed as
even more desperate, "It is memory which prevents the unhappy
individual from finding himself in his hope, and hope which prevents him from finding himself in his memory" (*E/O*, I, 223). If
there were no hope for a repetition, then he could sink contentedly
into the dream of memory. But perhaps the future will bring him
what his heart desires, perhaps this girl with the laughing eyes,
perhaps . . . . And yet he cannot live on in the anticipation of
this "perhaps." For this hope itself is shadowed by the unwavering
recognition that, no matter how it is fulfilled, it will pale in the
shadow of an experience which is already irretrievably lost and
gone.

Looking both to the future and to the past, the aesthete
recognizes his isolation. He realizes that he is ensnared in a hopeless oscillation. Hope calls up, and is cancelled by, memory. Memory stimulates hope, and is finally overcome by it. From memory
to an awareness of loss, to a hope for the return of that which is
lost, to a recognition of the futility of hope, to memory once again:
this is the agonizing wheel on which the aesthete is bound. Ensnared within this oscillation he recognizes his removal from time.
As with his earlier attempt to forge a unity with the world, once
again the aesthete is brought full circle. He begins by attempting
to concentrate his life in the fire of "the Moment." [19] But the fact
that he must *intend* this concentration brings about a fatal splaying of the moment. For what he desires is not any moment, but
the repetition of a moment of wholeness which trembles on the

limit of awareness. In the delicate touch of "the first," in the tingle of a new sensation, he feels the presence of this moment. He seeks it, wills it as a future possibility, and in so doing sets up the temporal diaspora. Both future and past recede farther and farther away, sealing him hermetically in the casket of his intending. He lives in a "now" without limit or distinction where it is always "an *idem per idem* . . . , no variety always a rehash!" (*E/O*, 1, 299). In this isolated moment (which is not "the Moment" he sought, but its polar opposite) he looks both ways, and recognizes that his retirement from time has been completed. He recognizes that he has in fact "no time at all."

> Alone by himself he stands in the wide world. He has no contemporary time to support him. . . . He cannot become old for he has never been young; he cannot become young, for he is already old. . . . He has no time for anything, not because his time is taken up with something else, but because he has no time at all (*E/O*, 1, 224).

vii. A Stranger and an Alien

And so the voyage is ended. After the deep sleep, the fitful dream, after the youthful quest of discovery, and after the agonized attempt to compress consciousness into the "flesh incarnate" of Don Juan: after all this, the aesthete is finally thrown up on the coast of despair. Now the laughter and excitement, the wine and the pretty faces, are all behind him.

> My soul is faint and impatient; in vain I prick the spur of pleasure into its flank, its strength is gone, it rises no more to the royal leap. Once pleasure had but to beckon me, and I mounted, light of foot, sound and unafraid. When I rode slowly through the woods, it was as if I flew; now when the horse is covered with lather and ready to drop, it seems to me that I do not move (*E/O*, 11, 40).

Awakening now on this distant coast, it seems to him as if the world itself has subtly altered. Only distantly in memory can he detect the ebb and flow of that passionate energy which brought him here. Now passion, movement, life—all are dead. Now he must adjust to a new life—the life of "a stranger and an alien" [20]

who must be content "to wander like an unquiet spirit, like a
ghost, amid the ruins of a world which is lost" (*E/O*, II, 223).

This was the world Kierkegaard surveyed when he looked
out over his life in the early 1840's. The years of dissipation—the
drunken evenings with friends like Jørgen Jørgensen, the brothel
visits, the chatter of café society—all this was over. True, these
excesses were not extraordinary for a young bachelor of Kierkegaard's wealth, and in May 1843 he will remark, "These pleasures
and excesses are perhaps in God's eyes not so scandalous, for it
was dread which led me to run wild" (IV A 107). But in any case,
now they were over and done with, and the landscape which
Kierkegaard viewed was the "dreary and disconsolate desert" of
Ahasuerus, the landscape of despair.

It is *despair* which is the very ambience of *Either/Or*, Volume I. It is this "sickness unto death" which enfolds the life-world
of the aesthete and is revealed implicitly in each one of his essays.
We can think of this first volume, then, as a laying out, as a laying
bare of the pathology of the sickness. In it we are offered a case
history and exhaustive description of symptoms.

Yet a complete diagnosis demands more than a simple enu-
meration of symptoms. Hence in this first volume, Kierkegaard is
also attempting to plot the etiology of despair—to chart its dy-
namics, describe its development, and isolate its source. In so
doing he keeps returning to *consciousness* as the ultimate patho-
genic factor. It is *consciousness* which is at once the source of the
sickness as well as its most outstanding symptom.

For what is despair but a kind of gigantism of consciousness?
And what is its evolution but the gradual enlargement of consciousness to such an abnormal size that it greets the victim of despair
wherever he looks, sealing him from the world, and robbing him
of the capacity ever to really *be* in any given moment? Moreover,
as we have seen, this disease comes about as a response on the
part of the individual to the very fact of consciousness. "Every
aesthetic view of life is despair"; yet the very choice of such an
aesthetic life-view is seen as motivated by the urge to overcome
consciousness. The aesthete wills to be unconscious, to be "flesh
incarnate," and in the moment of sensation to achieve that closure
which consciousness denies him. Yet the very fact that he *wills* the

destruction of consciousness is itself a contradiction. Instead of be-coming less conscious, he becomes more conscious. His project, originally designed to eradicate consciousness, is shipwrecked on the very fact of consciousness. In this way, it is *consciousness* which stands at the very heart of Kierkegaard's diagnosis of despair.

If the sickness is diagnosed in this way, then a possible ther-apy is suggested. For instead of denying the fact of consciousness, might we not accept it? And instead of consciously willing the destruction of consciousness, might we not expand it? If con-sciousness cannot be absorbed into flesh, might not it still be forged into will? As we shall see in succeeding sections, an at-tempted therapy of this sort is suggested by Kierkegaard in his characterization of the ethical act.

And so we come to the second volume of *Either/Or*.

VIII. *The Ethical Act: Choice*

"Behold, my young friend, this life of yours is despair," cautions the Judge, "It is as though you were caught and ensnared and could nevermore, either in time or eternity make your escape" (*E/O*, II, 209–10). Having said this, having diagnosed A's sickness as despair, the Judge now is in a position to prescribe a therapy. This therapy is the act of ethical choice.

We should recognize first that there is a distinction between an "aesthetic choice" and an "ethical choice."

> Your choice is an aesthetic choice, but an aesthetic choice is no choice. The act of choosing is essentially a proper and stringent expression of the ethical. . . . When one does not choose absolutely one chooses only for the moment, and therefore can choose something different the next moment. The ethical choice is therefore in a certain sense much easier, much simpler, but in another sense it is infinitely harder . . . . If you will understand me aright I should like to say that in making a choice it is not so much a question of choosing the right as of the earnestness, the pathos with which one chooses. Thereby the personality announces its inner infinity, and thereby, in turn, the personality is consolidated.
>
> (*E/O*, II, 170–71)

A so-called "aesthetic choice" is really no choice at all since it is made only for the moment. An "ethical choice" is a vow whose defining characteristic is its endurance and renewal in time. Thus made, and thus renewed, the passion of the choice serves to consolidate the personality. "The choice itself," the Judge points out, "is decisive for the content of personality, through the choice the personality immerses itself in the thing chosen, and when it does not choose it withers away in consumption" (*E/O*, ɪɪ, 167).

The victim of despair had permitted his life to be aesthetically dispersed into a multiplicity of different moods, projects, and emotions. Now he is to be the source of a radical act of self-integration. Just as earlier he had "contracted" despair, so now must he cure himself—for only he can perform the act of radical choice recommended by the Judge. It is then a *self-therapy* which the Judge is prescribing in his characterization of ethical choice.

But how is this therapy to be carried out? Every choice must be a choice of *something*. What is the object of ethical choice?

"And what is it he chooses?" asks the Judge. "He chooses himself, not in his immediacy, not as this fortuitous individual, but he chooses himself in his eternal validity" (*E/O*, ɪɪ, 215). The ethical choice is not a choice of this or that set of values, of this or that moral code. Rather it is a choice by the individual of himself. And as an act of self-choice it has two dimensions—one corresponding to the past (the facticity of the individual), and one corresponding to the future (the potentiality of the individual).

In choosing himself, the ethical man chooses a self which is quite definite and historical.

> He who chooses himself ethically chooses himself concretely as this definite individual. . . . The individual thus becomes conscious of himself as this definite individual with these talents, these dispositions, these instincts, these passions, influenced by these definite surroundings, as this definite environment. But being conscious of himself in this way he assumes responsibility for all this. He does not hesitate as to whether he shall include this particular trait or the other. . . . He has his place in the world, and with freedom he chooses his place, that is, he chooses this very place. He is a

definite individual, in the choice he makes himself a definite individual, for he chooses himself (E/O, II, 255–56).

In choosing himself the ethical man accepts his identity in all its concreteness. He is *this* person, born in *this* town, of *these* parents, at *this* time; *this* is his situation, and in choosing himself he accepts it unconditionally. Yet curiously, this very choice of the situation in all its concreteness transforms it. For by freely taking it on, it is transferred from the realm of necessity to the realm of freedom, "All that has happened to me or befallen me is by me transformed and translated from necessity to freedom" (E/O, II, 255). What previously was alien and unwanted, the ineluctable evidence of one's facticity is now penetrated with freedom. "He who lives ethically," the Judge remarks, "has seen himself, knows himself, penetrates with his consciousness his whole concretion" (E/O, II, 263).

This choice of oneself *in situ* has yet another dimension. For the fact that the ethical man chooses himself concretely involves a necessary transformation of his relation to the future—of his possibilities.

> He who chooses himself ethically has himself as his task, and not as a possibility merely, not as a toy to be played with arbitrarily. He can choose himself ethically only when he chooses himself in continuity, and so he has himself as a task which is manifestly defined (E/O, II, 262).

For the aesthete, the future and possibility are blank and open. They are, A admits in one of the diapsalmata, like the empty space into which a spider hurls itself.[21] But for the ethical man this empty space has been transformed into the firm outlines of a life-task. It is as if in discovering his identity in the act of ethical choice, the ethical man also discovered how this identity should be realized. Hence, while on the one hand the self he chooses is factual and past, on the other hand it is potential and future.

> Although he himself is his aim, this aim is nevertheless another, for the self which is the aim is not an abstract self which fits anywhere and hence nowhere, but a concrete self which stands in reciprocal relations with these surroundings, these conditions of life, this natural order (E/O, II, 267).

The self he chooses is of course himself. But this self includes vectors toward the future—gifts, talents, potentialities—and these also are included in the choice. By thus choosing the past in such a way that the future becomes definite the ethical man knits up the fracture in the tenses made evident in despair. Future flows out of past naturally and confidently; the personality is consolidated; the individual attains mastery over himself: "The fact that the individual sees his possibility as his task expresses precisely his sovereignty over himself" (*E/O*, II, 256).

Now it is just this aim of gaining "sovereignty over himself" which summarizes the ethical man's project. He *wills* now to penetrate his whole being with the consciousness of his choice.

> Only when in his choice a man has assumed himself, is clad in himself, has so totally penetrated himself that every moment is attended by the consciousness of a responsibility for himself, only then has he chosen himself ethically
>
> (*E/O*, II,252).

Now he is totally responsible for himself. All his past, all the facts of personal appearance and bodily disposition, all his hereditary gifts or deprivations, even all the things which have befallen him: all this tangled web of time past and given he accepts responsibility for, and thus transfers from the realm of necessity to freedom. Whereas the aesthete chose to deny consciousness in attempting to become "flesh incarnate," the ethical man seeks to "penetrate with consciousness his whole concretion." He contracts a never-varying "consciousness of a responsibility for himself" which penetrates even to the possibilities his facticity is heir to. In transforming these possibilities into tasks through an act of conscious choice the ethical man comes to consolidate his being. If the aim of the aesthete is to become pure flesh, then the aim of the ethical man is to become pure will.

IX. The Return to the World and Time

The first consequence of the ethical man's attempt to interpenetrate his life with consciousness is a new opening to the world.

> In the movement towards himself the individual cannot relate himself negatively towards his environment, for if

he were to do so his self is an abstraction and remains such. His self must be opened in due relation to his entire concretion; but to this concretion belong also the factors which are designed for taking an active part in the world. So then his movement is from himself through the world to himself (E/O, ii, 279).

The first prerequisite of ethical choice is the individual's acceptance of his present situation. This acceptance, which the Judge calls "repentance," forges a new unity between the world and the individual.

> He cannot relinquish anything in this whole, not the most painful, not the hardest to bear, and yet the expression for this fight, for this acquisition is . . . repentance. He repents himself back into himself, back into the family, back into the race, until he finds himself in God (E/O, ii, 220).

By the ethical man's choice the chrysalis of despair is sundered. Through his repentant acceptance of his past and his situation a new intimacy with the world is won. "Repentance," we are told, "puts the individual in the most intimate connection and the most exact cohesion with a surrounding world" (E/O, ii, 245).

This full-blown return to the world is one consequence of the ethical man's choice of himself. Yet a more startling consequence of this choice, and one far more difficult to trace, is the ethical man's correlative return to time itself. This return is sketched in Judge William's discussion of marriage.

Throughout the second volume Judge William uses marriage as a paradigm for the ethical life, and on the surface, at least, the reasons for the choice of such a paradigm are not readily apparent. Up to now we have spoken of the ethical life as grounded upon a choice of oneself, while marriage is founded upon a vow given to another. In the following passage Judge William describes the essential character of married love.

> Conjugal love has its foe in time, its triumph in time, its eternity in time, and so it would have its problems, even if I were to imagine it free from all socalled external and internal trials. Generally it has these too; but if one were to

interpret them rightly, one must observe two things: that
these trials are constantly inward determinations; and that
they constantly have in them the determinants of time. . . .
You may convince yourself of this more thoroughly by considering the predicates commonly applied to conjugal love.
It is faithful, constant, humble, patient, long-suffering, in-
dulgent, sincere, contented, vigilant, willing, joyful. All these
virtues have the characteristic that they are inward qualifications of the individual. . . . And they have reference to
time, for their truth does not consist in being once and for
all but in being constantly what they are. And by these
virtues nothing else is acquired, only they themselves are
acquired (*E/O*, II, 142).

Certainly most, if not all, the predicates of conjugal love would
find mention in any complete list of ethical predicates. Note the
characteristics which the Judge sees as common to these predicates:
(1) they are "inward qualifications of the individual," and (2)
they have "reference to time." These characteristics are also characteristics of ethical predicates. The ethical life is founded upon
an act of radical choice; marriage upon a vow. But both exhibit the
same substructure of assertion and renewal. A choice made for
the moment is "aesthetic" and really no choice at all. The very
essence of ethical choice is its endurance through time. It is then
a vow; its whole reality is found in "the inward qualification of the
individual" sustaining it through time. The reason Judge William
uses marriage as a paradigm of the ethical life is that marriage is
explicitly founded upon a vow, and hence makes clear the structure of assertion and renewal which supports the ethical life.

The ethical man's choice of himself is, then, a vow to himself. Moreover, it is by binding himself with a vow that he gains
a new intimacy with time. For it is the very substance of a vow
to be temporally extended; it only becomes itself through this
extension. While the aesthete was only vaguely aware of a temporal passage in the world around him, the ethical man now comes
to include time in his own person. Time becomes real for
the individual only when he wills that some inward qualification
shall remain constant through time (*E/O*, II, 140). Only when he

wills to be faithful or true, only when he gathers his life and stretches it upon the form of will, does he enter into time. Only then does he gain an "internal history" and thereby become fully "historical."

> When, however, it is a question of internal history every little moment is of the utmost importance. Internal history is the only true history; but true history contends with that which is the life principle of history, i.e. with time. But when one contends with time, then the temporal and every little moment of it acquires for this fact immense reality (E/O, II, 137).

Now every moment becomes full, every second gains tremendous significance. Contending in this way with time, the ethical man does not "kill" time but "preserves" it. The Judge concludes his discussion of the married man's "internal history" with these words.

> He has not fought with lions and ogres, but with the most dangerous enemy: with time. But for him eternity does not come afterwards . . . , but he has had eternity in time, has preserved eternity in time. He alone therefore has triumphed over time. . . . The married man, being a true conqueror, has not killed time but has saved it and preserved it in eternity. The married man who does this truly lives poetically. He solves the great riddle of living in eternity and yet hearing the hall clock strike, and hearing it in such a way that the stroke of the hour does not shorten but prolongs his eternity (E/O, II, 141).

x. The Ethical Ideal

While the aesthete attempted to overcome the void of consciousness by concentrating his life in sensation (by becoming "flesh incarnate"), the ethical man attempts to overcome this same void by penetrating his life with consciousness (by becoming pure will). He seeks to so enfold his life in consciousness that nothing is left out. All sensation, facticity, and possibility are plaited together in the service of will. He chooses himself, and in so choosing gains a "sovereignty over himself." And as we saw, this act of choosing brings with it a shattering of the hermetic life of despair and a return to the world and time.

We can think of the ethical man's choice of himself as a curious kind of marriage vow—a vow which marries him not merely to another person but to life itself. The Judge speaks of "the consolidation, the penetrating shudder through all thoughts and joints which marriage is, for after all it is truly a deed of daring" (*E/O*, II, 67), and this description might be just as aptly applied to the ethical man's choice of himself. For above all it is a "deed," an act which only the ethical man can perform for himself, an act by virtue of which *uno tenore* he seeks to free himself of despair. All the Judge's many appeals to A are founded on the presumption that by a single act of will, constantly renewed, the individual can cure himself of despair. By virtue of this act he becomes aware of a "consolidation," of a "penetrating shudder through all thoughts and joints," which transforms consciousness and cures despair. There is despair, and there is life; and between the two there is the healing act of choice whereby the individual once and for all "marries" himself to life.

The life on the far side of despair is described by the Judge in the closing pages of *Either/Or*, where he offers glimpses of his own existence as husband, father, and man of affairs. He admits that he too now and then comes to "subside into himself," permitting a "melancholy" [*Tungsind*] to gain ascendancy over him (*E/O*, II, 312). But swiftly the presence of his wife resuscitates him.

> When I am sitting thus lost and abandoned and then look at my wife walking about the room lightly and beautifully, always occupied, always with something to attend to, my eye voluntarily follows her movement, I participate in all that she undertakes, and it ends with my being again reconciled with time, finding that time acquires significance for me, that the instant moves swiftly (*E/O*, II, 312).

There is indeed something idyllic here in the Judge's description of his domestic life. It is filled with the rich tones, luminous atmosphere, and romance for the commonplace so characteristic of a Vermeer interior. The Judge tells how he returns from work to the beautiful tones of his wife's lullaby, how he enters to "hear the cry of the little one," which to his ear "is not inharmonious" (*E/O*, II, 329). There is a peace here, a feeling of time passing happily, of a harmony of the individual with his world which is quite touching. Here is the ideal of the ethical life: the husband, father, and man of affairs who has contracted a full commitment to life.

> His work is at the same time his calling, hence he works with pleasure. The fact that it is his calling brings him into association with other men, and in performing his job he accomplishes what he could wish to accomplish in the world. He is married, contented with his home, and time passes swiftly for him, he cannot comprehend how time might be a burden to a man or an enemy of his happiness; on the contrary, time appears to him a true blessing
>
> (*E/O*, II, 310).

This is indeed a touching picture. Yet it becomes even more touching when we recognize with a shock that it was precisely this ideal of life, this "or," that Kierkegaard himself relinquished in striding up the gangplank of a ship bound for Germany in the autumn of 1841.

xi. *The Cloister*

The Judge's life is really the contented bourgeois existence which Kierkegaard himself renounced in leaving Regine. In the letters of Judge William, Kierkegaard gives breath and movement to that ideal of life he hoped to attain with her. It was to be her health, we remember, which would cure his sickness. In becoming engaged to her he had already put behind him the aesthetic ideal of the 1830's. Now marriage would be the "or"—the first corridor of escape from the labyrinth of consciousness which had become so unbearable by 1840. Yet as we saw, this "or" proved to be a blind alley; Regine was revealed as no Ariadne, but only a pretty girl of seventeen.

Yet if all this is correct, note what it implies. It implies that when *Either/Or* was written Kierkegaard was already cognizant of the failure of the ethical ideal, that at the very time he was so glowingly describing the Judge's domestic life he also recognized its factitious character! What evidence do we have of such a recognition?

Five years later, in 1848, Kierkegaard reflects back upon the time when *Either/Or* was written. He writes,

> When I began *Either/Or* . . . I was as deeply under the influence of religion as ever I have been. I was so deeply shaken that I understood perfectly well that I could not possibly succeed in striking the comforting and secure *via media* in which most people pass their lives. . . . Personally I was very far from wanting to call existence back to marriage—I who religiously was already in the cloister, which thought is hidden in the pseudonym: Victor—*Eremita*.
>
> Such is the situation; strictly speaking *Either/Or* was written in a cloister . . . (*Point of View*, 18).

Yet if, as Kierkegaard says, he wrote *Either/Or* "in the cloister," if it is true that he stands with Victor Eremita *beyond* both the standpoints of the young man and Judge William, then it would follow that already in 1843 he was aware of the failure of the ethical ideal. Curiously enough, however, no clear recognition of the difficulties plaguing this view is offered in *Either/Or* or in the works which immediately followed. As we shall see, Kierkegaard seems to lose interest in the ethical ideal, and it is not until the *Postscript*, published three years later, that he offers a concise account of its failure. There he writes,

> The ethicist in *Either/Or* had saved himself through despair, abolishing concealment in self-revelation; but here was in my opinion a difficulty. . . . He made it appear that by despairing, in the very act of despair itself, as if *uno tenore*, he had been able to win himself. . . . He has indeed used a determination of freedom: to choose himself —which seems to lessen the difficulty. . . . But this avails nothing. When I despair, I use myself to despair, and therefore I can indeed by myself despair of everything; but when I do this I cannot by myself come back. In this moment of decision it is that the individual needs divine assistance.

> . . . By being there in passion and inwardness one will
> doubtless become aware of the religious—and of the *leap*
>
> (*Postscript*, 230–31).

As we have seen in past sections, the ethical project is grounded
upon the conviction that by a single act the individual can cure
himself of despair. In the passage above Kierkegaard points out
that this conviction is misplaced—that the victim of despair cannot break out of despair by *his own act*, but that he requires help
from beyond. Just so little as the aesthete could collapse consciousness into flesh, just so little can the ethical man attain closure
by becoming pure will. For pure will no less than pure desire requires consciousness as its infrastructure. When inclination and
will become coincident—when nothing is left to confront the self
as alien or other—at just this point does will itself become impossible. As Kierkegaard points out, "When I despair, I must use myself to despair." Yet if I am using myself, then I am not identical
with that self which is used. The very act of willing requires a gap
between the self which is willed and the self which wills. Thus it
is that consciousness can no more be forged into will than earlier
it could be collapsed into desire. As the foundational structure of
both will and desire, it evades identification with either.

The diaphanous void of consciousness remains, and with it
its labyrinth. The way out must then be in part a gift from beyond.
Self-therapy is impossible; divine assistance is required. Health, if
it comes, must come in the wake of what Kierkegaard will later
call a "thunderstorm"; it must be a "repetition," a thundering
crash of the eternal into time. Thus it is that the very failure of
the aesthetic and ethical projects dictates a final direction in which
Kierkegaard's quest is to be pursued. If consciousness can neither
be compressed into flesh in the moment of intense sensation, nor
be forged into will in the moment of ethical decision, nevertheless
it may yet be *shattered* by focusing its energies on something whose
very existence confounds consciousness. It is towards the discovery of this paradoxical something that the next segment of
Kierkegaard's pseudonymous authorship is directed.

5

REPETITION, FEAR AND TREMBLING

I. *Edifying Discourses*

Simultaneously with the publication of pseudonymous works in the early 1840's, Kierkegaard was also publishing a series of devotional works under his own name. A brief listing of the titles and publication dates of these works may prove enlightening.

TWO EDIFYING DISCOURSES (16 May 1843)
1. The Expectation of Faith
2. Every Good and Every Perfect Gift Is from Above

THREE EDIFYING DISCOURSES (16 October 1843)
1. Love Shall Cover a Multitude of Sins
2. Love Shall Cover a Multitude of Sins
3. Strengthened in the Inner Man

FOUR EDIFYING DISCOURSES (6 December 1843)
1. The Lord Gave, and the Lord Hath Taken Away
2. Every Good and Every Perfect Gift Is from Above
3. Every Good and Every Perfect Gift Is from Above
4. To Acquire One's Soul in Patience

TWO EDIFYING DISCOURSES (5 March 1844)
1. To Preserve One's Soul in Patience
2. Patient in Expectation

THREE EDIFYING DISCOURSES (8 June 1844)
  1. Remember Now Thy Creator in the Days of Thy Youth
  2. The Expectation of an Eternal Happiness
  3. He Must Increase, but I Must Decrease

FOUR EDIFYING DISCOURSES (31 August 1844)
  1. Man's Need of God Constitutes His Highest Perfection
  2. The Thorn in the Flesh
  3. Against Cowardice
  4. The Righteous Man Strives in Prayer with God and Con-
     quers—in that God Conquers

THREE DISCOURSES ON IMAGINED OCCASIONS (29 April 1845)
  1. What It Means to Seek God
  2. Love Conquers All
  3. The Decisiveness of Death

The first group of two discourses followed by three months the
publication of Either/Or, and Kierkegaard always thought of them
as "accompanying" his first pseudonymous work.[1] The second
group of discourses was published on the same day as Repetition
and Fear and Trembling, and the fifth group came out simultaneously with Philosophical Fragments and The Concept of Dread.
If we add to these three groups the Three Discourses on Imagined
Occasions, published simultaneously with Stages on Life's Way
in April 1845, the pattern becomes complete—each of the pseudonymous works had its accompanying set of discourses. Published
in Kierkegaard's own name, we would expect these discourses to
plot out Kierkegaard's position in contradistinction to that of the
various pseudonyms. Surprisingly enough however, we find that
the standpoint sketched in these discourses does not differ essentially from the standpoint of the pseudonyms. The author of the
Edifying Discourses, and the pseudonymous authors from Victor
Eremita to Johannes Climacus, all find their places on that curious
hermetic plateau beyond the aesthetic and ethical life-views, yet
short of the "higher immediacy" of faith.

The very titles of the edifying discourses suggest their content. From them we can read off a characteristic emphasis on pa-

tience and expectation. "The Expectation of Faith," "To Acquire One's Soul in Patience," "Patient in Expectation," "The Expectation of an Eternal Happiness": such titles as these bear witness not to the possession of either faith or the certitude of an eternal happiness, but rather to the expectation of both. As Kierkegaard is careful to point out in the prefaces which accompany these devotional works, they are not "sermons" [*Praedikener*] but "discourses" [*Taler*].[2] "Sermons" can only be given from a standpoint within faith, while "discourses" are suitable expressions for a standpoint anterior to faith. "Unless," Kierkegaard later remarks, "we are to have a confusion of tongues, the sermon must be reserved for the Christian-religious type of existence" (*Postscript*, 229). Not sermons, not written from a Christian standpoint within faith, these discourses "employ only ethically immanent categories," [3] and thus articulate a standpoint only "on the way" to faith—a standpoint which Johannes de Silentio will designate the "stage of infinite resignation."

The tone of these discourses is amply illustrated by this passage from one published in May 1843.

> There is a little word sufficiently familiar to the congregations even if not always heeded by them. . . . It is the word: at last; for so many of the sacred collects which are read in our churches end in this way: "and so at last be saved." The older man among us, who stands almost at the end, looks back in his thought over the way he has traveled . . . , he is weary and he says: "and so at last be saved." The younger, who even now stands at the beginning of the way, looks ahead in thought over the long road. In thought he experiences what is to come: the painful bereavements, the quiet concerns, the sad longings, the fearful anxieties; he is wearied at the thought and says: "and so at last be saved." It would indeed be a great gift if a man could rightly use this word; but no man learns this from another, but severally only from and through God. Therefore will we commit to Thee, Father in heaven, our heart and our thought, so that our soul may never be so ensnared by the joys of life or by its sorrows, that it forgets this liberating word (*Edifying Discourses*, 32–33).

The tone here is hushed, subdued, muted. We feel how distant the writer himself feels from salvation. If it comes, it will come "at last." Like the castle a long way off, it seems to lie at the end of a long road with many turnings. And now, feeling its remoteness, the writer cautions that we must remain expectant, careful not to become "ensnared by the joys of life or its sorrows." His advice to all those who stand with him beyond the illusory promise of the aesthetic and ethical life-views is to cultivate a spirit of *resignation*. We must, we are later told, bring ourselves to a position where we can say with Job, "The Lord gave, and the Lord has taken away. Blessed be the name of the Lord!" [4] Only then, when we have retired into the cloister by becoming aware of the vanity of the world, only then are we in a position to await expectantly the irruption of a faith which may or may not come.

It is startling how closely the standpoints of Kierkegaard's pseudonyms approximate this "stage of infinite resignation." The very meanings of their names help us locate them on this plateau. There is first of all Victor Eremita,[5] whose last name, we saw, located him "in the cloister." Next is Constantine Constantius, who, mired in his "constant constancy" cannot receive the thunderstorm of "repetition" which revives his young friend and restores him to life. Then too there is Johannes de Silentio, that "knight of infinite resignation," who can only stand "astonished" [forbauset] before the faith of an Abraham. Next is Vigilius Haufniensis, the pedantic psychologist, whose name is a Latin transcription for "the watchman of Copenhagen." Then there is Frater Taciturnus, that "taciturn" priest of the final stage anterior to faith. Finally, there is Johannes Climacus, who, although unable to make the movements of faith himself nevertheless lays out the ladder (Latin: climacus) leading to it. None of these pseudonymous authors pretends to have personal experience of faith, but all see it gleaming on the horizon. Thus, Constantine Constantius observes the irruption of faith in his young friend; Johannes de Silentio contemplates its Biblical expression in Abraham; Vigilius Haufniensis sees it as a possible cure for dread; Frater Taciturnus sees it as a possibility lying beyond both his own position and that of Quidam whose engagement is recounted; finally, Johannes Climacus sees faith as no more than the terminus of a ladder which he himself has failed to climb to its highest rung. Faith for all of them has the character of a much desired possibility, but not as an actuality they have experienced.

All of these pseudonymous authors could conceivably be members of that "fellowship of buried lives" described in *Either/ Or*, Vol. I. They all have renounced contact with life. They all in a sense "live *aphorismenoi* and *segregati*, like aphorisms in life, without community of men, without sharing their joys and their griefs." Yet their "despair," if we may call it this, seems less acute than that sickness we would normally associate with the *Symparanekromenoi*. Their cries of pain seem muted, perhaps not even cries of pain at all, and they do not seem to be "lost" in that odd way the aesthetes of *Either/Or* were "lost." It is as if they have neared the outer corridor of the labyrinth, have suffered through the crisis of their illness, and so find their despair not nearly so intense. Only in the characters that appear at a secondary level in these works (such as the Young Man in *Repetition*, or Quidam in *Stages on Life's Way*) do we feel despair tightened to the same pitch we associate with *Either/Or*. Both of these characters, modelled on Kierkegaard himself as a young man, carry with them the scars of that acute despair suffered by him in the late 1830's. They are once again, like the aesthetes of *Either/Or*, self-portraits of the artist as he was. But the principal pseudonyms, the putative authors of the books, seem to have moved beyond the experience of acute despair into a stage of resignation. They have become, as it were, *convalescents*.

Repetition

II. *Repetition: Constantine Constantius*

Repetition was published simultaneously with *Fear and Trembling* on October 16, 1843. Not long afterwards, Kierkegaard made the following entry in his journal.

> Repetition is and remains a religious category. Constantine Constantius cannot, therefore, get any further. He is clever, ironical, combats the interesting, but does not notice that he himself is stuck in it. The first form of the interesting is to love change; the second is to desire repetition,

but in self-sufficiency and with no suffering attached to it—
Constantine therefore is stranded on what he himself has
discovered, and the young man goes farther (IV A 169).

This entry gives us at once a glimpse of the two characters appearing in *Repetition*, as well as a brief statement of the central
problem of the book. The two characters are of course Constantine
Constantius—its pseudonymous author—and the nameless "young
man" with whom he corresponds. The central problem of the
book is whether (as Constantine puts it in the first paragraph) "a
repetition is possible" (*Repetition*, 3). Yet it would be too great
a simplification to contend that both characters are struggling
with the *same* problem. For as we shall see, each character formulates the problem in a different way, and it is precisely this difference in formulation which accounts for the failure of the first
and the success of the second.

"Inasmuch as for a long time," Constantine Constantius begins, "I have been engaged, at least occasionally, with the problem
whether a repetition is possible . . . , it suddenly occurred to me,
'Thou canst take a trip to Berlin, where thou hast been before,
and convince thyself now whether a repetition is possible and what
significance it may have' " (*Repetition*, 3). Part One of *Repetition*
recounts Constantine's visit to Berlin, and the failure of his attempt to realize "repetition." But it is by no means clear from the
beginning just what it is Constantine is trying to have *repeated*.
It is only towards the end of Part One, after Constantine has returned, disgruntled, from Berlin, that we learn what it was he
wished to have repeated. It was "contentment" [*Tilfredshed*].

Disillusioned with his visit to Berlin, Constantine remarks,
"Everyone who has thoroughly considered the matter will agree
with me that it is never granted to a man in his whole life, even for
so much as half an hour, to be absolutely content in all imaginable
ways" (*Repetition*, 74). Yet if one can never reach perfect contentment, nevertheless one can come very close to it. Constantine
then proceeds to describe in detail the occasion on which he came
closest to attaining real contentment. His description bears quoting
at length.

> Once I was very close to it. I got up in the morning
> feeling uncommonly well. The sense of well-being increased

out of proportion to all analogy during the forenoon. Precisely at one o'clock I was at the highest peak. . . . The body had lost all its earthly heaviness, it was as though I had no body. . . . My gait became a glide, not like the flight of a bird that cleaves the air and leaves the earth behind, but like the billows of the wind over a field of grain, like the yearning bliss of the cradling waves of the sea. . . . The whole of existence seemed to be as it were in love with me, and everything vibrated in pre-ordained *rapport* with my being. . . . Everything was enigmatically transfigured in my bliss, which was able to transform into its own likeness all things, even the observations which were most disagreeable and tiresome, even disgusting sights and the most fatal collisions (*Repetition*, 74–76).

Nowhere in all of Kierkegaard's published work do we find a more vivid description of that "moment of continuity" described earlier in Chapter 2. Yet it is precisely the recovery of this moment (now called "contentment") that is the aim of Constantine's trip to Berlin.

On an earlier visit he had been quite happy in Berlin. He had lived in a pleasant pension, dined in comfortable restaurants, and had enjoyed ample opportunities for satisfying his penchant for the theater. The high point of his earlier visit, in fact, had been a performance at the Königstäter Theater. At this performance he reached a summit of enjoyment paralleling his earlier experience of contentment.

> Thus it was I lay back in my loge, cast aside like the clothing of a bather, flung beside the stream of laughter and merriment and jubilation which foamed past me incessantly. I could see nothing but the vast expanse of the theater, hear nothing but the din in the midst of which I dwelt. Only now and then did I raise myself, look at Beckmann [one of the actors], and laugh so heartily that for very fatigue I sank down beside the foaming stream (*Repetition*, 63–64).

Once again, at the peak of his earlier visit to Berlin, Constantine had felt content. He decides to attempt to repeat the external circumstances of his earlier visit in hopes of recovering contentment. Sadly, his attempt proves futile.

Returning to Berlin on the first day of Lent he finds every-thing changed. The city seems greyer, deader than it was before. The wind is blowing now, and "the whole city is one cloud of dust" (*Repetition*, 40). He goes to his old pension and finds that there, too, time has brought its changes—his friend the concierge has married, and now proclaims the joys of marriage where earlier he had praised bachelorhood (*Repetition*, 39). Constantine decides to have a refreshment at his usual coffee house, and finds that it is now hot and stuffy (*Repetition*, 69). Wherever he goes he dis-covers that the actual place or experience fails to live up to its remembered surrogate. But perhaps in the Königstäter Theater things will be different; perhaps there he will be able to recover that enjoyment which highlighted his earlier visit. Alas, there also everything is changed. He cannot procure an empty box (as had been his custom) but must content himself with a place in the noisy crowd. He settles himself in his place, reflecting that the earlier audience was not as vulgar as the present one. And unhap-pily, a young girl he had admired at the earlier performance is no longer in attendance. Finally, when the footlights go up, he dis-covers to his acute disappointment that what before had seemed sparkling and witty now appears flat and dull. Recognizing that even the great Beckmann cannot make him laugh, he exclaims in disgust, "There is no such thing as repetition . . . Might exist-ence be more fraudulent than a bankrupt?" (*Repetition*, 68). In a rush of despondency he returns to his room, and within a few days takes leave of Berlin. "Repetition" has proved to be impos-sible; he arrives back in Copenhagen a chastened and sadder man.

Is "repetition" possible? Assuredly *not* for Constantine Con-stantius. His very specification of repetition, in fact, has entailed its impossibility; his formulation of the problem has denied it a solution.

Constantine is an aesthete—we shall meet him again in com-pany with Johannes the Seducer, Victor Eremita, the Fashion Designer, and the "young man" at the banquet in *Stages on Life's Way*. Being an aesthete (although a highly reflective one) Con-stantine's formulation of the problem of repetition is an aesthetic one. The familiar pattern outlined in *Either/Or* of desiring a *past* state as a *future* possibility is rehearsed once again in his project of repetition. He desires to recover the deliciousness of that past state of contentment, by repeating (if he can) the external conditions that produced it. But these conditions can never be repeated in their entirety, since both they and Constantine exist in time. Hence just as the aesthete's project in *Either/Or* "comes to grief upon time," [6] so Constantine's project of repetition meets shipwreck on the fact of change. The past cannot be repeated as future, and any projected repetition must inevitably be blocked by the difficulties elucidated in *Either/Or*. By giving the problem of repetition an aesthetic formulation, Constantine has made it into an insoluble puzzle. All his cleverness and intellectual acuity is to no avail. Returning from Berlin he complains, "And is it not true that the older one gets, the more deceptive life proves to be, that the shrewder one becomes and the more ways one learns to help oneself, the worse scrapes one gets into" (*Repetition*, 73). Realizing the impossibility of repetition he lapses into that slough of despair which sooner or later overtakes every aesthetic project.

> My home had become cheerless, precisely because it was the reverse of repetition, my mind was unfruitful, my troubled imagination was engaged in transmuting into the delights of Tantalus the memory of how richly the thoughts presented themselves on the former occasion, and this rank weed of memory strangled every weed at birth
>
> (*Repetition*, 69).

Constantine's descent into despair thus recapitulates the familiar progression outlined in *Either/Or*. But now we might ask, Is this all there is to Constantine's experiment of repetition? Is it no more than a retelling of the same story already told in far greater detail in *Either/Or*? Or are there subtleties in Constantine's character we have not detected?

It is perhaps too great a simplification to pass off Constantine as just another aesthete, and his experiment in repetition as the familiar aesthetic project. Constantine's story does not end with his return from Berlin, nor is his ultimate state one of despair. The remark quoted above to illustrate his despair was made *while he was still in Berlin*. If we follow him home to Copenhagen we can see how his state of mind undergoes a subtle change, how he moves beyond despair to a further standpoint. He describes this alteration in the first paragraph of Part Two.

> Some time passed. . . . A monotonous and uniform order was restored in my whole household economy. Everything which was not able to move stood in its precise place, and what able to go went its accustomed way—my parlor clock, my servant, and myself who with measured tread walked back and forth across the floor. For though I had convinced myself that no such thing as repetition exists, yet it is a sure truth that by firmness of purpose and by dulling one's talent for observation one can attain a uniformity which has a far more anesthetizing effect than the most capricious diversion, and which with time becomes stronger and stronger, like a formula of incantation. . . . Thus I lived, forgetting the world, as I thought, and by the world forgotten, when one day I received a letter from my young friend" (*Repetition*, 81–82).

The crucial phrases in this passage is, of course, the first one, "Some time passed. . . ." In the early sections of *Repetition* the reader finds it difficult to establish the temporal location of the narrator. Is Constantine recounting all this to us from the perspective of a week, a month, a year, five years? We do not know —for it is only as the story develops that we learn that all this is told from the perspective of probably several years. The experiment in Berlin took place a long while ago, long before Constantine began receiving letters from his young friend. Hence, both the experiment and its consequent despair are past history. "Some time passed . . . ," and this very passage of time has served to soothe Constantine's despair. In the meantime he has cultivated an "anesthetizing uniformity," and now feels almost happy in living isolated, "forgetting the world . . . , and by the world forgotten." What shall we call this hermetic stage beyond despair? Shall we liken it to the "stage of infinite resignation" later to be described by Johannes de Silentio? Or (with Kierkegaard) shall we call it "Stoicism"? [7] Whatever we call it we recognize that it is Constantine's *present* state—a move beyond the despair he remembers.

But we are not finished with Constantine just yet, for there is still the matter of these letters he ostensibly receives from the nameless Young Man in Stockholm. I say "ostensibly" because from the beginning we suspect that there is something not quite right about these letters. Note, for example, the following passage in which Constantine introduces them.

> The problem which baffles him [the Young Man] is neither more nor less than repetition . . . , whereas repetition is always a transcendence. It is lucky that the young man does not seek any enlightenment from me, for I have abandoned my theory, I am adrift. Repetition is too transcendent for me also. I can circumnavigate myself, but I cannot erect myself above myself, I cannot find the Archimedian point. . . . Even if he still were to desire my guidance, he would be seeking in vain. A religious movement I am unable to make, it is contrary to my nature. I am not inclined for this reason to deny the reality of such a thing, or to deny that one can learn a great deal from a young man. If he succeeds he will have no admirer more zealous than I
>
> (*Repetition*, 93–95).

This passage gives us a clear impression of the quality of Constantine's resignation, while at the same time illustrating the curious way in which he speaks of the Young Man. Constantine seems to know *too much* about him. In this and other passages he treats the Young Man more as a character in a play he has written than as an independent person. Finally, on the next to last page of the book we learn the truth. Constantine admits that he has indeed "brought him to birth" [8]—the Young Man is a creature of the imagination, created to explore the possibility of a religious repetition?

The basic dramatic situation proposed by *Repetition* now should be apparent. In recounting the failure of his journey to Berlin, Constantine has described the necessary failure of the aesthetic attempt at repetition. In Berlin he had tried to recover contentment, and had found (like the aesthetes in *Either/Or*) that all such attempts at recovery meet shipwreck on the fact of time. Unlike the aesthetes in *Either/Or*, however, this recognition does not prompt his retirement from the world in an inward-turning spiral of fantastic "recollection." On the contrary, he moves beyond the suffering of despair into a state of anesthetized resignation. It is from this state of resigned equilibrium that he now sets out to examine a wholly different sort of repetition. He invents the nameless Young Man, and through him imaginatively explores the possibility of a religious repetition. Thus in the second part of the book we find the so-called "problem of repetition" posed and solved within a different frame. Whereas in Part One repetition was examined within an aesthetic context, in Part Two it is examined within a religious one. It is this religious statement and solution of the problem we shall now investigate.

III. Repetition: The "Young Man"

The Young Man's first letters to Constantine evidence a state of quite palpable despair.

> My life has been brought to an *impasse*, I loathe existence, it is without saver, lacking salt and sense. . . . I stick my finger into existence—it smells of nothing
> (*Repetition*, 114).

> My mind is at a standstill, or rather I am going out of it. One moment I am tired and weary, yes, dead for sheer indifference; at another moment I am frantic and travel bewildered from one end of the world to the other, to find one person upon whom I could expend my wrath
> (*Repetition*, 115).

> I do not talk to anybody. . . . What good would it do if I were to say something? There is no one who would understand me. My pain and my suffering are nameless, as I am . . . (*Repetition*, 119-20).

The external cause of his despair is an unhappy love affair—a broken engagement with its attendant guilt. Yet as Constantine points out, the real source of the Young Man's despair lies much deeper. The unhappy love was only the outward correlative of an inward change. In reality he has become strangely ill in a spiritual sense; he has lost himself. The girl therefore "is not a reality but a reflection of the movements within him and their exciting cause" (*Repetition*, 92). He desires a "repetition," but not a worldly one. He does not want the girl back again, but desires a religious "repetition"—he wants himself back again.

He begins reading the book of Job, and immediately Job's conflict comes to exercise a peculiar fascination over his mind. He writes to Constantine on November 15th.

> If I had not Job! It is impossible to describe and to nuancer what significance he has for me, and how manifold his significance. . . . Every word of his is food and gladness and medicine for my ailing soul. Now one word rouses me from lethargy, so that I awaken to new disquietude; now it quiets the fruitless fury within me and puts an end to the horrible feeling of mute nausea produced by passion
>
> (*Repetition*, 121).

In the letters which follow it often seems as if Job's conflict has become the Young Man's.[9] Like Job sitting on his dungheap, the Young Man has run himself to a standstill. All worldly wisdom, all cleverness, all strategems and deceptions: all these have been exhausted. Yet in his exhaustion he still finds consolation in the story of Job's curious "repetition." He cannot conceive or understand how Job received everything double. Yet standing astonished before the fact of this "repetition" he finds consolation.

> When everything has come to a standstill, when thought is brought to a halt, when speech becomes mute, when the explanation in bewilderment seeks the way home —then there must be a thunderstorm. . . .
>
> So then there is such a thing as repetition. When does it come about? Well, that's not so easy to say in any human language. When did it come about for Job? When all conceivable human certitude and probability pronounced it impossible. Little by little he loses everything; therewith hope vanishes gradually in proportion as reality makes heavier and heavier claims upon him. . . . His friends, especially Bildad, know of only one way out, that by submitting to his chastisement he might hope to have a repetition in super-abundance. For that Job is not willing. Thereupon the plot

thickens, so that only by a thunderstorm can it be resolved. For me this narrative contains an indescribable consolation (*Repetition*, 132–33).

As the Young Man concentrates more and more of his energies on Job, it seems to him as if he were leaving his despair behind. At one point he remarks, "The frenzy of the fever is past, I am like a convalescent" (*Repetition*, 125). Like Constantine before him, he has reached a new plateau of emotional equilibrium. Calm, expectant, and drained of passion he observes that he is "expecting a thunderstorm."

> Here I stay—whether on my head or my heels I do not know; I know only this, that here I stay and that for a whole month I have remained *suspenso gradu* without drawing my foot towards me or making the least movement. I am expecting a thunderstorm . . . and repetition
>
> (*Repetition*, 135).

He remains in this state of attenuated expectancy only for a short time, when suddenly, with the violence of an August storm breaking the electric calm of late afternoon, the thunderstorm rolls over him.

> I am again myself, here I have the repetition, I understand everything; and existence seems to me more beautiful than ever. It came as a thunderstorm after all.
>
> I am again myself. . . . The discord in my nature is resolved, I am again unified. . . . Is there not then a repetition? Did I not get myself again, precisely in such a way that I must doubly feel its significance?
>
> It is over, my yawl is afloat. . . .
>
> The chalice of inebriation is again held out to me, already I inhale its fragrance, already I am sensible of its foaming music. . . . Hail to the solemn exultation of victory! Hail to the dance in the vortex of the infinite! Hail to the breaking wave which covers me in the abyss! Hail to the breaking wave which hurls me up above the stars!
>
> (*Repetition*, 143–46).

With these few lines of dithyrambic exultation the Young Man passes from our view. Nameless in coming, he vanishes just as nameless—a wraith, a ghost perhaps, assuredly a creature of Constantine's imagination; he slips away without offering us any interpretation of his curious experience of "repetition." For such an interpretation we must turn to Kierkegaard's *Papirer*.

IV. *Repetition: Kierkegaard*

In December 1843 *Repetition* was reviewed by J. L. Heiberg in a yearbook called *Urania*.[10] With characteristic penetration, the ruling potentate of Copenhagen's literary world observed that by the term "repetition" the author must have had in mind primarily the astronomical cycles of day and night, winter and summer. This comment was so silly that it prompted Kierkegaard to draft a reply to Heiberg on behalf of his pseudonym Constantine Constantius. Although never published, the reply now takes up fifty-four pages of Volume IV of the *Papirer*,[11] and offers a fascinating glimpse of Kierkegaard's own interpretation of *Repetition*.

Kierkegaard explains the relationship between Constantine and the Young Man in these words.

> The young man's problem was *whether repetition is possible*. It was as a parody of him that I [Constantine Constantius] made the journey to Berlin to see whether repetition was possible. The confusion consists in the fact that the most inward problem is here expressed in an outward way, as though repetition, if it were possible, might be found outside the individual, since it is within the individual it must be found, and hence the young man does exactly the opposite, he keeps perfectly still. Accordingly, the consequence of the journey is that I despair of the possibility and then step aside for the young man, who with his religious primitiveness is to discover repetition. So step by step he discovers repetition, being educated by existence.[12]

The story of Constantine's visit to Berlin is only a "parody" of the true religious repetition discovered by the Young Man. As Kierkegaard points out in this same *Papirer* draft, "Only two times is repetition said to exist, both times by the young man" (IV B 111). Yet if the central focus of the book is the Young Man's advance towards, and experience of, the moment of repetition, we should be in no doubt as to how radical Kierkegaard conceives this moment to be. He writes in the *Papirer*.

> When in defining repetition, one characterizes it as "transcendent," as "a religious movement by virtue of the absurd," "when one has arrived at the boundaries of the marvelous," when I say that "eternity is the true repetition," then I think I have expressed myself pretty intelligibly for the real reader of the book.[13]

All these definitions of repetition Constantine has used within the confines of the book itself.[14] In reiterating them here Kierkegaard wishes to emphasize the truly radical break made evident in the moment of repetition. It is a moment of violent cure, a "new birth" in Christian terminology, by virtue of which the individual virtually starts his life over.

Yet most importantly for our purposes, Kierkegaard sees this "new birth" as intrinsically a phenomenon of *consciousness*. In the letter to the reader which concludes *Repetition*, Constantine remarks,

> [The Young Man] explains the universal as repetition, and yet he himself understands repetition in a different sense; for while reality becomes repetition, yet for him his own consciousness raised to the second power is repetition [*bliver for ham den anden Potens af hans Bevidsthed Gjentagelsen*] (*Repetition*, 155–56).

This last clause is a peculiar one both in Danish and in English— the term *Potens* can mean in Danish "intensity," but here it carries the mathematical sense of "power" or "exponential number." Yet peculiar as this clause may be, Kierkegaard uses it no fewer than four times [15] in the *Papirer* draft mentioned above to describe what he means by "repetition." He spells out his meaning most precisely in this passage.

> In the explanatory letter it reads: "The young man explains it as his consciousness raised to a second power [*det unge Menneske forklarer det som den anden Potens af hans Bevidsthed*]." That quite well ought to be the most definite expression for the fact that repetition is conceived

by me as a development; as consciousness raised to the second power is indeed no insignificant repetition [*thi Bevidsthedens anden Potens er jo ingen intetsigende Gjentagelse*], but a repetition such that the new has absolute significance in relation to the foregoing, is qualitatively different from it (IV B 117).

The change of repetition, which we have been told is "a religious movement by virtue of the absurd," is now characterized as a change within consciousness—a transformation by which consciousness is "raised to a second power."

While he was writing *Repetition*, Kierkegaard inscribed the following Latin motto in his journal.

Nullum exstitit magnum ingenium sine aliqua dementia [16]

It might well stand as a motto over *Repetition*, for if any theme is fundamental to this book it is the theme of religious madness. It is already anticipated in Part One, where Constantine, in speaking of the man "who knows how to keep silent," remarks,

For him there will come an instant when it is as though he were about to lose his reason. But this is only a moment, though it is a dreadful moment. It is like the fever which comes on of nights at half past eleven or twelve, and at one o'clock one works as buoyantly as ever (*Repetition*, 27–28).

The man "who knows how to keep silent" becomes the Young Man, who, awaiting the breaking of the thunderstorm, "sits perfectly still." The "fever" we recognize as the Young Man's despair, and the "dreadful moment" is none other than the moment of repetition. Whereas Constantine can only suggest the possibility of such a moment and then draw back from it, the Young Man can welcome it as his saving cure. It is he, not Constantine, who can achieve the thunderstorm which breaks only *after* "everything has come to a standstill, when thought is brought to a halt, when speech becomes mute, when the explanation in bewilderment seeks the way home."

In *Repetition* Kierkegaard is offering a structured account of the stages that culminate in the "divine madness" [17] of repetition.

The Young Man runs through all three stages: despair, a moment of quiet resignation when "the fever is past," and finally—repetition. Constantine, lacking the "religious primitiveness" of the Young Man, can only run through the first two and thus remains a "convalescent." Marooned on the plateau of resignation he stands with Kierkegaard hopefully looking forward to the cure of repetition. And like Kierkegaard, he recognizes that this repetition he desires is only a possibility; it has no more actuality than the wraithlike figure of the nameless young man whom he himself creates. And so, as *Repetition* closes, the outlines of Kierkegaard and his pseudonym merge; both stand anxiously awaiting a moment of madness which will bring in its train a new order of consciousness—a consciousness no longer hermetically sealed in the cloister of resignation, but a consciousness "raised to the second power," a consciousness which will assure their passage across the "boundaries of the marvelous" into that transfigured world the far side of despair, a consciousness which will enable them to exultantly proclaim with the Young Man, "Hail to the breaking wave which hurls me up above the stars!"

Fear and Trembling

Published on the same day as *Repetition*, *Fear and Trembling* was the second of the two to be written.[18] It shows its maturity in the Biblical story on which it focuses, as well as in the axis of psychological conflict which provides its structure.

In one of the letters in *Repetition* the Young Man observes, "Job's significance is that the border conflicts incident to faith are fought out in him" (*Repetition*, 130). This is a highly acute observation about Job, who is after all neither a saint nor a hero of faith. It is appropriate that he should be the Biblical focus of *Repetition*, whose concern is precisely these "border conflicts." But now in *Fear and Trembling* Kierkegaard is pressing an exploratory foot over the "boundaries of the marvelous" into the proper territory of faith itself. It is only proper that Job should recede into the background while Abraham takes his place. For Abraham is beyond the "border conflicts"; he is a *faithful* man; he is the very paradigm of faith—the "knight of faith." In shifting his focus from

Job to Abraham, Kierkegaard moves from a consideration of the boundaries of faith to a consideration of its center.

This advance is further reflected in the central psychological conflict around which the book is organized. Gone is the interest in despair which motivated the recounting of Constantine's experiment in Part One of *Repetition*. Gone too is the interest in the ethical life-view which motivated the long discussions of *Either/Or*, Volume II. Now the lines are clearly drawn: *either* resignation or faith; either the anguished hesitation of a Johannes de Silentio, or the mad confidence of an Abraham. The conflict which had been obscured in *Repetition* by the ambiguity of Constantine's position is now sharply delineated, "the knight of infinite resignation" stands face-to-face with "the knight of faith."

v. The Knight of the Cloister

"I have no faith at all," admits Johannes de Silentio, "I am by nature a shrewd pate, and every such person has great difficulty in making the movements of faith" (*Trembling*, 42). Yet if Johannes cannot make the movements of faith, he can at least describe their character. Hence, as he tells us in the Preface, his project is one of rescuing faith from those system-builders who would go beyond it. His intention is to draw with great precision what he calls "the boundary of the unknown land" [*det ubekjendte Lands Graendse*] (*Trembling*, 174), although he himself is unable to overstep that boundary. Hegel and his camp followers had argued that faith was an "immediacy" to be left behind by the advance of knowledge.[19] It is Johannes' intention to show that they were wrong, to demonstrate that "faith is not the first immediacy but a later one." [20]

In this role he naturally becomes a modern day defender of the faith. Hegel had made faith too easy, had underestimated both it and the difficulties through which it is achieved. In an age when everyone was trying to make things easy, Johannes de Silentio (like the later pseudonym Johannes Climacus) [21] sees his task as making things more difficult. Faith is achieved only when the individual has passed through an anterior "stage of infinite resignation." Only when the individual has made "the cloister movement," has personally attained a state of "infinite resignation," only then is he in a position to make the converse movement of return—the movement of faith.[22] "The infinite resignation," Johannes points out, "is the last stage prior to faith, so that one who has not made this movement has not faith" (*Trembling*, 65–66). The cloister of infinite resignation becomes the last stopping point on the road to faith, the narrow passage through which all who aspire to faith must pass.

Having attained this final stage, Johannes is a fit guardian of the passage to faith. A self-styled "knight of infinite resignation," he guards the boundary of "the unknown land" turning back all those who are unprepared to participate in its mysteries. Before continuing, the traveler must tarry awhile in the cloister, following Johannes in making the movements of infinite resignation and thus preparing himself for the journey ahead. Note how Johannes describes these movements.

> For the act of resignation faith is not required, for what I gain by resignation is my eternal consciousness, and this is a purely philosophical movement which I dare say I am able to make if it is required, and which I can train myself to make, for whenever any finiteness would get the mastery over me, I starve myself until I can make the movement (*Trembling*, 69).

This movement we have met before in Judge William's call to his young friend to "despair." It is a call to shift one's spiritual energies in the most radical way from the external to the internal world. One must come to realize the truth of the prophet's words: "Vanity of vanities . . . all is vanity!" One must despair of ever finding happiness in the world, recognize with Constantine Constantius that repetition is impossible, and join Victor Eremita in the cloister. Having cut the sinews of interest joining one to the world, having "starved" oneself almost as primitive peoples fast in preparation for a mystical initiation, one is now in a position to advance towards faith. The cloister door has clanged shut behind.

Johannes de Silentio is, then, the knight of the cloister, the guardian of the rites and privileges of this *Atre Périlleux* on the way to faith. Yet it is interesting to note with what ambivalence he regards his sojourn here. On the one hand, he describes it as a state of not unpleasant equilibrium.

> In the infinite resignation there is peace and rest . . .
> (*Trembling*, 64).
> I can well endure living in my way, I am joyful and
> content, but my joy is not that of faith, and in comparison
> with that it is unhappy . . . (*Trembling*, 45).
>
> But for the man also who does not so much as reach
> faith life has tasks enough, and if one loves them sincerely,
> life will by no means be wasted, even though it never is
> comparable to the life of those who sensed and grasped the
> highest (*Trembling*, 192).

These passages remind us of Constantine's description of his own
state of suspended animation after his return from Berlin. The
cloister of infinite resignation, we feel, is not such a bad place in
which to rest. For here the fever of despair is past; the ragged edge
of hysteria has receded into the distance. An equilibrium has been
established and now we wait—like convalescents in a well-run and
not uncomfortable sanitorium.

Yet still it is a sanitorium, and it is impossible to blunt the
recognition that there is a fuller, more vital life awaiting on the
outside. And so in Johannes' remarks we detect an edge of regret,
of dissatisfaction, of a hope for something better. He writes,

> And yet it must be glorious to get the princess, . . .
> the knight of faith is the only happy one, the heir apparent
> to the finite, whereas the knight of resignation is a stranger
> and an alien [*en Fremmed og Udlaending*].[23]

The last phrase, "a stranger and an alien," we have met before. It
was applied by Judge William to the desperate plight of his young
friend (see above Chapter 2, Section VII), and still earlier in the
Papirer Kierkegaard had used the term "stranger" to describe himself (see above Chapter 2, Section IX). Hence, no matter how stable
and pleasant the cloister of resignation may seem, we recognize in
its walls and buttresses the familiar outlines of that labyrinth
Kierkegaard knew so well. The walls may seem less grey, their
angles less stark, but still they are there, and beyond lies the "unknown land," that world of light and laughter which forever
beckoned in the distance.

Ensconced in the cloister, Johannes looks both ways. Towards the world at large, he watches the approach of pilgrims along the way of faith, and warns them of the preparatory exercises they must undergo before proceeding further. Looking in the other direction, he measures the approach of knights strong and bold, who have dared penetrate the "unknown land," have entered the Sacred Castle, and now are returning to the world. Their eyes fired with the "divine madness," these "knights of faith" have freely "assumed the burden of the paradox" (*Trembling*, 107), and now are wending their way back to the world. Among them is found Abraham.

vi. *The "Knight of Faith"*

By faith Abraham went out from the land of his fathers and became a stranger in the land of promise. He left one thing behind, took one thing with him: he left behind his earthly understanding, and took faith with him—otherwise he would not have wandered forth but would have thought this unreasonable.[24]

What so impresses Johannes about the Biblical story of Abraham is the awful isolation which the old patriarch freely accepted in his willingness to sacrifice Isaac. For in leaving Sarah and his kinsmen, Abraham "went out from the land of his fathers" not only in a physical but also in a moral sense. The ethical expression for his contemplated act is "murder" (*Trembling*, 38). In leaving the tents of his people he also left behind him the accumulated moral wisdom of the race which would damn to all eternity this act he contemplated. He had chosen to go (in Nietzsche's words) "beyond good and evil," and in this unknown country on the far side of our ordinary moral concepts he could expect no understanding or sympathy. He had chosen to venture out beyond justification, beyond even human speech, into the silence of the desert. As Johannes expresses it, he was "an emigrant from the sphere of the universal" (*Trembling*, 178).

The more Johannes considers Abraham, the less he is able to understand him. "Humanly speaking," Johannes writes, "he is mad, and cannot make himself understandable to anyone. And yet it is the mildest expression to say that he is mad." [25] A person like Abraham who goes out beyond all human concepts, all standards of right and wrong, who believes the impossible, a person like this we call "mad." "Venerable father Abraham," Johannes intones, "Thou who first didst know that highest passion, the holy, pure and humble expression of the divine madness which the pagans admired—forgive him who would speak in praise of thee, if he does not do it fittingly" (*Trembling*, 30). And so Johannes proceeds not to understand Abraham, but to praise him. He stands aghast before him, for Abraham appears to have visited lands and climes the ordinary man has entertained only in his dreams. Johannes cannot take even the first step towards understanding him. As he exclaims again and again, he can only stand "astonished" [*forbauset*] before him (*Trembling*, 50). "One cannot weep over Abraham," remarks Johannes, "one approaches him with a *horror religiosus* as Israel approached Sinai" (*Trembling*, 92).

Yet if Johannes can never understand this *horror religiosus*, he can at least come to understand what he cannot understand. What is the anatomy of Abraham's mad belief? What is the impossible that he believes? Johannes explains it in this way.

> But what did Abraham do? He arrived neither too soon nor too late. He mounted the ass, he rode slowly along the way. All that time he believed . . . He climbed the mountain, even at the instant when the knife glittered he believed that God would not require Isaac. He was indeed astonished at the outcome, but by a double-movement he had reached his first position, and therefore he received Isaac more gladly the first time. . . . He believed by virtue of the absurd; for all human reckoning had long ceaséd to function. . . . To be able to lose one's reason, and therefore the whole of finiteness, of which reason is the broker, and then by virtue of the absurd to gain precisely the same finiteness—that appals my soul . . . (*Trembling*, 47–48).

Abraham believes that he will receive Isaac back again, and he believes this "by virtue of the absurd." He believes it, as Johannes is careful to point out, not against probability or expectation (*Trembling*, 80). Rather he believes it against the recognition of its impossibility; he believes it against, in spite of, all "human calculation." God has called Isaac; Abraham has acknowledged His call; and, as father and son climb Mount Moriah, Isaac is as good as dead. And yet Abraham believes.

There is then a duality to this faith of Abraham. He believes "by virtue of the absurd," and he believes against the background of an "infinite resignation." If Abraham had not first resigned himself to Isaac's loss, if he had simply *hoped* for his rescue, he would not have been the paradigm of faith we venerate. But his faith is no despairing hope. It consists in holding fast an absurd belief against the background of a thoroughgoing resignation. Abraham makes a "double-movement." He *resigns* and *believes* in the self-same instant. He does not first make the movement of resignation, and only later the movement of faith. Rather he makes them simultaneously, and it is this duality, this holding fast to the finite at the same time one pushes it away—it is this which "appals" Johannes.

This singular double movement becomes the hallmark of the knight of faith. Johannes admits that he has never met such a knight, at least outside of literature, but nevertheless he can paint imaginatively this unforgettable portrait of him.

I candidly admit that in my practice I have not found any reliable example of the knight of faith . . . , but I can well think of him. Here he is. . . . The moment I set eyes on him I instantly push him from me, I myself leap backwards, I clasp my hands and say half aloud, "Good lord, is this the man? Why he looks like a tax collector!" One can discover nothing of that aloof and superior nature whereby one recognizes the knight of the infinite. He takes delight in everything, and whenever one sees him taking part in a particular pleasure, he does it with the persistence which is the mark of the earthly man whose soul is absorbed in such things. He tends to his work. . . . He takes a holiday on Sunday. He goes to church. . . . In the afternoon he walks to the forest. He takes delight in everything he sees, in the human swarm, in the new omnibuses, in the water of the Sound; when one meets him on the beach road one might suppose he was a shopkeeper, taking his fling. . . . On the way home he reflects that his wife has surely a little warm dish prepared for him, e.g. a calf's head, roasted, garnished with vegetables. . . . He lives as carefree as n'er do well. . . . With infinite resignation he has drained the cup of life's sadness, he knows the bliss of the infinite, he senses the pain of renouncing everything, the dearest things he possesses in the world, and yet finiteness tastes to him just as good as to one who never knew anything higher . . . , he has the sense of enjoying it, as though the finite life were the surest thing of all. And yet, and yet the whole earthly form he exhibits is a new creation by virtue of the absurd (*Trembling*, 52–56).

This portrait, of course, has been painted before. We recognize it immediately as the earlier-described "married man" of Judge William's encomiums in the second half of *Either/Or*. The "married man" appears again (still *married* we note), yet now in the depths of his eyes we detect something different. For previously he had achieved his "marriage" to life unaided. He had won it in the instant of ethical choice when individual and world, past and future, had been fused in a new continuity. Now he seems slightly different: a humility, a softness, an understanding of worlds beyond and terrors accepted has taken the place of the Judge's narrow vision. He has been "married" this time not by his own act, but by a movement from beyond, by an unveiling of the mystery, by a sharing in the "divine madness." By his own effort the knight of faith can renounce the world, and by renouncing, join Johannes in the cloister. But by himself he can go no further; by himself he cannot so much as place a step over the "boundaries of the marvelous." For this passage something more is required. Johannes writes,

It is about the temporal, the finite, everything turns in this case. I am able by my own strength to renounce everything, and then to find peace and repose in pain. . . . But by my own strength I am not able to get the least of the things which belong to finiteness, for I am constantly using my strength to renounce everything. By my own strength I

am able to give up the princess. . . . But by my faith, says
that marvelous knight, by faith I shall get her in virtue of
the absurd (*Trembling*, 70–71).

It is from this miraculous passage that our hero Abraham has returned.

We can then detect in *Fear and Trembling* a subtle shift in
focus from that of the earlier written *Repetition*. Instead of examining a Biblical personage on the edge of faith (Job), Kierkegaard
now chooses to examine a personage close to the center of faith
(Abraham). In addition, the standpoint of "infinite resignation"
has been clarified as the last and necessary stopping-point on the
way to faith. But with these allowances, it is remarkable how much
alike in perspective and theme the two books are. Both are written
from the perspective of the *Edifying Discourses*; that is, from a
standpoint which looks forward to faith as a much desired possibility, but which is nevertheless *anterior* to faith. Side by side with
the author of the *Edifying Discourses*, Constantine Constantius
and Johannes de Silentio find their places on that curious hermetic
plateau beyond the aesthetic and ethical life-views, yet short of
the "higher immediacy" of faith.[26] All three have made the movements by which the world, and all the affective ties of the world,
have been put behind them. Each of them stands "a stranger and
an alien" looking back at a world they have outgrown. And all, on
the very extremities of their individual life-horizons, detect the
presence of another world—a world lighter, and freer, and more
intense than any world they have ever known.

It is their preoccupation with the difficulties of passage to
this other world which constitutes the common theme of the two
pseudonymous works. Both offer the roughest of sketches of this
passage. Constantine invents his Young Man, and then charts his
prodigy's encounter with the thunderstorm of repetition; Johannes
paints the portrait of the imaginary knight of faith he admits he
has never met. Both of these invented characters (removed by
two imaginative levels from the real author of both books) explore
tentatively the difficulties of passage. And both, curiously enough,
find that the price of passage is the loss of sanity. To complete the
passage the mind must be shocked, consciousness jarred to such

an extent that it shatters, leaving as jagged fragments the individual's prior concepts, opinions, categories, prejudices. The Young Man must feel his mind explode in the thunderstorm of repetition which "raises consciousness to a second power"; Abraham must leave his earthly understanding behind and become "mad" in a worldly sense. If sanity must remain a *conscious* sanity—that is, a "dreadful still life"—then perhaps insanity is preferable; in substance, this is the thrust of Kierkegaard's thought in these works which immediately followed *Either/Or*.

Yet one cannot help but leave these works with the feeling that the heart of the mystery still lies concealed. For one does not know as yet just what is "mystery" and what is not. Certainly some sort of divine grace must accompany the passage to dementia. But to what extent is the passage dependent on grace, and to what extent is it still a function of human effort? In the final analysis we know very little about this miraculous passage after reading *Repetition* and *Fear and Trembling*. For how is consciousness to be "raised to a second power?" All we know is that the Young Man considers the story of Job, somewhat later experiences repetition, and then vanishes from our view. And how too does one become divinely "mad" to the stature of an Abraham? When we encounter Abraham he has already achieved dementia; all we know is that he believes. Is there then nothing further the knights of infinite resignation can do but wait expectantly for a call from beyond? Or is there perhaps an additional wonder to be contemplated, a further movement to be made, before they are welcomed into the company of the knights of faith? Then too there is the unamplified announcement in *Fear and Trembling* that the knights of faith "have assumed the burden of the paradox"? What is this magic paradox whose assumption brings in its train the divine madness of faith? These are the questions we are left with at the close of *Repetition* and *Fear and Trembling*. Madness has been suggested as the ultimate cure for consciousness, but the catalyst of madness has not been identified. For a fuller revelation we must await the discussion of "the Paradox" in Kierkegaard's next book.

6

PHILOSOPHICAL FRAGMENTS

During the middle and late years of his authorship Kierkegaard often remarks on his peculiar need of Christianity, and on how attractive it is to a person of his quite singular mind-set. In 1850 he observes,

> My need of Christianity is so great (both on account of my sufferings and my sins and my frightful introspection [*Indadvendthed*]): that is why I am not understood. And so many times I have been afraid of making life all too serious for others; therefore, I am very careful (x^2 A 459).

Earlier he has remarked how he felt himself so strangely drawn towards Christianity,[1] how a certain "exhausted decrepitude" of a peculiarly Kierkegaardian sort was "required to feel a real need of Christianity" (viii^1 A 663). Then in the *Postscript* he points out how "Christianity fits perfectly into the picture." "Subjectivity culminates in passion," he remarks, "Christianity is the paradox, paradox and passion are a mutual fit, and the paradox is altogether suited to one whose situation is to be in the extremity existence" (*Postscript*, 206). As we read these remarks, and as we follow the progress of Kierkegaard's authorship in the published works of the mid-1840's, we feel how extraordinarily appropriate Christianity (at least as Kierkegaard interpreted it) was to his search for a cure to the sickness of consciousness. Consider, for example, *Philosophical Fragments*.

By the time this book was published in June of 1844 Kierkegaard's search had reached a crucial juncture. It had already become apparent that consciousness could neither be compressed into flesh in the moment of intense sensation, nor be collapsed into will in the moment of ethical decision. In his last pseudonymous works Kierkegaard had entertained the possibility that consciousness might yet be shattered in a moment of divine madness. In *Repetition* and *Fear and Trembling* he had suggested the possibility of a miraculous passage to faith which would be accomplished in the moment of repetition. But the vehicle of transit for this passage had not been conceived, nor had the agency which would shatter the veil of consciousness been identified. It is at just this point that Christianity appears on the scene. In the twin Christian concepts of "the Moment" and "the Paradox" Kierkegaard had found what he was searching for. "The Moment" of Christian rebirth—the "fullness of time"—replaced the moment of repetition whose praises Constantine Constantius had sung. And in "the Paradox" of God's entry into time in Christ, Kierkegaard had found that thought which defied thinking, had found the event the very contemplation of which would assure the destruction of consciousness. These two concepts define Kierkegaard's notion of Christianity as he presents it in the *Fragments*. One is forced to ponder whether, if Christianity had lacked these two incendiary notions, Kierkegaard would have paid it the least attention.

1. *"The Moment"*

On the title-page of *Philosophical Fragments* appears the following three-part question.

> Is an historical point of departure possible for an eternal consciousness; how can such a point of departure have any other than a merely historical interest; is it possible to base an eternal happiness upon historical knowledge?
>
> (*Fragments*, iii).

It would be incorrect to say that the *Fragments* attempts to answer this question. It does not. Rather it attempts to suggest how this question can be seen as the touchstone for distinguishing between two quite different philosophies of life—the Socratic and the Christian.

"From the standpoint of the Socratic thought every point of departure in time is *eo ipso* accidental, an occasion, a vanishing moment" (*Fragments*, 13). The Socratic doctrine of *anamnēsis* had taught that each individual possessed the truth within him; all learning, according to this doctrine, was only a process of recollecting a truth already known. In this framework the teacher (namely Socrates) became merely the occasion for a person's achievement of self-knowledge. Thus Socrates could speak of himself as a midwife whose thought had no positive content, who only functioned to aid others bring to birth a truth already contained within them. But if one only requires an "occasion" to come into possession of the truth, then the temporal point of departure—the actual identity of this occasion—becomes indifferent. If one can learn the truth just as well from a servant girl as from a Socrates, if one likewise can learn it just as well this week as next year, if one's learning of the truth wipes clean the past years of error, if all this be true, then of course the significance of the individual occasion vanishes in the haze of an indefinite recollection.[2] Kierkegaard puts it this way.

> The temporal point of departure is nothing; for as soon as I discover that I have known the Truth from eternity without being aware of it, the same instant this moment of occasion is hidden in the Eternal, and so incorporated with it that I cannot find it so to speak, even if I sought it; because in my eternal consciousness there is neither here nor there, but only an *ubique et nusquam* (*Fragments*, 15–16).

The Socratic standpoint presupposes an undifferentiated temporal continuum. Since every moment is equally important (or equally unimportant) one's location in time becomes an *ubique et nusquam*. But what if one chooses to answer the fundamental question in the other way? What if one chooses to assert that an historical point of departure is possible for an eternal consciousness? What if one assumes that "the moment in time must have a decisive significance"?[3]

Such an assumption, Kierkegaard demonstrates with a few masterly strokes, is the ground premise of Christianity. Beginning with this single assumption of the decisive importance of the Moment, Kierkegaard manages to derive in skeletal form the whole Christian framework. His derivation can be briefly represented in the following steps.

Assumption: If the moment in time is to have decisive significance, then . . .

1] The individual did not always possess the truth (p. 16).

2] He must have come into possession of the truth (p. 17).

3] The teacher must have given him not only the truth but also the condition for possessing it (p. 18).

4] The teacher must not be another human being, but rather "*the God*" (p. 18).

5] The learner's state must have come about through the learner's freedom; the deprivation of truth could not have come about by an act of God or by accident (p. 18).

6] The learner's state is "*sin*" (p. 19).

7] The teacher saves the learner from his own self-imposed bondage; he is "*Redeemer*", "*Saviour*", and "*Judge*" (pp. 21–22).

8] The teacher's act is "*atonement*" (p. 21).

9] The learner's acceptance of the truth in the Moment makes him "a new creature." This change is called "*conversion*," the "*New Birth*" (p. 23).

10] The moment is the "*Fullness of Time*" (p. 21).

The niceties of this derivation need not concern us.[4] What is important to note is Kierkegaard's contention that the whole of Christianity is predicated upon the existence of the Moment. If the Moment does not exist, then (as he is careful to point out again and again) "we remain at the Socratic standpoint" (*Fragments*, 18). Only Christianity, he emphasizes, makes such a claim concerning a temporal point of departure for an eternal consciousness.[5] This claim becomes the defining characteristic of Christianity—the touchstone which distinguishes it from other life-views.

Of course Kierkegaard had his own reasons for singling out the Moment as the touchstone of Christianity.

> In the *Moment* man becomes conscious of the new birth, for his antecedent state was one of non-being. Had his preceding state in either instance been one of being, the moment could not have received decisive significance for him, as has been shown above. While then the pathos of the Greek consciousness concentrates itself upon Recollection, the pathos of our project is concentrated upon the Moment (*Fragments*, 25–26).

This moment of rebirth is a shattering, a convulsion in the soul. Note the violence of the metaphors Kierkegaard uses to describe it.

> When the seed of the oak is planted in earthen vessels, they break asunder; when new wine is poured in old leathern bottles, they burst; what must happen when the God implants himself in human weakness, unless man becomes a new vessel and a new creature! But this becoming, what labors will attend the change, how convulsed with birth-pangs! (*Fragments*, 42–43).

How these two passages remind us of earlier Kierkegaardian moments! We recall Judge William's description of the ethical act—of that moment when "by the individual's intercourse with himself he impregnates himself and brings himself to birth" (*E/O*, II, 263). And we remember the Young Man's exultation in *Repetition* over the onslaught of the thunderstorm which enabled him to exclaim, "I am again myself, here I have the repetition, I understand everything, and existence seems to me more beautiful than ever." The possibility of there being a sudden crook in time, a fracture, an instant of appalling violence when the individual was, as it were, born anew—the possibility of such a moment had preoccupied Kierkegaard from the very first. How fitting, how natural then, that at a crucial juncture in his authorship he should turn to "the Moment" of Christian theology. It fitted perfectly into that web of memory and expectation which constituted his life in the middle 1840's; it articulated his hope for an exit from the labyrinth, and (most importantly of all) it answered to his own experience. The Moment—the "fullness of time" of Christian theology—became the last of a series of names for that moment of continuity which Kierkegaard knew and which we examined in Chapter 2. It was the moment of passage when the threshold was left behind, when the harsh outlines of the world of the square melted into the softer forms of the world of the circle, "Rejoice, and again I say, Rejoice!"

II. *"The Paradox"*

There should be little doubt now of the true identity of the Moment discussed in *Philosophical Fragments*. Nor should there be any doubt of the essential mystery involved in its occurrence. By his own efforts the individual cannot bring about the Moment. Like the earlier discussed moment of repetition it comes as a gift from beyond, as a stirring of the breeze "which blows from the Groves of Mamre to the eternal habitations," and Kierkegaard is careful to make this clear in the *Fragments*. In the last citation noted above he speaks of the Moment as that instant when God "implants" himself in a human life. And earlier he has pointed out that a fundamental distinction between the Christian and the Socratic standpoints lay in the fact that, for the Christian, the learner receives not only the truth, but also the conditions for appropriating the truth, directly from the hand of God (*Fragments*, 18). In the Moment, the individual crosses the threshold into faith "in virtue of the condition he himself receives from the God" (*Fragments*, 131). The Moment has an undeniable air of mystery; it witnesses the arrival of grace—the instant when the "unfound door" is opened from the other side.

All this has been apparent since the first discussion of the Moment in *Repetition*. But what was left indefinite both in that work and in *Fear and Trembling* is the precise extent of the mystery of grace. From Johannes de Silentio we learn the necessity of making the movement of infinite resignation before venturing across the "boundaries of the marvelous." And from both Johannes and Constantine Constantius we learned to suspect that our sanity would be the price of passage across the threshold. But just how we are to lose our sanity, what further steps we are to take preparatory to the arrival of grace, all this up to now has been left indefinite. In the *Fragments*—and more precisely in Kierkegaard's discussion of "the Paradox"—it gains greater definition.

It is impossible to understand Kierkegaard's description of the Paradox without first becoming familiar with the subtle web of meaning he spins around the terms "Reason" (*Forstanden*), "existence" (*Tilvaerelse*), and "Faith" (*Troen*). For it is within this web, lurking like a spider in a dark corner, that the Paradox has its home.

By "Reason" Kierkegaard means that agency which carries out the movements of discursive thought in mathematics, the sciences, and in everyday life. The activity of Reason is "thinking" (*Taenkning*). We should be careful not to read into his use of the term *Forstanden* any tendency to invoke the Kantian distinction between *Vernunft* and *Verstand*, for Kierkegaard means us to take this word in its straightforward, everyday sense.[6] The meaning he attaches to the term "existence" (*Tilvaerelse*) is equally straight forward for a Dane, but for the English-speaking reader it requires a brief explanation. The Danish infinitive form "to exist" is *at vaere til*, while the infinitive "to be" is *at vaere*. Thus contained within the very etymology of the Danish word for "existence" (*Tilvaerelse*) is the notion of being in time—of being "*til*" —and it is this meaning Kierkegaard wishes to attach to the term. Each of these first two terms ("Reason" and "existence") is used in but one sense apiece in *Philosophical Fragments*, while the third term, "faith" (*Troen*), has a double sense—an ordinary, everyday sense (translated as "belief" in the present English edition), and a privileged, religious sense (translated as "faith").[7] The religious sense we are familiar with from *Fear and Trembling* (it is the same "faith" which Abraham exemplifies), while the ordinary "belief" sense of *Troen* is introduced for the first time in *Philosophical Fragments* for reasons soon to be made clear.

These then are the individual meanings Kierkegaard gives to these terms. More important than their individual meanings, however, is the contextual frame in which they are woven.

In Chapter III of the *Fragments* Kierkegaard argues that all discursive thought *begins* with existence, and does not *reach* it by a train of inference. He writes,

> Generally speaking, it is a difficult matter to prove that anything exists. . . . The entire demonstration always turns into something very different and becomes an additional development of the consequences that flow from my having assumed that the object in question exists. Thus I always reason from existence, not toward existence, whether I move in the sphere of palpable, sensible fact or whether I move in the realm of thought. I do not for example prove that a stone exists, but that some existing thing is a stone. The procedure in a court of justice does not prove that a criminal exists, but that the accused, whose existence is given, is a criminal (*Fragments*, 49–50).

In order to go about its work Reason must assume the existence of that about which it reasons; if existence is not presupposed at the beginning it can never be produced by a movement of thought; thinking *begins* with existence and does not move towards it. But certainly, a philosopher might object, do we not have criteria enabling us to distinguish between existence and non-existence? Would we, for example, be inclined to believe in the existence of something which could not be apprehended publicly, in different situations, by different observers? Kierkegaard never takes up explicitly the question of existence criteria, but his answer to such an objection is not difficult to frame—it would point out the correctness of the hypothetical philosopher's admission that "we *believe* in the existence of something." For Kierkegaard's whole argument is that ultimately we must *believe* in existence, we cannot know it. No matter what existence criteria we may formulate, we must still *believe* in their legitimacy. And if we choose to say that legitimacy itself has criteria, then our belief only retreats to a second level. This is precisely the thrust of Kierkegaard's long discussion in the Interlude section of the *Fragments* regarding the uncertainty of all historical knowledge (*Fragments*, 97–107). The present or past existence of any individual or object, he emphasizes, is never certain, never an object of knowledge, but only of belief.[8] Certain knowledge can be found within the structures of logic and mathematics,[9] but outside their precincts, in the coming-into-being and passing-away of life in the world, here we must be satisfied with *belief*.

Consider now how this exposition of the interdependence of existence and belief undercuts the stability of that conscious world which Reason has constructed. We have already been instructed in *Fear and Trembling* how Reason is the "broker" of "the whole of finiteness." Now the stability of this finite whole has been brought into radical question. For it is Reason which has populated this whole with supposed real, existent entities—Reason is constantly making inferences about rocks and criminals and philosophers—and now the existential reality of all these entities has been questioned. The traditional solipsistic cut has been made. The foundation of Reason, thinking, even the whole common-sense world, the foundation of this gigantic structure of knowledge, probability, prejudice, and habit has been undermined at its deepest level. Little is now needed to make the whole edifice collapse. Little—or perhaps a lot?

As we noted above, Reason may very well have its existence criteria. It may establish ground rules for the sorts of things which can properly be said to exist, and these general rules and criteria will aid the individual in articulating and organizing his conscious world. But what if the individual were asked to believe in the existence of something, which, by the rules and criteria of Reason can never come into existence? Then would not the individual have to choose between his belief and his Reason? And what might be the object of such a belief which would confound Reason? Might it not be God?

Many religious persons (and many who are scarcely religious at all) proclaim their belief in the existence of God. But by their proclamation they mean the existence of God in some extra-spatiotemporal sense. They mean that God exists *beyond* the world, or *above* the world, or in the *depth* of the world; but they certainly do not mean that He lived and died in the world as we live and die. The mere application of tensed verbs to God would strike many as offensive; God did not live and then die—He is eternal, atemporal. Yet, according to Kierkegaard, Christianity makes precisely this claim. Christianity claims that God came into time like any of us, that He was born of a woman, traveled in the world under the guise of a servant, taught among us, and was finally killed (*Fragments*, 130). But how can this be? "God," Kierkegaard points out in the *Fragments*, "is not a name but a concept." [10] To hold that God came into time in this way is as insane as it would be to assert that one saw the British Constitution walking down the street.[11] Such a belief cannot be made to jibe with Reason. It offends Reason and its criteria. It is finally not even a "belief" at all, rather it is the substance of "faith" (*Troen*).[12]

Existence, the *possible* which through a freely acting cause became *actual*, is the object of "belief" (*Troen* in its unprivileged sense); the paradox of God's entry into time in Christ, the *impossible* become *actual*, is the object of "faith." The Paradox is then an event—the proclaimed flesh and blood existence of God. It is this event which challenges the sovereignty of Reason. "Reason," Kierkegaard writes, "will doubtless find it impossible to conceive it, could not of itself have discovered it, and when it hears it announced will not be able to understand it, sensing merely that its downfall is threatened" (*Fragments*, 59). Threatened thus, Reason can respond in either of two ways. If it refuses to renounce sovereignty, if the accumulated patterns of thought and decision are not put to the side, then we have the "offended consciousness."

> The offended consciousness holds aloof from the Paradox, and the reason is: *quia absurdum*. . . . Reason says that the Paradox is absurd, but this is mere mimicry, since the Paradox is the Paradox, *quia absurdum*. The offended consciousness holds aloof from the Paradox and keeps to the probable, since the Paradox is the most improbable of things . . . (*Fragments*, 65).

"Offense" (*Forargelse*) is one possible response to a confrontation with the Paradox. "Faith" is the other.

> But how does the learner come to realize an understanding with this Paradox? We do not ask that he understand the Paradox, but only understand that this is the Paradox. How this takes place we have already shown. It comes to pass when the Reason and the Paradox encounter one an-

other happily in the Moment, when the Reason sets itself aside and the Paradox bestows itself. The third entity in which the union is realized is that happy passion to which we shall now assign a name. . . . We shall call this passion: Faith (*Fragments*, 72–73).

The happy confrontation of Reason and the Paradox eventuates in Faith—the setting aside of Reason and its structures in favor of the revelation contained in the Paradox. And when does this happy confrontation occur. It occurs in the Moment.

> How does the learner then become a believer or disciple? When the Reason is set aside and he receives the condition. When does he receive the condition? In the Moment (*Fragments*, 79).

We have now come almost full circle. Reason has been shown to be dependent on *belief* for its assumptions concerning *existence*. The existence of God in time has been revealed as the event which confounds *Reason*, and has been designated *the Paradox*. Finally, the setting aside of Reason in *the Moment* has been identified as the movement which culminates in *faith*. Only one more arc is needed to complete the circle. Kierkegaard remarks in regard to the appropriation of the Paradox.

> Unless the God grants the condition which makes it possible to understand this, how is it to be supposed that the learner will be able to discover it! But that the God himself gives this condition has been shown above to be a consequence of the *Moment*, and it has also been shown that the Moment is the Paradox.[13]

The Moment is the Paradox, the two halves of the circle now join. The Paradox is God's entry into time. Yet it is precisely this intrusion of the eternal into time which constitutes the Moment. God entered time in the person of Christ, but he also enters into time in every moment when an individual sets aside his Reason in confrontation with the Paradox. God's first entry constituted the Paradox—that Moment of divine instantiation which would prove to be the "occasion" (in the Socratic sense) for all future Moments. Yet in these successive Moments God is not absent.

Rather he is there "giving the condition," just as he gave the original condition for man's salvation by becoming flesh in Christ. Each Moment then witnesses the divine dispensation, each reduplicates the first Moment. And just as God's first entry into time is paradoxical, so are all future entries.[14] Faith itself is para-doxical, a miracle, and as Kierkegaard observes, "all that holds true of the Paradox also holds true of Faith" (*Fragments*, 81). Finally we are brought back again to the Moment, revealed now as sharing an identity with the Paradox, a still point where man's freedom and God's grace intersect.

Kierkegaard's description of the Paradox as the last guardian of the passage to faith reminds us of Nicholas of Cusa's similar formulation. For Cusa described the "Wall of Paradise" which conceals God from human sight as made up of the "coincidence of opposites," its gate guarded by "the highest spirit of reason who guards the way until he has been overcome." [15] Like Cusa, Kierkegaard sees the way to faith as guarded by the "spirit of reason." He speaks in the *Postscript* of "faith's crucifixion of Reason," [16] and in the last pages we have seen how this crucifixion is carried out on the cross of the Paradox.[17] The paradox becomes a kind of Medusa's head upon which the individual must gaze before proceeding across "the boundaries of the marvelous." True he can turn away in offense, and if he does, faith will remain for him always an unexplored region. But if he gazes long and hard, if he concentrates all the resources of his mind and will on this unthinkable thought, and finally if the "condition" is forthcoming from the hand of God; if all this takes place, he can look forward to a violent shattering of his conscious world. The familiar and tiresome outlines of his previous life-world will disintegrate, and in their place will arise the gentler forms of the life-world of faith. The last door will have been opened. The labyrinth escaped.

Early in the *Fragments* Kierkegaard remarks that the supreme passion of all thinking is to "discover something that thought cannot think." [18] Whether this indeed be a fair description of thinking remains problematical, but it well describes Kierkegaard's intention in the *Fragments*. In this odd little book he has been trying to find just such a curiosity of reflection—a thought which defies thinking. For if such a thought could be discovered, it would prove to be the nemesis of thinking; concentrated upon such a thought, thinking would tremble, lurch, and finally shatter—leaving behind as bits and pieces the fragments of an earlier order of experience. From our past studies it should be evident why Kierkegaard desired the destruction of thinking. For it was *thinking* which was his enemy. Thinking was the ever-wakeful demon which robbed him of all immediacy, made it impossible for him to forget himself even in sleep, and spun the diaphanous membrane of consciousness. It was this activity of *thinking*, this bare fact of *being conscious*, which caused Kierkegaard such suffering. The tracing and retracing of familiar passageways, the endless confrontations with the stale air and "midnight shapes" of his own imagination, the impossibility of ever escaping his own tiresome self—this was the secret suffering which lay behind his authorship and prompted him in the *Fragments* to pursue the death of consciousness. Seen in the light of Kierkegaard's longstanding search for an exit from the labyrinth, a cure for consciousness, what is sometimes opaque in *Philosophical Fragments* becomes transparent. More importantly, seen in this light the peculiar attenuation of the picture of Christianity presented in the *Fragments* becomes comprehensible.

As we noted at the beginning of this chapter, the twin concepts of the Moment and the Paradox define the picture of Christianity sketched in the *Fragments*. But now we should observe how strangely tensed the Christian picture becomes through Kierkegaard's emphasis on these two concepts. True, all the standard Christian tokens appear on the board, but the game appears to be being played for a different end. What, for example, do we learn in the *Fragments* of Christian teaching? What suggestion do we get of the possibility of a Christian ethic? Is it correct to suppose that the anatomy of Christian belief can be reduced to the bare skeleton Kierkegaard offers? [19] The twin concepts of the Moment and the Paradox have been emphasized to such an extent that Christianity becomes not so much a way of life, as a highly esoteric mental therapy. The whole emphasis of Kierkegaard's treatment of Christianity in the *Fragments* is on the radical shift of consciousness experienced in the Moment. All the complications of Christian belief are reduced to a concentration on the unthinkable thought of the Paradox which eventuates in the Moment. Having become ensnared in the web of Kierkegaard's personal quest, Christianity is drawn into an unfamiliar form. What before was familiar and inviting, becomes terrifying, shocking, offensive. The magnitude of Kierkegaard's need, it would seem, at least partly shaped the form of its satisfaction.

7

THE CONCEPT OF DREAD

Philosophical Fragments and *The Concept of Dread* are in more than one respect companion volumes. Published on the 13th and 17th of June 1844, respectively, it was Kierkegaard's original intention to have them go forth under his own name—early drafts of the title pages list "S. Kierkegaard" as author.[1] In the published versions, however, the title pages were altered to list Johannes Climacus as author of *Fragments* and Vigilius Haufniensis as author of *Dread*. Although pseudonymous in form, these works cannot be called truly "pseudonymous" in the same sense as *Either/Or* or *Repetition*. Neither Johannes Climacus nor Vigilius Haufniensis have the actuality and dramatic thickness characteristic of the earlier pseudonyms. In *Philosophical Fragments*, for example, we learn next to nothing about Johannes Climacus,[2] and in the Preface to *Dread* Kierkegaard admits that "Vigilius Haufniensis" is more properly an anonym than a pseudonym.[3] These pseudonyms seem thin and wraithlike in comparison with a Judge William or a Constantine Constantius. If we deign to call them pseudonyms, we must not forget that they are perhaps the thinnest to be found in Kierkegaard's marionette theater.

Their thinness is in great measure explained by the tasks Kierkegaard set for them. In earlier works the pseudonym itself was the center of interest. Through it Kierkegaard was able to present a human life-view in all its richness and immediacy. Instead of telling us about a particular person and his life-view, Kierkegaard gave us that person nakedly revealed in his diaries, letters, and essays. The pseudonym became the vehicle—the very means—by which Kierkegaard communicated to his reader both the richness of a particular life-view, and also the wide spectrum of diversity characterizing different life-views. It was for this reason that the aesthete A, or Johannes the Seducer, or Judge William were such highly textured, such fully actual, pseudonyms. To a lesser extent the same thing might be said of Constantine Constantius, the Young Man, or Johannes de Silentio—they all have, if not the breath of life, at least a verisimilitude thereto. But in these works from June of 1844 the life-view of a particular character or character-type is no longer the center of interest. The focus has now shifted to an explicitly philosophico-theological frame. On their most manifest level both *Fragments* and *Dread* are orthodox philosophico-theological dissertations—the first offering a thorough-going comparison of two metaphysical frameworks (Christianity and Speculative Idealism), and the second offering (in the words of the title-page) "a simple psychological deliberation in the direction of the dogmatic problem of original sin." [4] With such a task set for it, the pseudonym soon finds itself superfluous. For with the focus now shifted from the life-view of the supposed author, to the problem he takes up, the pseudonym is left without a *raison d'être*. Thus, after paying lip-service to the device of pseudonymity in the prefaces of both works, Kierkegaard quickly abandons it and proceeds to write the books as they were originally planned—that is, as philosophico-theological utterances of Søren Kierkegaard.

Yet it is not on the philosophico-theological level that these two works from June of 1844 are ultimately companion volumes, nor is it on this level that they are most effectively understood. It is indeed true that under the pseudonyms Johannes Climacus and Vigilius Haufniensis Kierkegaard has assumed the costume and language of the philosopher/theologian. Yet it would be a sad deception if we permitted this costume and this language to conceal from us a deeper level—a level of probing and questioning closer to that locus of secret suffering which animates Kierkegaard's authorship. Consider, for example, *Philosophical Fragments*.

It is difficult to imagine a more abstrusely philosophical work. In the Interlude section Johannes Climacus discusses with great acuteness such concepts as "necessity," "possibility," "existence," and "becoming," while, in an earlier part, he has surveyed the status of traditional arguments for the existence of God, and has considered the relation of speculative philosophy to Christianity. From one perspective these discussions seem so arid and technical. What could be drier than a discussion of the relation between "possibility" and "necessity"? Yet, if the last chapter has shown anything, it has shown that the unifying theme of the *Fragments* is Kierkegaard's intention to isolate the agent of cure, to discover that narrow passage which leads out of the labyrinth to faith. As we have tried to show, it is this intention which relates the comprehensive discussions of "the Moment" and "the Paradox" to the more metaphysical discussions of "existence" and "belief." The fabric of philosophical discussion in *Fragments* is stretched over a level of deep personal concern, and it is by first penetrating to this level that we can most effectively understand the work in its totality.

We turn now to *The Concept of Dread*, a book which by Kierkegaard's own admission is the driest and most dogmatic of the pseudonymous group.[5] We should warn the reader in advance that in examining *Dread* our interest will not focus on Kierkegaard's well-known discussion of the so-called "dogmatic problem of original sin." Rather, we shall search below the surface discussion of dogmatics to that level of personal concern which links *The Concept of Dread* with the earlier and later pseudonymous works. There are always two levels to Kierkegaard's discussion in *Dread*. On the manifest level he is apparently seeking to make some contribution to the theological discussion concerning the dogmatic problem of original sin. Yet as the book proceeds we come to see another level, a more private level, on which our discussions of past chapters find their relevance. Here we find Kierkegaard once again returning to earlier concerns, once again retracing conceptually the evolution of his illness, once again describing the psychic contents of "that dreadful still life." Viewed on this level, what is perhaps the driest and most pedestrian of Kierkegaard's works turns out also to be the most harrowing.

1. *The Heterogeneity of Dread*

The term "dread" (*Angest*) [6] is not a new one to the reader who has followed our discussion up to this point. In Chapter 2 it was pointed out how the experience of dread was (by Kierkegaard's own admission) an important factor in his personal descent into despair. As we remember, in 1843 he singled out dread as the cause of his "going astray" in the late 1830's, remarking in his journal that his sins "perhaps in God's eyes are not so scandalous, for it was dread which led me to run wild." [7] Then too we recall how in *Either/Or* Kierkegaard plotted the stages of his descent into despair, how he described the progression from dread through the "immediate stages of the erotic." Dread, we recall, was there indicated as the energy behind Don Juan's pursuit. As the first manifestation of the dawning consciousness, it was the motivating force behind the movement from "dreaming," to "seeking," to "desiring"—that fated movement which (according to Kierkegaard) inevitably terminates in the sickness of despair.

Hence in turning to *The Concept of Dread* we already know more than a little about dread—we know its origin in Kierkegaard's biography, and we know how it was treated in his first pseudonymous work.

On the final page of *The Concept of Dread* Kierkegaard speaks of dread as a peculiar kind of "hypochondria" (*Hypochondre*), and amplifies his meaning by offering in a footnote a passage from Kant's pietist friend, Johann Georg Hamann.

> It is therefore in a higher sense that Hamann employs the word "hypochondria" when he says: "This dread which we experience in the world is the only proof of our heterogeneity. For if we lacked nothing, we should do no better than the pagans and the transcendental philosophers who know nothing of God and like fools fall in love with this precious world; no homesickness would attack us. This impertinent uneasiness, this holy hypochondria, is perhaps the fire whereby we sacrificial animals must be salted and preserved from the decay of the passing age." [8]

Two years earlier, in 1842, Kierkegaard inscribed the same passage
in his journal with the additional comment, ". . . a remark which
I can use, although he [Hamann] has neither understood it as I
wish to understand it, nor has he thought further about it. . . ." [9]
We can imagine with what surprise Kierkegaard came across this
passage, and with what a personal meaning he would endow it.
For here was corroboration from another individual of the "holy
hypochondria" he himself had felt, and here too was an explanation of its significance which fitted perfectly with his own reflections. Dread is the proof of man's heterogeneity. Animals and
plants cannot feel dread since they lack consciousness,[10] and it is
consciousness (we learned in *Either/Or*) which is the source of
dread. But if dread be the proof of man's heterogeneity, it is also
the source of his torture. Being conscious, man can never sink
down into the sleep of flesh. For this "impertinent uneasiness,"
this "homesickness" for another world, assures his estrangement
from the earth. This is Hamann's suggestion as to the significance
of dread, and it is around this kernel of suggested meaning, informed and amplified by prior experience and reflection, that
Kierkegaard spins his discussion of "the concept of dread."

ii. *The Concept of Dread*

As Kierkegaard suggests on the title page, the principal dogmatic problem with which his "concept of dread" is meant to deal
is the problem of man's Fall. Broadly speaking, this problem takes
the following form: If man ever was truly innocent, how then did
he become guilty?

There are two possible solutions to this problem lying at
different ends of the spectrum of freedom and necessity. The first
solution would teach that man's Fall was preordained by God,
that sin came into the world by necessity. The second would
teach that man fell owing to an act of abstract *liberum arbitrium*
on man's own part. Kierkegaard rejects both of these extreme solutions, calling the first a "self-contradiction," and the second "a
nonsense to thought" (*Dread*, 45). Yet having rejected both extremities, he is faced with the necessity of carving out his own
solution somewhere between. This he does by suggesting "dread"
as a third term, a state of "trampled freedom" (*Dread*, 45) lying

midway between the poles of freedom and necessity, a condition mediating guilt and innocence.

> Innocence is ignorance. In his innocence man is not determined as spirit but is soulishly [sjelelig] determined in immediate unity with his natural condition. Spirit is dreaming in man . . .
>
> In this state there is peace and rest, but at the same time there is something else, which is not dissension and strife, for there is nothing to strive with. What is it then? Nothing. But what effect does nothing have? It feeds dread. This is the deep secret of innocence, that at the same time it is dread. Dreamingly the spirit projects its own reality, but this reality is nothing, but this nothing constantly sees innocence outside itself.[11]

Innocence is not an equilibrium state, but a transitional one. Qualified already by a tremor of consciousness, it is not the deep sleep of the purely animal, but the fitful slumber, the dream-stirred sleep of consciousness aborning. Kierkegaard continues.

> Dread is a qualification of the dreaming spirit, and as such it has its place in psychology. When awake, the difference between myself and my other is posited; sleeping, it is suspended; dreaming, it is a nothing vaguely hinted at. . . . Dread is a *sympathetic antipathy* and an *antipathetic sympathy.* . . . One speaks of a sweet dread, a sweet feeling of of apprehension, one speaks of a strange dread, a shrinking dread, etc. . . . If we observe children, we find this dread more definitely indicated as a seeking after the adventurous, the tremendous, the mysterious. . . . This dread belongs so essentially to the child that he cannot do without it; even though it alarms him, it yet captivates him by its sweet feeling of apprehension.[12]

In this passage we see the core of Kierkegaard's reinterpretation of the traditional presentation of man's Fall. The orthodox framework of innocence and guilt is replaced by a Kierkegaardian framework of gradations of consciousness. Innocence is no longer a mythic Eden; rather it is the infantile dream state out of which the child carves the distinction of self and world. The Fall now becomes not an historical event hidden in the origins of the race, but rather a psychological event endlessly repeated in the lives of individuals. It is for this reason that Kierkegaard will later point out in *Dread* that each individual recapitulates in his own life Adam's mythic Fall (*Dread*, 32). Each man rehearses in his own life the awakening of consciousness, and the "homesickness" this brings in its train. What in more traditional language we have called "original sin," becomes now the drawing of the veil of consciousness between individual and world. How characteristic of Kierkegaard it is that he should locate the agony of the post-lapserian world not in man's expulsion from the Garden and the necessity of his subsequent suffering and death in the world, but rather in the simple fact of human consciousness! As we saw in *Either/Or*, it is man's awareness of this consciousness, made known to him first in dread, which leads him through "the immediate stages of the erotic" into the labyrinth of despair. And it is this same evolution which Kierkegaard hints at in his connection of "sinfulness" and "sensuousness," and in his contention that "sensuousness corresponds proportionally with dread" (*Dread*, 58). Faced with the fact of his own consciousness, spurred on by dread, man seeks to submerge himself in the sensuous, to become pure flesh. But, as we have seen, this only serves to heighten his consciousness. Again and again the cycle repeats itself, until man becomes lost in despair. In that moment he can look back to a prior innocence, realizing that the wages of sin are not death but the conscious still life of the sickness unto death.

And perhaps in that moment he can realize too that he himself is the source of this sickness whose first symptom is dread. Dread feeds on nothing (*Dread*, 38), but it is man himself who secretes nothing. "If man were a beast or an angel," Kierkegaard writes, "he would not be able to be in dread, and the greater the dread the greater the man. . . . Man himself produces dread" (*Dread*, 139). Not an immediate unity, but a synthesis to be achieved, man feels dread. This dread—the characteristically human sickness—establishes man's heterogeneity with all of nature in his identity as "spirit" (*Aand*). For dread springs from the relation of spirit to itself and to its situation.

> Everything turns upon dread coming into view. Man
> is a synthesis of the soulish and the bodily. But a synthesis is
> unthinkable if the two are not united in a third factor. The
> third factor is spirit. . . . And how is spirit related to itself
> and to its situation? It is related as dread. Spirit cannot do
> away with itself, even less can it grasp hold of itself, so long
> as it has itself outside of itself. Neither can man sink down
> into the vegetative life, for he is determined as spirit. He
> cannot flee from dread as he loves it; really he does not love
> it for he flees from it.[13]

In this way Kierkegaard has embroidered Hamann's notion
of the heterogeneity of man made evident in dread. Man is spirit,
Kierkegaard tells us, and as spirit he exhibits none of the closure
common to nature. Lacking closure, always aware of the diaphanous membrane of consciousness, man feels his estrangement as
dread. The traditional structure in which the problem of original
sin is discussed is replaced by a Kierkegaardian frame of reference
defined by these three notions of "spirit," "consciousness," and
"dread." In this second framework the Fall is interpreted as a
recurrent event in the drama of the individual life, following from
man's identity as *spirit*, invited by *dread*, and culminating in that
agony of *consciousness* which Kierkegaard knew so well. It was
perhaps this second framework which Kierkegaard had in mind
when he told us in 1842 that he understood Hamann's observation
in his own special way.

III. *Dread: The Encounter with the Void*

Even the most casual reader of *The Concept of Dread* cannot fail but be struck by what its translator calls its "unevenness of
style." [14] For long stretches Kierkegaard drones on in the academic
style of the lecturer, pedestrianly worrying obscure points of ethico-
theological doctrine and psychology. Then suddenly the style
changes, the slightly condescending expression of the lecturer is
replaced by the more anxious visage of the individual sufferer,
passion replaces dispassion; it is at these times, Lowrie remarks,
that Kierkegaard dives to "great depths" (*Dread*, ix). We should
not be surprised to learn that what Kierkegaard finds at these

"great depths" are none other than relics of that life-world we surveyed in Chapter 2.

There is first of all Kierkegaard's description of the experience of dread.

In a passage already cited [15] Kierkegaard has linked dread with *nothing*. He has remarked how nothing "feeds dread," how it is nothing which is at once dread's source and focus. "If then we ask what is the object of dread," he remarks in a later passage, "the answer as usual must be that it is nothing. Dread and nothing regularly correspond to each other." [16] On still other occasions Kierkegaard will link dread both with the future and with possibility. "The possible corresponds precisely to the future," he will write, "for freedom the possible is the future; and for time the future is the possible. Corresponding to both of them in the individual life is dread" (*Dread*, 82). From such passages as these we might glean some indication as to the real identity of dread— that is, we might begin to suspect that in describing "dread" Kierkegaard is really describing that confrontation with the void we detailed in Chapter 2. The following passage, offering perhaps Kierkegaard's most vivid characterization of the experience of dread, lends confirmation to our suspicions.

> One may liken dread to dizziness. He whose eye changes to look down into the yawning abyss becomes dizzy. But the reason for it is just as much his eye as it is the precipice. For suppose he had not looked down.
>
> Thus dread is the dizziness of freedom which occurs when the spirit would posit the synthesis, and freedom then gazes down into its own possibility, grasping at finiteness to sustain itself. In this dizziness freedom succumbs. Further than this psychology cannot go (*Dread*, 55).

In likening dread to dizziness Kierkegaard brings us very close to his own experience of dread—an experience grounded in his confrontation with the void of consciousness. This dread cannot be identified with an agoraphobia, with an anxiety over the extent of physical space. Rather it is the individual's dizziness, his swoon, over the "enormous extension" of inner space. He looks within, there to be confronted with the awful void thrown up by consciousness. Part of this void is of course consciousness' voyage into the future, its imagination of possibilities more terrible than any actuality. And part too of this void is a corollary awareness of what Kierkegaard calls "the alarming possibility of being able" (*Dread*, 40). The sins and crimes, but also the heroism and good works, which lie within the realm of possibility alarm the individual who would see himself reflected in them. Consciousness turns inward, and finds in its most private lair only an absence, a void. This is man's sickness, but also his nobility as a creature of freedom. Man learns that he is no-thing, but only a possibility of becoming. The result of this confrontation with the inward void is the "dizziness" of dread.

In describing dread Kierkegaard is of course describing his own encounter with the void. But this is not all. For in describing one particular variety of dread—the "daemonic" or "dread of the good"—he offers a vivid portrayal of the polarity of good and evil, value and disvalue, stimulated by this encounter.

"The daemonic [*det Daemoniske*]," Kierkegaard observes, "is the confined [*det Indsluttede*], the daemonic is dread of the good." [17] Again and again in his journals we have seen Kierkegaard complain over the *Indsluttethed*, the "confinement," which seals him from the world and time, and which he can never succeed in breaking through. "No, no my *Indsluttethed* cannot be broken," he complains in 1848, "at least not now. The thought of wanting to break it occupies me so much, at every moment, that it merely sets itself more and more fast" (VIII[1] A 645). Now this same *Indsluttethed* becomes a defining characteristic of one variety of dread. Kierkegaard continues.

The daemonic is unfreedom which would shut itself off. . . . The daemonic is the confined and the unfreely revealed. . . . Freedom is precisely the expansive [*Udvidende*]. It is in opposition I would employ the word "confined" for "unfreedom." Commonly a more metaphysical term is used for evil; it is called the negative. The ethical expression for it is precisely (if one observes its effect in the individual) the confined. The daemonic does not confine itself with something, but is self-confined, and therein lies the profundity in existence, that unfreedom precisely makes a prisoner of itself. Freedom is constantly communicating . . . , unfreedom becomes more and more confined and wants no communication.[18]

As Kierkegaard continues in succeeding pages to describe "dread of the good," the polarity set up between communication and non-communication, between freedom and unfreedom, becomes more explicit. The polarity between continuity and discontinuity is established as the fundamental polarity.[19] "The good" [det Gode] is said to mean continuity,[20] while the daemonic dread of the good takes joy in continuity's absence. All that remains is for one final aspect of the daemonic to be sketched. This is, of course, its "vacuousness" or "tediousness."

> The daemonic is the vacuous, the tedious. . . . The continuity which corresponds to the sudden is what one might call extinction. Tediousness, extinction, is in fact a continuity in Nothing. . . . Freedom is quietness in continuity; the opposite of this is the sudden. . . . The vacuous or tedious in turn characterize confinement. . . . Thus the whole definition of this concept is rounded out, for the form of vacuity is precisely confinement.[21]

The daemonic is now revealed as an existence willfully lived out in the desert of nothingness. It is a continuity in Nothing. It is confinement, noncommunication, tediousness, extinction, death.

There should be little doubt in any reader's mind regarding the true identity of the state described here as the daemonic or dread of the good. For once again Kierkegaard is describing that state of paralysis and vacuity which he knew so well, and which in Either/Or he called "despair." In reading these passages we are returned once again to the world of the aesthete A, Johannes the Seducer, and the mysterious brotherhood of the Symparanekromenoi —that "fellowship of buried lives." And this, of course, is as we would expect it to be. In Either/Or Kierkegaard traced the movement from dread to despair. In The Concept of Dread he has returned to the same ground, once again pointing out dread as the source of the pathogenesis, and once again describing the terminal symptoms in much the same phrases as those used earlier in Either/Or.

Yet allowing for this similarity, we can still detect one chief difference in the later treatment. This concerns what we might call Kierkegaard's recognition of the *willfulness* of despair.

Kierkegaard calls despair "the daemonic" or "dread of the good" and in so doing implies that there is something *willful* about it. "The daemonic does not confine itself with something," he has told us, "but is self-confined, and therein lies the profundity in existence, that unfreedom makes a prisoner of itself." Yet if unfreedom really does "make a prisoner of itself," then should not despair be seen as a sickness which does not befall its victim, but is rather willfully contracted by him? And if dread be a "hypochondria," then might not the ultimate stage of dread—the daemonic (despair)—be constituted in part by an odd variety of self-enjoyment? Might it be that Kierkegaard (at least in part) actually enjoyed his suffering and sickness?

Certain comments from his journal lead us to treat such a supposition with respect. For example, in 1848 he writes, "I have in my melancholy yet loved the world, for I have loved my melancholy" (VIII[1] A 641). And later on the same year, in recollecting his earlier love affair, he writes, "I was unhappy in my love; but I cannot think of myself as happy unless I were to become another person. But I was blissful in my unhappiness. . . . There is a melancholy in everything in my life, but also again indescribable bliss" (IX A 65). This odd ambivalence, this masochistic bliss which Kierkegaard felt in the immensity of his suffering, was part and parcel of that suffering. In a highly curious way he seemed to enjoy the stifling air of that labyrinth, which at the same time, he so desperately sought to escape. A British psychiatrist, Rudolph Friedmann, has remarked of him,

> With Kierkegaard [Friedmann has already said that the name means "churchyard" or "cemetery" in Danish] there was an indivisible union between name and personality. The black drapery of introversion, the fatal perfume of white funeral roses, and the loneliness of the heaths of Jutland, clung to him. Only those who have been chosen for loneliness can understand loneliness, the autistic wandering through the streets, the flowering of the personality which takes place amidst the dark avenues of the night alone

and without friends, the caressing of the cold windows of life with passionate and yet hopeless, withdrawn lips. . . .[22]

In these words Friedmann has caught something startlingly true about Kierkegaard, a brief reflection off the dark side of the Kierkegaardian moon. For no matter with what passion Kierkegaard describes the wonders of faith, and no matter with what eager expectation he looks forward to the discovery of the "unfound door," we recognize that there is another side to him which seeks not escape, but perpetual incarceration in the still life of the labyrinth. Kierkegaard may press his passionate lips to the windows of life, but we recognize that they are just as quickly withdrawn and pursed in the definite gesture of refusal. It is this duality of seeking and refusal, of the desire for faith combined with a twisted joy in the suffering of non-faith, which introduces another intentional level under the picture of the Kierkegaardian quest we have presented. This is the meaning of his designation of despair as "the daemonic." He is advising us that if dread be the "holy hypochondria," we should not let its holiness conceal its darker side—that side constituted of the hypochondriac's fatal infatuation for the perfume of disease. In these brief passages near the conclusion of *The Concept of Dread* Kierkegaard has dared reveal this darker side, has dared risk a penetration to the most private level of his psyche, there to discover yet another aspect of that void which both alarmed and fascinated him. It is the encounter with this void on a multitude of levels which constitutes the existential background to Kierkegaard's definition of "the concept of dread."

IV. Summary

If in the past we have lacked a special term for describing that awareness which lay at the very center of Kierkegaard's life-experience, now in "dread" we have such a term. "Dread," described as it is in the passages quoted above, specifies with great precision the ambivalence of Kierkegaard's struggle with consciousness. Dread is "a sympathetic antipathy and an antipathetic sympathy," a careful blending of terror and fascination. In his youth Kierkegaard knew dread in its most sympathetic disguise as "a seeking after the adventurous, the tremendous, the mysterious,"

as a mixture of curiosity and trepidation which we often associate
with children. It was perhaps a more innocent dread of this sort
which prompted him in 1837 to remark, "Yes, I believe I would
give myself to Satan so that he could show me every abomination,
every sin in its most dreadful form—it is this inclination, this
taste for the mystery of sin" (II A 599). Innocent as it may have
been at the time, he recognized later that it was a dread of this
sort which accounted for his "going astray," for the doomed experiment in hedonism which culminated in his entry into the still
life of despair. Awaking on despair's distant shore he recognized
that dread now had changed masks, and wore not the playful
visage of childhood adventurousness, but rather the snake-entwined
countenance of "the daemonic." Dread now invited him to inhale
in great draughts that sickly-sweet aroma of white funeral roses,
the perfume of despair, to lie down in his labyrinth prison and
embrace forever its sickness, its emptiness, its death; to accept once
and for all a life of *Indesluttethed* whose only continuity was "a
continuity in Nothing." He listened to its invitation, he considered
its plea, and then drew back, aware that what he heard was the
voice not of life but of death. Yet drawing back he was still at-
tracted, withdrawing from the void he could not forget it, and it
is the ambivalence of this attraction tensed against repulsion which
is recorded in these sections of *The Concept of Dread*.

In examining dread Kierkegaard has been examining once
again both the evolution of his sickness, as well as the symptom-
atology of its final stage. *The Concept of Dread* thus plays a part
in a continuing effort at diagnosis, and in this role it recapitulates
many of the discussions of *Either/Or*, Volume I. Moreover, if we
turn to consider *Dread's* companion volume—*Philosophical Fragments*—the parallel between *Either/Or* and these twin works of
June 1844 is even more apparent. For just as in *Either/Or*, Volume
II, Kierkegaard considered a possible therapy for consciousness, so
in *Philosophical Fragments* he investigated the possibility of a
religious cure. Where earlier the "ethical act" was entertained as
the catalyst which would break the chrysalis of despair, now the
individual's confrontation with the Paradox is postulated as per-
forming a similar function. In a very real sense, then, we may think
of the twin works *Philosophical Fragments* and *The Concept of*

Dread as two parts of a later-day attempt to play out again the drama of *Either/Or*—this time in a philosophico-theological setting rather than a literary one. Although the language and costumes of the pseudonyms have changed, the underlying pattern remains fixed. Health confronts sickness, continuity confronts discontinuity, the world of the square confronts the world of the circle. The more things change within Kierkegaard's marionette theater, the more (it would seem) things remain the same.

This fixity, moreover, this strange recurrence of the pattern presented for the first time in *Either/Or*, is not restricted to these two works from June of 1844. For as we shall see in the next chapter, such a pattern of sickness and cure—of a deficient mental state juxtaposed against a healthy counterpart—is a common characteristic of all the pseudonymous works we have investigated thus far. It was such a characteristic we had in mind when earlier we remarked that Kierkegaard often seems not to be writing different books at all, but only to be rewriting the same book in different ways.

8

STAGES ON LIFE'S WAY

1. *Interlude*

In following the course of Kierkegaard's authorship from *Either/Or* through *The Concept of Dread* we are reminded often of the truth of Rasmus Nielsen's observation concerning his friend. Again and again in the works which flowed from Kierkegaard's pen in the early 1840's we have seen evidence of what Nielsen called his "*apriori* nature." The story of Kierkegaard's early authorship is not one of development but of repetition. It is not a story of the sequential examination of different themes and materials, but of the circular return again and again to the same theme and body of material. To introduce a metaphor, we can think of these works not as individual links lying end to end in a linear chain, but rather as slightly eccentric loops piled one atop the other.

This is not to say that no progression at all is evident in these works. On the contrary, in preceding chapters we have traced just such a progression. From the aesthete's unsuccessful attempt to compress consciousness into flesh, to the ethical man's equally unsuccessful attempt to collapse consciousness into will, to the agonizing search for a catalyst of madness which would shatter consciousness: this is the progression past chapters have illuminated. Yet allowing for this progression, the final impression we take from these works is one not of development but of circularity. Again and again in these works we have watched the same mental landscape pass before our eyes with only minor alterations. We have watched in these works not a kaleidoscopic change from pattern to pattern, but rather a *repetition* of the same pattern under different names.

We encountered this pattern for the first time in reading Kierkegaard's *Papirer*. Here it was revealed in its purest form as a polarity between continuity/discontinuity, health/sickness, summer/winter, the world of the circle/the world of the square. At isolated moments we saw Kierkegaard's winter world illuminated by brilliant shafts of sunlight. In these socalled "moments of continuity" he knew the lifting of the veil of consciousness. There was, we saw, at the very center of Kierkegaard's experience an intense polarity between two states of consciousness: one deficient and empty, the other exhilaratingly full.

In *Either/Or* this pattern was given its most exhaustive exemplification in the contrast between the aesthetic and ethical lifeviews. In the first volume of *Either/Or* we saw how the aesthetic life-view ultimately leads to the sickness called "despair." This sickness, whose evolution is charted in the admissions of Johannes the Seducer and the young aesthete A, closely resembled Kierkegaard's own sufferings as recounted in the *Papirer*. It in turn was juxtaposed against an imagined healthy state represented by Judge William, who prescribed the "ethical act" as a cure for A's despair. In this framework Kierkegaard's "dreadful still life" became despair, its ideal counterpart became the happy "marriage to life" of Judge William, and the moment when the second replaced the first, "the moment of continuity," became the "ethical act."

In succeeding works this same pattern reappeared under various guises. In *Repetition*, for example, the sickly or deficient state of consciousness is represented by Constantine's inability to achieve "repetition." The fulfilled state is here only hinted at as that condition the fictitious Young Man will enjoy after his experience of "repetition." Turning to *Fear and Trembling*, we find that certain elements in the pattern have been altered, but not sufficiently to conceal its essential form. The deficient state of consciousness is now represented by the muted, less hysterical, despair of Johannes de Silentio—that self-styled "knight of infinite resignation"—who conjures up the health represented by Abraham.

Although altered in certain ways, the polarity between sickness and health, between the world of the square and the world of the circle, still remains.

Finally, in the twin philosophico-theological works from June of 1844 the pattern is once again repeated. The deficient state is exhaustively described in *The Concept of Dread*. Just as earlier in *Either/Or* Kierkegaard had plotted the evolution from "dread" to despair, so in *The Concept of Dread* a similar movement is charted. "Dread" is now seen as the original state of mankind—a state anterior to either innocence or guilt which develops by the addition of will into a more desperate state called "dread of the good." This latter state, characterized by tediousness, vacuity, and *Indeslut-tethed*, we recognize as despair under a new name. Against this deficient state is juxtaposed the health of "faith"—described now but briefly in the concluding chapter of *The Concept of Dread*. The passage from one conscious state to the other—from sickness to health—is examined in *Philosophical Fragments* where the notions of the Paradox and the Moment play crucial roles. Here, in *Dread's* companion volume, the healthy state maintains its identity as "faith," while the "moment of continuity" is now stressed as "the Moment"—that instant when the individual, in forfeiting his reason on the cross of the Paradox, undergoes a conversion and becomes divinely mad. Whereas in *Either/Or* the ethical act was postulated as the agent of cure, now the individual's confrontation with the Paradox comes to fulfill a similar function. The triad of sickness, health, and moment of cure is again complete.

Another way of viewing this pattern is to see it as a parallel expression of that duality of focus we saw to be characteristic of the early "studies" in the *Papirer*. There, we recall, Kierkegaard's search was seen to have a double focus. Not only did it involve an outward-directed canvassing of alternative life-views, but it also involved an inward-directed exploration of some of the "multiplicity of shadows" which constituted Kierkegaard's own person. In the pseudonymous works the outward focus finds expression in the discussions of the imagined state of health—in Judge William's description of the bliss of marriage, in the Young Man's joy over "repetition," in Johannes de Silentio's breathless description of the life of the "knight of faith." Within these same works the inward focus finds expression in the exhaustive description of psychic illness: In the persons of the aesthete A, Johannes the Seducer, Constantine Constantius, and Johannes de Silentio we detect shadowy reflections of Kierkegaard's own sickness—latter-day actors in the costumes of the Master Thief, Faust, and Ahasuerus.

By the spring of 1845 Kierkegaard's search for health was entering a new phase. Its results up to this time had been disappointing in the extreme, and by now its circular character was becoming readily apparent. With agonizing regularity the inward and outward foci kept presenting repetitive pictures. Whenever Kierkegaard looked outward, whether in glancing at the blissful married life of the Judge or in considering with Constantine the Young Man's "repetition," his hopes inevitably appeared clothed in the same garments. And when he looked inward, whether in describing the despair of the aesthete or in characterizing more formally the quality of "the daemonic," the outline of that dreadful still life remained unchanged. Like a prisoner who, failing to find an exit on his first circuit of the cell, continues to circle its walls, so Kierkegaard continued to circle the walls of his labyrinth. With each circuit a new work fell from his pen, joining its predecessors as yet another witness to the quality of his torment. The "unfound door" remained "unfound," the labyrinth impenetrant.

Kierkegaard's despair over this continual and fruitless oscillation is given expression by a note in his personal copy of *Either/Or*. Apparently with great care, he underlined the following phrases from the 75th diapsalm.

> *Vainly I strive against it. My foot slips. My life is still a poet's existence.* What could be more unhappy? I am predestined; fate laughs at me when suddenly it shows me *how everything I do to resist becomes a moment in such an existence* (IV A 217).

He is enough of a poet to *imagine* the exaltation of the Young Man in the throes of "repetition," or *imaginatively* to sketch the outlines of a Judge William or a "knight of faith." But imagining is not living, and, to the Young Man's rapturous paean to the "breaking wave which hurls me up above the stars," we must oppose Kierkegaard's complaint from the year 1844.

> At the present time I suffer much from the dumb nausea of thoughts. There is a dread over me; I cannot say what it is that I cannot understand. Just as Nebuchadnezzar, I must pray not only for an explanation of the dream but also that someone will tell me what it was I dreamed
>
> (v A 71).

Against the occasional escape of one or more of his imagined creations from despair and its pain, we must oppose Kierkegaard's continued suffering. In 1844 he observes, "At this time I am so indolent that I care for nothing" (v A 48), and later on the same year he complains that "so long as I live, I live in contradiction" (v A 68). Yet perhaps his mental state during these years is best summarized by an entry from 1845. "The burden remains continually the same; but every time one tiredly calls: What time is it?—comes the reply: an eternity!" (vi A 135). Yet "if the burden remains continually the same"—if the search for health had brought about in Kierkegaard's own life no lasting or important results—then it is not surprising that at just this time doubts would begin appearing concerning the very legitimacy of the search. It had been many years since Kierkegaard set out from Gilleleje on the "path" he claimed to have discovered. Many years had passed with no surcease of torment. Given the apparent fruitlessness of the search it was only natural that questions would begin arising concerning its significance and value. What was the meaning of the confinement [*Indesluttethed*] and melancholy [*Tungsind*] which never left him? Were these only idiosyncratic phenomena, symptoms of a diseased mind, or did they have another significance? Why had they so afflicted *him*? These were the questions Kierkegaard was asking in the mid-1840's, questions whose answers he was seeking in a number of different directions.

A cluster of *Papirer* entries from the mid-1840's dealing with the problem of "the exception" attest to one direction in which the search was pursued.[1] His visit to a doctor in 1845 to determine whether his suffering might have a medical origin gives evidence of another direction.[2] Yet certainly the most interesting result of Kierkegaard's questioning concerning the meaning of his suffering can be located in the works themselves. And of all the works there is one—published in the spring of 1845—in which this questioning becomes explicit. It is to this work, entitled *Guilty?/Not Guilty?*, that we now shall turn.

II. *Guilty?/Not Guilty?*

The work we read today under the title *Stages on Life's Way* is a composite of two smaller works. The first third, including the aesthetic symposium and Judge William's dissertation on marriage, was originally intended to be published in its own right under the title *Vrangen og Retten* (*The Right Side and the Wrong Side*). The last two-thirds, made up of Quidam's diary and Frater Taciturnus' commentary on it, was also designed as an independent work bearing its present title, *Skyldig?—Ikke-Skyldig?* (*Guilty?/Not Guilty?*). Only at the last moment did Kierkegaard change his mind and decide to publish the two under a single title. It was at this last stage that he added the title *Stadier paa Livets Vej* (*Stages on Life's Way*), the preface by Hilarius Bogbinder, and repaginated the final drafts of both works to agree with his new plan.[3]

The first part, *Vrangen og Retten*, is essentially a repetition of *Either/Or*—a fact which Kierkegaard himself later points out in the *Postscript*.[4] Instead of the lone aesthete of *Either/Or*, we now have five; instead of Judge William's three letters to his young friend we now have a single essay on marriage. But these are only differences of detail, and, in all essentials, the later work only duplicates the former: the aesthetic life once again confronts the ethical life; Judge William praises marriage while the aesthetes deprecate it; the reader is once again invited to choose between "either/or." Since this first part of *Stages on Life's Way* adds so little to our knowledge of either the aesthetic or ethical life-views, it will be put to the side in favor of the more interesting second part. For it is in *Guilty?/Not Guilty?* that Kierkegaard takes up in earnest questions which long have lain in the background of his authorship, questions which concern the very meaning and legitimacy of both the authorship and the search for health which spawned it.

Guilty?/Not Guilty? was a long time in the writing. Unlike Kierkegaard's other works which were written in an uninterrupted flow over a short period of time, *Guilty?/Not Guilty?* was composed in starts and stops over a period which stretched from May 1843 to March 1845—a period which embraced the writing of *Repetition, Fear and Trembling, Philosophical Fragments, The Concept of Dread*, as well as twenty-one devotional addresses. It was written, then, as a counterpoint to these other works, taking up and articulating a region of concern which lay in their background from the very beginning. In this regard, Kierkegaard's first mention of it on 17 May 1843 is revealing.

> I have just begun a story entitled: *Guilty?/Not Guilty?* It will naturally contain things which may astonish the world; for in the last year and a half I have experienced more poetry than all the novels put together . . .[5]

The reference here to the "last year and a half" refers of course to Kierkegaard's break with Regine and to his subsequent reflections on this break, while those "things which may astonish the world" are his revelations concerning the intricacy of the affair as well as the magnitude of his suffering over it. It is not surprising then that the dramatic skeleton of the completed *Guilty?/Not Guilty?* is the tale of a young man's broken engagement and its concomitant suffering. In relating this story Kierkegaard's psyche splits (so to speak) in two. He becomes first of all a young man suffering from an unhappy love affair. Called Quidam (Latin: "a certain one"), this young man recounts in a series of diary entries the growth and subsequent denouement of a love affair which duplicates in many details the story of Kierkegaard's own involvement with Regine.[6] These diary entries serve as an occasion for the remarks of Frater Taciturnus, Kierkegaard's second *alter ego*, a humorous metaphysician who attempts to disclose the meaning of the young man's suffering. *Guilty?/Not Guilty?* is perhaps the most starkly autobiographical of all of Kierkegaard's works. With it (as we shall see in future sections) the pseudonymous authorship takes a highly significant turn, a turn which uncovers regions of concern and knots of questions which up to now have lain in obscurity.

III. *Quidam's Diary*

Quidam's diary opens on a somewhat threatening note. In considering whether he should propose marriage to his new-found love he asks,

> Ought a soldier of the advanced guard be married?
> Dare a soldier on the frontier (spiritually understood) take
> a wife, a soldier on duty at the extremest outpost, who is
> fighting day and night against the robber bands of an innate
> melancholy? (*Stages*, 188).

The clouds of melancholy threaten. The terrors and alarms of his
own spiritual life dissuade Quidam from moving closer to his beloved. Her youth and gaiety must not be shadowed by bringing
her into contact with such dark thoughts. But it is just this youth
and gaiety which is so attractive. Perhaps her girlish spontaneity,
her health, can cure his sickness? A bit later he exclaims rhapsod-
ically.

> The first kiss—oh what bliss! A girl joyful in heart,
> happy in youth! And she is mine. What are all gloomy
> thoughts but a cobweb, and what is melancholy but a mist
> which flies before this reality, a sickness which is healed by
> the sight of this health, this health which indeed is mine
> since it is hers who is my life and my future. Wealth she
> does not possess . . . , but she can say as an apostle said to
> the impotent man, 'Silver and gold have I none; but what
> I have, that I give thee, arise and be strong' (*Stages*, 201).

On this confident note he asks for his beloved's hand. Her father
agrees to the match and within a few days the banns are announced. Their affair has entered a new stage; now they are an
engaged couple.

They follow the prescribed motions of the engagement ritual.
He accompanies her to parties; they walk together; he reads sermons to her. At least to an external observer's gaze, all seems to
be proceeding naturally. But within himself Quidam feels a
gathering malaise, a disturbance in the blood. He writes,

> What is this? What does it mean? I am as deeply
> moved as the forest in its anxious flutter against the coming
> storm. What presentiment is this which oppresses me? I
> no longer recognize myself. Is this being in love? Oh no! . . .
> The clouds gathering over my head are religious crises
> (*Stages*, 200).

A bit later he reveals more of the nature of these socalled "religious crises."

> I am not actually a religious individual; I am only a possibility of such a thing. . . . When one is able to comprehend the religious need so profoundly that one might even do well to call for the priest, and one has a philosophic scepticism completely corresponding to it, the prospects are not exactly the best (*Stages*, 242).

Stretched between "religious need" and "philosophic scepticism" Quidam sees himself as "the most frightful thing of all, an eternal torment: a personal existence which is unable to unite itself in a conclusion" (*Stages*, 220). So stretched, it is not surprising that his fiancée's girlish innocence soon becomes distasteful to him. She is *too* innocent, *too* happy, *too* immediate in her tastes and interests. "If she were unhappy," he remarks, "it would help. But this childlike happiness, this lightness in the world which I cannot understand and with which I cannot sympathize deeply and essentially" (*Stages*, 210). What before had been attractive now becomes detestable. As the gap between the two widens, Quidam turns inward to more private concerns.

"Before I was engaged to her," reflects Quidam, "my life was like a painful inquisition of myself, then I was interrupted and summoned out to the most dreadful decision; and when I am through with that, if ever I am, then I can begin again with myself where I left off" (*Stages*, 240). Soon he comes to feel his "painful inquisition" to be related to both his "religious need" and also his melancholy. He recognizes his melancholy as a sickness, but he also speculates that perhaps this sickness may yet culminate in a state of religious health. And so he comes to cherish his melancholy.

> But the strange ideas of melancholy I do not give up; for these I call pulls—if only I follow them and hold out, they lead me to the eternal certainty of the infinite. In my loneliness therefore these ideas are dear to me, even though thy affright me; they have the utmost importance for me and teach me (*Stages*, 345).

It soon becomes apparent that the road which led to a happy marriage has been lost, and whether by choice or necessity Quidam now finds himself on another road, a road of loneliness whose final destination remains unknown.

It is not long before the outward characteristics of the affair make manifest this change in Quidam's interior life. The two lovers argue, are reconciled, and then argue again. Finally the break is made; the ring is given back, the engagement terminated. But curiously this termination of the affair only serves to heighten its intensity for Quidam. At one point the girl has remarked that she would surely die if Quidam left her. This remark remains in his memory long after, and torments him with the thought that he may have her suicide on his conscience. He is conscious of her all the time, yet careful not to betray his interest. He inquires of her health through third parties, watches her from hidden locations, yet never permits her to become aware of his concern for her. Although he has parted from her he cannot forget her, and this is the source of his suffering.

Having forsaken his single chance for a normal life, Quidam's anguish becomes more intense. His present existence seems empty, dead, drained of meaning and vitality. Invoking the familiar language of despair, he complains,

> There is no change of seasons for me, as in me there is no change (*Stages*, 322).

> My suffering is boring. In fact I am still constantly engaged in expounding this nothing, and the scenery is unalterably the same (*Stages*, 319).

> I am a lost wayfarer, I am like one who has come into a strange land where people talk a different language and have other customs (*Stages*, 290).

He feels himself tormented by the total deficiency of the present when juxtaposed against the past. Pathetically, he compares himself to a wounded mussel.

> So it is a mussel lies on the seashore; it opens its shell in search of nutriment, a child sticks a twig into it, so that it cannot shut. Finally the child grows tired of the play and

would pull the twig out, but there remains a splinter. And the mussel shuts its shell; but deeply within its shell it suffers and cannot get the splinter out (*Stages*, 354).

"In search of nutriment" he had opened himself to the love of his fiancée. Once opened in this way, he can never succeed in quite closing his shell again. For the memory of the release he had enjoyed with her, remains within as a splintered token of his past. Yet tormented as he is by this memory, he is all the while expectant of something to come. He calls himself a "lookout" (*Stages*, 327), and in the following passage, remarks how he longs to see the end of his quest.

> Oh, in loneliness I have never wished for death. I do not understand how men can suddenly become torpid enough to wish for death. For me, on the contrary, the more it grows dark about me, the more I wish to live, in order to hold out by myself, to see if my enthusiasm was an empty word or a power, whether it was the strong drink which foams of itself or penny beer, which foams indeed—but by a foreign admixture (*Stages*, 347).

He feels drawn towards this unknown destination while at the same time doubting the legitimacy of the call which attracts him. Is his enthusiasm a genuine religious vocation or is it only an affect of a morbid temperament? Is it the "strong drink which foams of itself" or only the "penny beer which foams indeed—but by a foreign admixture"? Has he sacrificed his happiness on the altar of melancholy, or is this sacrifice a necessary one on the road to religious salvation? Finally, it comes down to a question of *meaning*.

> If there were any man I could turn to, I would go to him and say, "Oh please supply a little meaning to me in my bewilderment." The most dreadful meaning is not so dreadful as meaninglessness, and this is the more terrible the more meaninglessly it smiles (*Stages*, 329).

What causes Quidam such distress is the tormenting thought that his rejection of his beloved, of his last possibility for a normal life, will prove to be without significance. Perhaps he should have stayed with her; perhaps his quest is an illusion. "What is my life but a striving after wind?" he complains, "My existence is nothing but *molimina*, useless effort" (*Stages*, 354).

IV. *Frater Taciturnus' Commentary*

Quidam's appeal for a man who can "supply a little meaning" is answered in the person of Frater Taciturnus. In a long commentary on Quidam's diary the Frater offers a framework in which the young man's suffering may be interpreted. Within the terms of this framework his suffering is made both comprehensible and significant.

Frater Taciturnus begins his commentary with the following schematic presentation of the young man's predicament.

> One perceives at once the fanatic enthusiast, and an enthusiast he is to become, but in another sphere. So time passes, he forms his resolve, but the erotic factor has not received due attention. Then he is in for it, and he conceives the situation ethically, whereas the religious possibility is constantly the deepest thing in his soul. . . . The ethical now becomes clarified to him in reality, and he comes to grief. The offense he did her was not in breaking off, but it was that with such a view of life he wanted to be in love. The stages [*Stadier*] were arranged thus: an aesthetic-ethical life-view in illusion, with the dawning possibility of the religious; an ethical life-view which condemns him; he sinks back within himself—and there he is where I would have him (*Stages*, 34).

This passage marks the first appearance of the famed structure of "stages on life's way" [*Stadier paa Livets Vej*] in Kierkegaard's work, and we should note that it is introduced for the express purpose of explaining the young man's predicament. The "stages" are stages in the young man's development, and at least at this point, are given no further metaphysical status. By postulating this framework of stages Frater Taciturnus proposes to explain the significance of Quidam's suffering. For Quidam, we learn a bit later, is "an enthusiast, and an enthusiast of a peculiar sort" (*Stages*, 367). His enthusiasm is not directed toward the erotic—toward the infinitely subtle play of mind and feeling involved in creating and savoring erotic moods—nor is it enthusiasm of an ethical sort which would find its natural outlet in the life of action. Rather it is a *religious* enthusiasm. Beyond the attractions of both the aesthetic and the ethical, Quidam is "impelled by the intensity of the spirit towards the religious" (*Stages*, 381). He can no longer sink down into the vegetative immediacy of romantic courtship. This time is past for him; to use his own words, he is "too old," his "twenty-five winters" have aged him an eternity beyond the "sixteen summers" of his fiancée (*Stages*, 247). He exists on the far side of the "time of immediacy" (*Stages*, 377), yet short of religious maturity. But as Frater Taciturnus points out, "If it is true that the time of immediacy is past, then the thing is to win the religious, nothing intermediate is of any avail" (*Stages*, 377).

The locus of Quidam's torment is thus found to lie in his identity as a religious "possibility" who has not in actuality reached the full-blown religious stage. His torment is a self-torment arising from his having stopped halfway.

> It is now easily seen what the religious person must mean by self-torment. The thing is to discover *by oneself* the whole possibility of danger, and *by oneself* to discover every instant its reality . . . , but the thing is at the same time to be joyful. In what does this self-torment consist? It consists in halting halfway. It does not consist therefore in first stage above mentioned, but it consists in the fact that one is not able to press through to joy. And this is not comic, says the religious person, nor does it exist in order to draw aesthetic tears, for it is culpable, and one *shall* press through. Everyone who does not get through is himself to blame.[7]

In Quidam's case his self-torment takes the form of a mixture of melancholy and confinement (*Indesluttethed*). Frater Taciturnus goes on to interpret these sufferings as symptoms of his struggle towards the religious. He writes,

> Confinement [*Indesluttethed*], however, can signify various things. His confinement is essentially a form of melancholy, and again melancholy in his case is the con-

densed possibility which must be gone through with in the
experience of a crisis if he is to become clear to himself in
the experience of the religious. . . . His confinement is in
fact neither more nor less than the condensed anticipation
of the religious subjectivity. . . . His confinement is a pres-
age of a higher life. . . . Confinement therefore can hardly
be taken away from the confined individual, and properly
he must be healed religiously in himself. This is the most
abstract form of confinement when it is the anticipation of
a higher life in the condensation of possibility. . . . From
this standpoint of possibility one can strive after religious
transparency, and this is what he must do.[8]

As the Frater pronounces in such authoritative tones his diagnosis
of Quidam's "case," we are reminded of the labors of earlier diag-
nosticians. For Judge William also proposed to comprehend his
young friend's predicament, and Constantine Constantius spoke
in equally confident tones of the "crisis" his Young Man was ap-
proaching. The Frater, however, exhibits a characteristically new
attitude towards his patient's affliction. Unlike Judge William and
Constantine Constantius he views the sufferings of his patient as
intrinsically natural, and even valuable. "Suffering," he points out
in quoting Pascal, "is the natural state of the Christian, just as
health is that of the 'natural man' " (Stages, 416). Quidam's suffering is interpreted as a symptom of the ascent to the "higher
life" of "religious transparency." As the Frater points out, Quidam's melancholy "is a crisis anticipatory of the religious experience" (Stages, 389). Indesluttethed and melancholy have meaning,
they are not pathological phenomena, but markers on the way to
faith. Man was planned by God for the highest, remarks the
Frater, even though attaining this highest may involve severe suffering (Stages, 426). As a hallmark of incipient religiosity the
suffering which afflicts Quidam is not a morbid phenomenon but
a symptom of his approach to the final stage. Soon Quidam will
have achieved his passage, will have "pressed through to joy."

Frater Taciturnus is himself ignorant of the precise details
of this "joy." He cautions us often that he himself is not a religious
person; he has not passed beyond the "metaphysical," has not

achieved even the status of a Quidam.[9] Yet ignorant of the precise details of the religious experience, the Frater is not ignorant of its form. Its source, he tells us, will lie in what religious people call "the forgiveness of sins" (*Stages*, 433f), and its form will be that of a "second immediacy" [10] more vivid than the first, an immediacy attained only when the individual, after having severed all ties with the world, has in fact become "another man" (*Stages*, 435). This "second immediacy" is that state of salvation towards which Quidam is tending, a state lying beyond both Quidam's and the Frater's present standpoints. It is the hope of reaching this "higher life" which the Frater holds out to Quidam in his need. This is his answer to Quidam's appeal for someone who can "supply a little meaning to me in my bewilderment."

v. The Meaning of Suffering

It is precisely this overriding concern with *meaning* which marks off *Guilty?/Not Guilty?* from the earlier pseudonymous works. This can be seen most clearly by comparing *Guilty?/Not Guilty?* with an earlier work, *Repetition*, which it parallels both in theme and structure.

As in *Guilty?/Not Guilty?* the principal theme in *Repetition* was one of unhappy love—of a young man's broken engagement and its attendant suffering. The story of this unhappy love was related in the Young Man's letters to Constantine, who comments on them just as later Frater Taciturnus comments on Quidam's diary. Moreover, if we turn to consider the true identity of the "young man" figure in both stories, the parallel becomes even stronger. For just as the Young Man in *Repetition* turns out on examination to be a fictitious character invented by Constantine, so too does Quidam turn out to be a product of the Frater's imagination.[11] Both figures are invented by the narrators of the two stories to explore standpoints they themselves are unable to reach —that is, in the case of Constantine to explore the possibility of a religious "repetition," and in the case of the Frater to examine the sufferings of a religious "enthusiast." The theme of both works is one of unhappy love, while the common structure of both is that of a "thought-experiment." [12]

Yet it is against the background of this commonality of

theme and structure that the fundamental difference between the two works can best be seen. For while in *Repetition* the focus of interest lies in the actual experience of repetition, in *Guilty?/Not Guilty?* the center of concern becomes the *meaning* of Quidam's sufferings. It is not insignificant that the earlier work carries the Young Man through the actual experience of repetition, while the later work leaves Quidam in an ambiguous state of anticipation. In *Guilty?/Not Guilty?* the actual experience of religious salvation recedes into the background. For although the Frater explains that such a salvation, such a "second immediacy," awaits Quidam at the end of his spiritual quest, he also points out that "the religious existence is a constant history of suffering" (*Stages*, 415). How long must the religious individual endure his suffering before he "presses through to joy"? Is this suffering a lifelong sickness, or is it a more temporary phenomenon? To these questions the Frater has no ready answers, principally because his concern rests not on the outcome of Quidam's suffering but on its *meaning*.

Whether or not the Young Man in *Repetition* was justified in leaving his fiancée was not a question that seriously concerned Constantine Constantius. His concern (and indirectly the concern of the whole book) was "with the problem whether a repetition is possible" (*Repetition*, 3). Yet it is precisely this first question which is central to the ponderings of Quidam and Frater Taciturnus. The full title of the later work is *Guilty?/Not Guilty?: A Story of Suffering*, and we are to take at least part of Quidam's suffering to reside precisely in the ambiguity of his guilt. For how is his rejection of his beloved to be interpreted? He tells us that it was a necessary act springing from melancholy. It was melancholy, he maintains, which stood between him and a happy marriage. But what is the meaning of this melancholy? Does it spring from nothing more profound than a morbid temperament? If so, then Quidam must accept guilt for the needless wounding of his fiancée. Or are these "strange ideas of melancholy" really symptoms of his religious maturity? Are they perhaps "pulls" (as he calls them) which draw him towards a "higher life"? If so, then his rejection of his beloved gains a certain justification. Like Abraham's act, it becomes a sacrifice, a necessary act of self-denial on the way to religious fulfillment. The question "Guilty?/Not Guilty?" thus hinges on the meaning of Quidam's act of rejection. But as we have seen, the question of the meaning of this act cannot be disentangled from the more general question concerning the meaning of Quidam's suffering as a whole. Hence it is the concern with meaning—and more precisely the meaning of suffering—which stands at the very center of *Guilty?/Not Guilty?*. Whereas in the earlier work an escape from suffering, an imagined cure in the experience of "repetition," occupies the center of attention, in the latter work suffering itself—its meaning or non-meaning—now becomes the focus of interest.

But why is such a change in emphasis of such crucial importance? Why does it mark, as we indicated above, "a highly significant turn" in Kierkegaard's pseudonymous authorship? To answer this question we must turn to a revealing passage from the *Concluding Unscientific Postscript*. In commenting upon the integral relationship which obtains between a religious view of life and the acceptance of suffering, Johannes Climacus remarks.

> Viewed religiously, it is necessary to comprehend suffering and to remain in it, so that reflection is directed upon the suffering and not away from it. . . . A poet is often a sufferer in existence, but what we reflect upon is the poetic productivity which is thereby brought about. The existing poet who suffers in his existence does not really grasp his suffering, he does not penetrate more and more deeply into it, but in his suffering he seeks away from the suffering and finds ease in poetic production, in the poetic anticipation of a more perfect, a happier, order of things. . . . But back from the enchantment of the poetic productivity and the wishful imaginative order of things, back from the identification with the poetic character, the poet and the actor turn to the suffering of reality, which they cannot grasp. . . . The poet can explain (transfigure) the whole of existence, but he cannot explain himself, because he will not become religious and grasp suffering's secret as the highest life form
> (*Postscript*, 397–98).

In light of the number of times Kierkegaard complains bitterly in his journals over his identity as "only a poet," [13] this passage becomes highly significant. For does not the description offered here of the poetic enterprise ring especially true when applied to Kierkegaard's own early production? Consider now this whole, long search for a cure—for an exit from the labyrinth of consciousness —which we have followed from the earliest *Papirer* studies through *The Concept of Dread*. What is it but "a way of escape," a "wishful invention," an attempt to "find ease in poetic production, in the poetic anticipation of a more perfect, a happier, order of things"? Think now of the warm tones in which the Judge's "marriage to life" was sketched in *Either/Or*, Volume II, or of the equal tenderness with which Johannes de Silentio *imagines* how a knight of faith might appear. Likewise, think of the eagerness with which Constantine Constantius *imagines* the manic joy of the Young Man's experience of repetition, or of the excitement with which Johannes Climacus or Vigilius Haufniensis describe the exhilaration of faith. What are these constructions but repeated attempts on Kierkegaard's part to *escape*, repeated moves not to "grasp his suffering," not to "penetrate more and more deeply into it," but rather ways of evading it by anticipating imaginatively "a happier order of things."

When in past chapters we spoke of Kierkegaard's desire "to escape from the labyrinth of consciousness," we did not use this term "escape" idly. For the fundamental life-outlook we saw revealed in the *Papirer* studies, that life-outlook which moulded the early phases of Kierkegaard's authorship, was predicated upon the possibility of *escape*. Magical in its core, it was founded on the conviction that a key, a magic talisman, a miraculous agent of cure, could be found which would permit *escape*. It was the constancy of this single life-outlook under the welter of different themes and pseudonyms which produced that curious oscillation found in the early works. Sickness and health, the world of the square and the world of the circle, an examination of the deficient state juxtaposed against an imagined cure: this was the polarity within which that oscillation took place. Now, in *Guilty?/Not Guilty?* this oscillation is slowly being brought to a close. With the recognition that the sickness of consciousness cannot be escaped, the earlier cycle of questioning winds to a close, to be replaced by a new cycle which up to now has lain in shadow. Whereas the primary concern of the first cycle lay in finding an escape from suffering, the essential interest of the second cycle lies in "penetrating more and more deeply into it" so as to grasp its meaning. We are watching here the replacement of one fundamental life-outlook by another. The early magical view of life begins to crumble as its key premise (that escape or cure is indeed possible) is revealed as more and more unlikely. In its place we observe rising a new view which sees life as a perpetual torment—a suffering without remedy —whose meaning resides precisely in the enormity of the suffering. To use Kierkegaard's own vocabulary, a "religious" view of life comes to replace a "poetic" one.

In *Guilty?/Not Guilty?* this transposition has not yet been accomplished, and therefore it must be seen as a transitional work. Although the center of interest has shifted from the actual experience of salvation, to a concern with the *meaning of suffering*, nevertheless, the possibility of an escape in this life is still entertained in the Frater's glowing description of the "second immediacy" of faith. In Kierkegaard's next work, *Concluding Unscientific Postscript*, this last escape hatch is closed, and faith becomes now the expectation (not the actuality) of an "eternal blessedness." It is in this work that the question of meaning finds its response in the pronouncement that "truth is subjectivity," and it is here that Kierkegaard's new life-outlook is given its first exhaustive specification. Once again invoking Kierkegaard's own vocabulary, we might say that the *Postscript* is the first work of the pseudonymous group to be genuinely "religious."

9

CONCLUDING UNSCIENTIFIC
POSTSCRIPT

Of all Kierkegaard's works, the *Postscript* is perhaps the most difficult to understand in a short compass. Four hundred eighty pages long in the original Danish edition, it is a hodge-podge of different themes, ideas, comments, and opinions. Here we find, for example, a forty-page appendix entitled, "A Glance at a Contemporary Effort in Danish Literature," sandwiched between two chapters discussing the notion of "subjective truth." Here is irony and humor, a bit of Biblical exegesis, tight conceptual analysis, and at many points prose of great passion and beauty. Here in fact is almost everything we would *not* expect to find after glancing at the oddly systematic table of contents. Yet it does not take the reader long to recognize that the systematic character of the table of contents is meant facetiously (part of the joke of calling a 480-page work a "postscript" to a work of 164 pages),[1] and that a systematic argument is the last thing Kierkegaard has in mind. More impressionistic than logical, its development is not linear but angular. We keep moving around a particular life-outlook, seeing it from different angles, looking at its different aspects, investigating and reinvestigating its central problem. Given this angular character of the *Postscript*, it is imperative at the outset to understand clearly the identity of its central life-outlook.

Let me say without further ado that this life-outlook is of course that of Quidam of the *Stages*, and that the central problem investigated in the *Postscript* is Quidam's problem—the meaning

of suffering. Yet Quidam's problem is preeminently also Kierkegaard's problem, and so the most effective way to comprehend it
(and the life-perspective out of which it grew) is to turn, not back
to *Stages on Life's Way*, but rather to other published and unpublished works of this period. For at just this time Kierkegaard
introduces into both his published and unpublished writings an
idea of the most far-reaching importance. In his growing preoccupation with the strange Pauline notion of "the thorn in the flesh"
(*Paelen i Kjødet*) he reveals that life-outlook which lies at the
very heart of the *Postscript*. Virtually unknown to English-speaking readers, it is this notion above all which best summarizes the
mature religious outlook that Kierkegaard was developing in the
middle and late 1840's.

1. *"The Thorn in the Flesh"*

On October 2, 1855 Kierkegaard collapsed in the street and
was taken to Frederiks Hospital, where he died on the eleventh of
November. During the intervening weeks he was visited almost
daily by his boyhood friend, Emil Boisen, who made a transcript
of their conversations. The following excerpt is taken from Boisen's
notes.

> *Thursday:* He was very weak; his head hung down on his
> chest, and his hands trembled. He fell into a doze; coughing
> woke him. . . . I asked him whether he could collect his
> thoughts or whether they were confused. Most of the time
> they were clear, but sometimes at night they wandered.
> Whether he could pray in peace to God: "Yes, that I can."
> Whether he still had anything to say: "No; yes, remember
> me to everyone, I was much attached to them all, and tell
> them that my life is a great, and to others unknown and
> incomprehensible suffering. It all looked like pride and vanity
> but it was not. I am no better than others, I said that and
> never anything else. I had my thorn in the flesh [*min Pael
> i Kjødet*], and so I did not marry and could take no position;
> yet I am a theological *Candidat* and had a public right and
> was well-sponsored. I could have gotten anything I wanted,
> but in its place I became the exception [*Undtagelsen*]." [2]

Although this is Kierkegaard's last mention of "the thorn in the flesh," it should come as no surprise to readers of his journal that on his death-bed he should choose such a phrase for characterizing that "great, and to others unknown and incomprehensible suffering" which was his life. For often during his last ten years we find him attempting to make sense of his suffering in terms of this curious New Testament notion. He uses it for the first time in an entry written contemporaneously with the publication of the *Postscript* in February 1846.

> *This is how I have understood myself in my whole literary work:*
>
> I am in the deepest sense an unhappy individuality which from the earliest years has been nailed fast to some suffering or other bordering upon madness, which must have its deepest ground in a disproportion between soul and body. . . . Perhaps because of the strained relation between soul and body my mind has received a tensile strength that is rare.
>
> [Kierkegaard goes on at this point to tell about his unsuccessful visit to a doctor to see if his suffering might be alleviated by medical means.]
>
> From that moment I made my choice. That sad discord with its attendant suffering (which undoubtedly would have driven most of those with sense enough to understand it to suicide) I have looked upon as my thorn in the flesh, my limit and my cross; I have looked upon it as the high price at which the Almighty God sold me an intellectual power which has found no equal among its contemporaries. . . .
>
> During my work I have also constantly believed that I learnt to understand better and better God's will in regard to me: that I bear the agony with which God laid the reins upon me and so perhaps achieve the exceptional [*det Overordentlige*] (vii¹ A 126).

Here he talks of the "thorn in the flesh" as a "disproportion between soul and body." The following year he will describe it in terms more reminiscent of Quidam's discussion of those "strange ideas of melancholy" which drew him towards a "higher life."

Oh, the thorn in the flesh has broken me once and for all in a finite sense—but eternally speaking I spring all the higher. Perhaps that is right. Perhaps God prefers a man who is sick and nurses the thorn, and who is neither cured nor eternally helped. . . . With the help of the thorn in my foot I spring higher than anyone with sound feet (VIII[1] A 156).

Again in 1848 he will reiterate this theme in describing how the thorn has prevented him from becoming "worldly."

As far as I am concerned, I have had a thorn in the flesh from my earliest years. Were that not so I should have been very worldly. But that I cannot be however much I might wish it (IX A 208).

And again in 1852 a similar complaint.

About Myself

June 19 Understanding myself to be fundamentally different from others, also with a thorn in the flesh, in great inner suffering I became an author.

Thus I held out year after year in spite of suffering. . . .[3]

Yet nowhere in all these passages mentioning his "thorn in the flesh" does Kierkegaard give us a clear description of it. It has prevented him from marrying and from seeking an official position; it is, he calls it, "my limit and my cross"; it has "broken" him "once and for all in a finite sense," and perhaps has made it possible for him "to achieve the exceptional." Yet after all these allusions to it, the reader is still very much left in the dark as to its true identity. For a clearer picture the published works must be consulted.

Several months before the publication of *Stages on Life's Way* Kierkegaard wrote a short edifying discourse entitled, "The Thorn in the Flesh." Taking as its text II Corinthians 12:7, this discourse focuses on an explication of the Pauline phrase which forms its title. In the second verse of this chapter Paul has reported his transport "whether in the body or out of it" up into "the third heaven." In the seventh verse he comments upon his experience of revelation in the following manner.

And lest I should be exalted above measure through the abundance of the revelations, there was given to me a thorn in the flesh, the messenger of Satan to buffet me, lest I should be exalted above measure.

Note the way in which Kierkegaard interprets this verse.

The thorn in the flesh, then, is the contrast to the unspeakable blessedness of the Spirit. . . . Blessedness is lost, it recedes farther and farther; alas it was unspeakable to possess, the pain is unspeakable because it cannot even express its loss, and memory can do nothing except faint in impotence! To have been carried up into the third heaven, to have been hidden in the bosom of eternal blessedness, to have been enlarged in God—and now to be tethered by the thorn in the flesh in the thralldom of temporal existence (*Edifying Discourses*, IV, 61).

Against the "thralldom of temporal existence" the victim of the thorn in the flesh opposes a desperate nostalgia for "blessedness." Kierkegaard continues.

That apostolic expression ["the thorn in the flesh"] not only suggests the desertion, the suffering of the separation which is even more terrible than that of death, because death only separates a man from the temporal and so is a deliverance, while this separation shuts him out from the eternal, and so is an imprisonment, which again leaves the spirit sighing in the fragile earthen vessel, in the straitened room, in spiritual exile; for the home of the spirit is in the eternal and the infinite. That very instant everything begins again from the beginning. He who has been outside of the body now returns to the body; but this condition of thus being within himself, is not the condition of freedom and the emancipated spirit. So the unspeakable blessedness is passed, the harvest song of rejoicing is silent, again there must be sowing with tears, the spirit must again sit oppressed, must again sigh, and only God knows, what the sigh does not know, whether or not the harp of joy will again be tuned in the secret places of the soul. The man is returned to himself (*Edifying Discourses*, IV, 62–63).

It is in passages like this that Kierkegaard comes closest to transforming prose into poetry. Nor is it difficult to understand why Kierkegaard's passion should crest on such a passage as this. For in Paul's experience of being "carried up into the third heaven," Kierkegaard has found an apostolic correlate to his own experience of bliss. And in the Pauline notion of the "thorn in the flesh" he has found a tool for interpreting his own estrangement. Note how precisely the mood (and at points even the language) of this passage duplicates earlier entries in the *Papirer*. Where in this passage Kierkegaard speaks of "that very instant [when] everything begins again from the beginning. He who has been outside the body now returns to the body . . . ," earlier in the *Papirer* he has complained of that moment when "oh so sadly, I wake up again and just so sadly begin to see exactly the unhappy relativity in everything." [4] The experience of communion which cannot last, but which must be carried in memory as a counterpoint to the deficiency of the present moment: this experience, as past chapters have revealed, was characteristically Kierkegaardian. Stretched between two worlds, he suffered from a "total spiritual incapacity . . . coupled with a consuming longing, with a spiritual passion." The phrase, "the thorn in the flesh," thus comes to stand for a characteristic suffering, the torment of a life in time lived against the background of an experience of "unspeakable blessedness."

In speaking of his suffering as the "thorn in the flesh" Kierkegaard means to indicate the passion which supports it. On the one hand, it is the *bereavement* of an existence lived out in time against the background of a memory seething with eternality. But more than this it is also the uncertainty of *expectation*. At the end of the passage cited above, we note the assertion that "only God knows, what the sigh does not know, whether or not the harp of joy will again be tuned in the secret places of the soul." But we should mark that the uncertainty is not concerned with whether the "harp of joy" will again be tuned in *this* life. Rather it is concerned with the expectation of a "blessedness" in the life beyond. Paul has been given "a thorn in the flesh" lest in *this life* he "should be exalted above all measure." And likewise for Kierkegaard the focus of expectation now moves beyond this world. Part of the torment of his expectation is indicated in a journal entry from 1847.

The way of tribulation remains equally dark to the very end—it must be a different way which little by little gets lighter. Neither does one know when the change will come nor exactly whether or how much nearer one has come to it (for that cannot be known in the dark). But one believes that the change will come, and then with the blessedness of eternity. When the child in the dark room waits for the door to be opened and all the hoped for glory to show itself, then even at the last second before the door is opened it is just as dark as before. . . . So the child endures in patience; for to make a noise for fear of being forgotten is, he knows quite well, to spoil everything. Oh, but it is so hard for a man to hold out thus and set everything upon the last moment, we should so much like it to show itself little by little (vIII[1] A 191).

The change may come, but if it comes it will come only in "the last moment." And so the "thorn in the flesh" comes to stand for the torment of a life not only oppressed by the "thralldom of the temporal" but also tantalized by the expectation of an "eternal blessedness." Like a child in the dark, Kierkegaard stands in expectation of a change which can come only at the terminus of "the way of tribulation" which is life.

The suffering denominated by the phrase "thorn in the flesh" is therefore constituted of an amalgam of bereavement and expectation—bereavement over the loss of an "eternal blessedness," and expectation of its recapture in a life beyond. It was this suffering (this *passion*, if you will) which made of Kierkegaard "the exception," which prevented him from marrying and seeking an official position, which "broke" him "once and for all in a finite sense." But most important, it was this suffering which formed the life-background to the writing of the *Postscript*. If we are asked from what existential perspective this work was written, we must reply that it springs from the perspective of an author tormented by a "thorn in the flesh."

II. *Johannes Climacus*

"I am anything but a devilish good fellow at philosophy," announces the pseudonymous author of the *Postscript*, Johannes

Climacus, "I am a poor, individual existing man, with sound natural capacities, not without a certain dialectical dexterity, not
entirely destitute of education. I have been tried in life's *casibus*
and cheerfully appeal to my sufferings" (*Postscript*, 548). Johannes
never tells us what these "sufferings" are, yet their identity is not
difficult to guess. For Johannes too, it would seem, has felt the
pang of the "thorn in the flesh."

At the very climax of a critical discussion in the *Postscript*,
Johannes makes reference to the "thorn in the flesh."

> The Apostle Paul mentions the religious suffering in
> one of his epistles, and in that connection one will also find
> that the suffering becomes a sign of the blessedness. I refer
> of course to the passage in the Epistle to the Corinthians
> about "the thorn in the flesh." He states that it happened
> once, whether he was in the body or out of the body he does
> not know, that he was caught up into the third heaven. . . .
> What evidence did the Apostle retain to assure him of the
> reality of the experience? A thorn in the flesh—that is, an
> experience of suffering. . . . The religious individual sus-
> tains a relationship to an eternal blessedness, and the sign
> of this relationship is suffering, and suffering is its essential
> expression—for an existing individual (*Postscript*, 406–407).

If the defining characteristic of the "religious individual" is that
he "sustains a relationship to an eternal blessedness," then we
must recognize that Johannes himself falls under such a definition.
For earlier, in setting out the fundamental intent which motivated
his writing of the *Postscript*, he admitted his own "infinite interest
in an eternal blessedness."

"I, Johannes Climacus," he wrote, "born in this city and now
thirty years old, a common ordinary human being like most people,
assume that there awaits me a highest good, an eternal blessedness
[*en ewig Salighed*]. . . . I have heard that Christianity proposes
itself as a condition for the acquirement of this good, and now I
ask how I may establish a proper relationship to this doctrine." [5]
It is because Johannes himself is interested in an "eternal blessedness" that he has chosen to concern himself with Christianity.
"Christianity," he continued, "proposes to bestow an eternal bless-

edness upon the individual man, thus presuming an infinite interest as *conditio sine qua non*" (*Postscript*, 19). It is this "infinite
interest" which is the *conditio sine qua non* of the Christian life,
and also the source of Johannes' concern with Christianity. More
significantly for our purposes, it is this "infinite interest in an
eternal blessedness" which marks off Johannes' existential perspective as a "religious individual" and, concomitantly, a sufferer
from the "thorn in the flesh." This can be seen most clearly by
considering the outlines of the life-view presented by Johannes
in the *Postscript*. With little alteration it duplicates that bitter-
sweet amalgam of bereavement and expectation surveyed in the
last chapter.

"Our whole earthly existence is a kind of sickness" (*Postscript*, 403), remarks Johannes, while at another point observing,
"The poor existing individual is confined to the straitjacket of
existence" (*Postscript*, 172). In another section he offers the following observation which reminds us immediately of the passage
from Kierkegaard's journal cited above. "Let me rather know from
the beginning that the road may be narrow, stony, and beset with
thorns until the very end; so that I may learn to hold fast to the
absolute *telos*, guided by its light in the night of my sufferings"
(*Postscript*, 362). How reminiscent this passage is of "the way of
tribulation" described by Kierkegaard in his journal, a way which
(we recall) remained "equally long and equally dark to the very
end." Such a view of existence as a "sickness," a "straitjacket," a
path "narrow, stony and beset with thorns until the very end"—
such a view contains much of the "bereavement" characteristic of
an outlook which saw life as a kind of "spiritual exile." Johannes
uses almost the very same phrase in later describing the religious
person as "a stranger in the world of the finite," as a man "who
lives in the finite but does not have his life in the finite" (*Postscript*, 367). The tone of these passages is hushed, subdued, muted
—a tone befitting the description of a bereaved state; as we shall
see, Johannes' bereavement goes not unmixed with expectation.

In a later passage he characterizes existence as "a period of
courtship," as "an enthusiastic venture in uncertainty" (*Postscript*,
355). And of course, the aim of the "courtship" is that "eternal
blessedness" which hovers on the limits of awareness at the end
of time. It is because "an eternal blessedness cannot be possessed

in time . . . that the whole of time and of existence should be the period of striving" (*Postscript*, 355–56). Against the prospect of this future blessedness, the present "period of courtship" becomes tumescent with expectation. Eternity, we learn, is translated for the existing individual into the mode of futurity; the eternal becomes the "future life" (*Postscript*, 272–73). As futurity, the individual's relation to eternity, to an "eternal blessedness," becomes one of expectation, "In the life of time the *expectation* of an eternal blessedness is the highest reward" (*Postscript*, 360). And so in time an individual can never attain an "eternal blessedness" although he may indeed *expect* it. But his expectation may be illusory. He may be wrong, and so his relation to an eternal blessedness must necessarily be an uncertain one: "It is really too much to ask," remarks Johannes, "that anything subject to expectation should be made definitely certain" (*Postscript*, 379).

But now Johannes's characterization reaches a crucial turn. For if the individual's relation to the eternal is inevitably uncertain and expectant, then what should be the vehicle of this relation? What could it be but passion? "It is only momentarily," writes Johannes, "that the particular individual is able to realize existentially a unity of the infinite and the finite which transcends existence. This unity is realized in the moment of passion [*Lidenskabens Øjeblik*]" (*Postscript*, 176). It is through passion (*Lidenskab*) that the individual is related to the eternal, and it is only in passion that he truly exists.

> The utmost tension of human subjectivity finds its expression in the infinite passionate interest in an eternal blessedness (*Postscript,* 51).

> In the infinite passionate interest for his eternal blessedness, the subject is in a state of the utmost tension, in the very extremity of subjectivity (*Postscript*, 52).

> All idealizing passion is an anticipation of the eternal in existence so as to help the individual to exist (*Postscript*, 277).

To *exist*, on Johannes' view, means to permit the uncertain illumination of a future life to penetrate the vacant precincts of the present one. To use a metaphor of his: to exist is to drive a team

of horses, one infinitely fast and the other excruciatingly slow—
"Eternity is the winged horse, infinitely fast, and time is a worn-
out jade; the existing individual is the driver" (*Postscript*, 276).
In this conflict between time and eternity is born the individual's
existence, "The apprehension of the distinction 'here' and 'here-
after' is at bottom the apprehension of what it means to exist"
(*Postscript*, 506). It is such a view of existence as an intersection
of time and eternity, as a life-long bereavement tensed against
expectation, that Johannes offers in the *Postscript*, and it is this
view which identifies his perspective as a victim of the "thorn in
the flesh."

III. *Subjective Truth: The Meaning of Suffering*

Johannes Climacus and Kierkegaard, then, both share an
identity as victims of the "thorn in the flesh." Yet with due consideration we can see that this identity must be shared with a
third. For is not the Quidam of *Stages on Life's Way* equally
eligible for membership in this select fraternity of fellow sufferers?
The characteristic *bereavement* of Kierkegaard and Johannes over
the emptiness of the present—over life as a "spiritual exile," a
"sickness," a "straitjacket"—is echoed by Quidam's complaint
over a present life where "there is no change of seasons" and where
he has become "a lost wayfarer." And the *expectation* of Kierkegaard and Johannes is likewise echoed in Quidam's intention to
"hold out" in order to see whether his enthusiasm was genuine or
ersatz. All three feel the attraction of a future state, and strain
towards it from a present which is dead and empty. The identity
of this future state for Quidam is unknown (Frater Taciturnus
tells us that it is a "second immediacy" attained in this life, but
Quidam does not know this), while for Johannes and Kierkegaard
this state is that "eternal blessedness" achieved at the end of time.
But for all three the characteristic life outlook of bereavement
mixed with expectation is the same. And for all three, this similarity of outlook dictates a similar problem.

Are Quidam's "strange ideas of melancholy" really "pulls"
towards a "higher life"? Will the "infinite interest" of which
Johannes makes so much, finally eventuate in that "eternal blessedness" for which he yearns? Will that "consuming longing," that

"spiritual passion," of which Kierkegaard speaks find its consummation at "the last moment" when "the door is opened"? These questions are only various specifications of that critical problem which confronts any variation of the life-outlook denoted by the phrase "the thorn in the flesh." For as Johannes has pointed out in the *Postscript*, Paul uses this phrase to denote a relation of *significance* between his present suffering and a future bliss. "The religious individual," remarked Johannes, "sustains a relation to an eternal blessedness, and the sign of this relationship is suffering." Thus it is that the critical problem concerns the *meaning* of *suffering.* All the questions noted above could be answered affirmatively if it were possible to state unequivocally that the present state of suffering was a *sign* of the future state of fulfillment. But can an individual ever reach a standpoint from which such an assertion can be made? Consider this passage from the *Postscript.*

> In the eternal blessedness itself there is no suffering, but when an existing individual establishes a relation thereto, this relationship is quite rightly expressed through suffering. If an existing individual, through knowing that this suffering means the relationship, were capable of elevating himself above the suffering, then he would also be able to transform his status from that of an existing individual to that of an eternal being; but this he will scarcely wish to attempt. But if he cannot do this, he is again in the situation of suffering, because this knowledge must be held fast in the medium of existence. In the same moment the perfection of his joy will fail of being complete, as it must always fail when it must be had in an imperfect form. . . . But at the same time that an individual suffers religiously, he cannot in his joy over the significance of this suffering as a mark of the relationship transcend the suffering; for the suffering is rooted in the fact that he is separated from his blessedness, but also signifies that he has a relationship to this blessedness, so that to be without suffering means to be without religion (*Postscript*, 404–405).

We must be careful about the word "knowledge" in this passage. For the sense of the passage is that a "knowledge" about the significance of one's suffering is impossible to attain. The gaining of such knowledge, such certainty, would require that the existing individual transform himself into an eternal creature. Yet finite and temporal as he is, he must content himself with what Johannes calls a "militant certainty"; that is, "a certainty not achieved by the struggle becoming weaker, and in fact illusory, but only by its becoming stronger" (Postscript, 203). Such a knowledge which "must be held fast in the medium of existence," might better be called by another name. Kierkegaard himself has suggested such a name; it is "subjective truth."

"Here is such a definition of truth," writes Johannes in the Postscript, "an objective uncertainty held fast in an appropriation-process of the most passionate inwardness is the truth, the highest truth attainable for an existing individual" (Postscript, 182; italics are Kierkegaard's). Yet without some qualification this definition of truth is silly. For can the "objective uncertainty" of there being life on Mars ever function as "the highest truth attainable for an existing individual"? Of course not. For this definition to be given sense a further specification must be made concerning the object of the "truth." Johannes has made this specification a few pages earlier in distinguishing between "essential" and "accidental" knowledge, and in asserting that "subjective" or "essential" truth finds a home in the former.

> All essential knowledge relates to existence, or only such knowledge as has an essential relation to existence is essential knowledge. All knowledge which does not inwardly relate itself to existence, in the reflection of inwardness, is, essentially viewed accidental knowledge (Postscript, 176).

> The question here is about essential truth, or about the truth which is essentially related to existence, and that it is precisely for the sake of clarifying it as inwardness or as subjectivity that this contrast is drawn (Postscript, 178).

Hence, the definition of truth as "subjectivity" is not meant to have universal application; it characterizes one variety of truth— "essential truth," or truth which has direct relevance to an individual's existence. But what does it mean to assert that this variety of truth is "inwardness" or "subjectivity"? Consider the following citations.

In an attempt to make clear the difference of way that exists between an objective and a subjective reflection, I shall now proceed to show how a subjective reflection makes its way inwardly in inwardness. Inwardness [*Inderligheden*] culminate in passion [*Lidenskab*] (*Postscript*, 177).

Suffering [*Lidelse*] is precisely inwardness
(*Postscript*, 256).

Spirit is inwardness, inwardness is subjectivity [*Subjectivitet*], subjectivity is essentially passion, and in its maximum an infinite, personal, passionate interest in one's eternal blessedness (*Postscript*, 33).

Given such statements as these we may feel confident in setting up the following equation: *inwardness = passion = suffering = subjectivity*. Moreover, all these terms only articulate in slightly different ways what is "in its maximum an infinite, personal, passionate interest in one's eternal blessedness." The contention is that "subjective truth" is buttressed by nothing more than this "infinite interest," and that a "subjective" reflection can only take place within the fabric of such an interest. This becomes even clearer when we glance at the portrait of the subjective thinker painted in the *Postscript*.

"The subjective thinker," Kierkegaard asserts, "has the task of understanding himself in his existence" (*Postscript*, 314). But note carefully the arena in which this task is to be carried out.

Similarly there is required for a subjective thinker fantasy and feelings, dialectics in existential communication, together with passion. But passion first and last
(*Postscript*, 312–13).

While objective thought is indifferent to the thinking subject and his existence, the subjective thinker is an existing individual essentially interested in his own thinking, existing as he does in his thought. His thinking has therefore a dif-

ferent type of reflection the reflection of inwardness, of possession, whereby it belongs to the subject and to no other
(*Postscript*, 67–68).

The subjective thinker has only a single scene, existence. . . . His scene is—inwardness in existing as a human
being (*Postscript*, 319–20).

Abstract thought is disinterested, but for an existing
individual, existence is the highest interest. An existing individual therefore has always a *telos* and it is of this *telos*
that Aristotle speaks when he says that theoretical thought
differs from practical thought (*Postscript*, 278).

The primary characteristic of the subjective thinker is then his
passion. He is *interested* in his own existence, and this interest is
at once the source and guide of his thought. It is this interest, this
personal passion, which determines his scene—that is, "inwardness
in existing as a human being."

But note what all this indicates. If the distinguishing mark
of the "subjective thinker" is his passion, and if (as Johannes further argues) "human passion culminates in the pathetic relation
to an eternal blessedness" (*Postscript*, 345), then the "subjective
thinker" becomes only another disguise for the victim of the "thorn
in the flesh." To be interested in one's own existence means to be
interested in one's own healthy existence—a health to be found
only at the end of time in the form of an "eternal blessedness."
The cultivation of this interest becomes the very definition of "subjectivity," [6] and we have already seen that it is precisely this subjectivity which is the truth. But given inwardness as the "scene"
of the subjective thinker's activity, it becomes apparent that the
whole idea of "understanding oneself in existence" takes on a new
interpretation? For what could such an understanding be but a
"knowledge" of the meaning of that selfsame suffering which is
the substance of inwardness. We have moved to a position where
a wholesale translation of terms can be carried out: the "subjective
thinker" is revealed as a victim of the "thorn in the flesh"; "subjective" or "essential" truth is disclosed as only another name for
that "knowledge" of suffering's meaning which "must be held fast

in the medium of existence"; and the subjective thinker's task of understanding himself in existence becomes now that "grasping" of suffering's meaning—that "penetrating more and more deeply into it"—which we alluded to in the last chapter.

This translation of terms is helpful, for it substitutes one framework of comprehension for another, less accurate one. As long as we talk of a "subjective *thinker*" whose task is "to *understand* himself in existence," and as long as we talk about a "subjective *truth*" or a "*knowledge*" of suffering's meaning, we may be misled into believing that Kierkegaard is describing some *intellectual* activity. This is precisely what makes the discussion here so confusing. For Kierkegaard is using the language of intellect— speaking of "thinking," "truth," "understanding," and "knowledge,"—to describe something which is nonintellectual. The central question being asked is whether a particular kind of sufferer can have any knowledge or certainty concerning the meaning of his suffering. Kierkegaard's answer to this question is a resounding "No!" With regard to the question of meaning the victim of the "thorn in the flesh" is finally thrown back on his passion. To Quidam's question, to Johannes' question, to Kierkegaard's own question, there is finally no satisfactory answer within the realm of intellect; there is only passion. For such a sufferer "truth is subjectivity," and by "subjectivity" Kierkegaard means pure passion, rigid and unflinching interest in what he calls (and what seems so foreign to our modern ears) an "eternal blessedness." It is the hope for this blessedness—for this cure—which is the only "answer" available to the sufferer in his need. Yet such a passionate hope is not exchangeable, the gossamer thread of expectation is too ephemeral for the transfer from one person to another, and so each must spin with his own thread the tent of his illusion, just as each must die alone. The "truth," the "knowledge," that Kierkegaard is here describing bears no relation to its epistemological cousins. Fabricated not of intellect, but of passion, it is the ambiguous evaluation of life's meaning and end which grows out of the stuff of life and must be held firm in the ebb and flow of experience. The maxim "truth is subjectivity" springs not from the philosopher's study, but from the personal agony of a "thorn in the flesh."

IV. "And now faith's strife!": A New Portrait of the Knight of Faith

There exists no alleviation for the "thorn in the flesh"; one cannot *know* that the suffering has meaning although one can *believe* it. Yet it is precisely the ambiguity of this meaning which inflames the religious individual's passion. The object of his passion is the idea of an "eternal blessedness," which, in its very ambiguity comes to play a strangely hypnotic role—removed to the farthest reach of time, haloed in mystery, it yet attracts, and by attracting succeeds in transforming the whole of life.

"What the conception of God or an eternal blessedness is to effect in the individual," writes Johannes, "is that he transform his entire existence in relation thereto, and this transformation is a process of dying away from the immediate" (*Postscript*, 432). Shaken in his most inward parts by this yearning, this desperate nostalgia, the religious man takes up a new stance with respect to the world around him. In setting up "an absolute direction towards the absolute *telos*," he cuts the nerve of desire which joins him to the finite.

> In his immediacy the individual is rooted in the finite. But when resignation has convinced itself that he has acquired the absolute direction toward the absolute *telos*, all is changed, and the roots have been severed. He still lives in the finite, but he does not have his life in the finite. His life has, like that of other human beings, the various predicates of a human existence, but he is in them as one who is clothed in the borrowed garments of a stranger. . . . Just as the dentist has loosened the soft tissues about a tooth and cut the nerve, so the roots of his life in the finite have been severed (*Postscript*, 367).

In reordering the direction of his life the religious man takes up a stance of fundamental and irrevocable estrangement vis-à-vis the world around him. In the following passage, Johannes describes this estrangement in metaphors of the greatest power.

> This [transformation] occurs slowly, but finally he will feel himself absolutely imprisoned in the absolute concep-

tion of God; for the absolute conception of God does not consist in having such a conception *en passant*, but consists in having the absolute conception every moment. This is immediacy's check, the death verdict which announces its annihilation. Like the bird which flits carelessly here and there, when it is imprisoned; like the fish which fearlessly cleaves the waters and makes its way among the enchanted regions of the deep, when it lies out of its element on the dry ground—so the religious individual is confined; for absoluteness is not directly the element of the finite creature. And as one who is sick and cannot move because he feels pain everywhere, and as one who is sick and cannot keep from moving as long as he lives, although he feels pain everywhere—so the religious individual lies fettered in the finite and the absolute conception of God. . . . The religious man lies in the finite like a helpless child

(Postscript, 432).

We must not forget that in the sentence which begins this passage (and which we quoted a few lines above), the so-called "conception of God" is identified with the "conception of an eternal blessedness." Thus it is the priority of the religious man's yearning for this ultimate state which brings about a transformation in his existence. Rigid in his single-minded attention to this ideal, he becomes imprisoned by it like a captured bird or a fish out of water; it is this ideal which gives the "death verdict" to his immediacy and decrees that he must "lie in the finite like a helpless child." Such is the transformation wrought by the religious man's passionate nostalgia for an "eternal blessedness."

We would be poor critics indeed if we did not notice the close and obvious similarity between this state of estrangement, called "religiousness A" in the *Postscript*, and that earlier "stage of infinite resignation" described by Johannes de Silentio in *Fear and Trembling*. Both states are brought about by a movement of resignation in which the individual cuts all the affective threads joining him to the finite world. Both states, moreover, are preparatory, transitional ones, which must be run through before a final stage can be reached. Just as in *Fear and Trembling* we learned that the "stage of infinite resignation" was a necessary one on the

way to faith, so in the *Postscript* we learn that "religiousness A"
must be plumbed to its depth before there can be any possibility of
a participation in "religiousness B"—the paradoxical, distinctly
Christian, form of religiosity.[7] The ultimate stage in both cases is
called by the same name, faith, but here the similarity ends. For
in *Fear and Trembling* faith was seen as a completed state in which
the individual could find equilibrium, as an ultimate state of consciousness which could be attained at one point—*uno tenore*. Now
in the *Postscript* it is given a very different characterization. This
change in the description of the ultimate state is of course evidence of a change in attitude which separates the two works by
a far greater distance than the three years which separate 1843
from 1846. This change warrants our closest attention.

Towards the close of the *Postscript* Kierkegaard once again
takes up a description of that "knight of faith" earlier described
in *Fear and Trembling*. In a footnote, his pseudonym Johannes
Climacus casts a glance back at the earlier work, and makes this
highly significant observation.

> Such a "knight of faith" was depicted in *Fear and
> Trembling*. But this picture was only a daring and somewhat
> reckless anticipation, and the illusion created was gained by
> presenting this knight in a state of completeness, and hence
> in a false medium, instead of in the medium of existence
> (*Postscript*, 447 footnote).

Painted in the fantastic medium of imagination rather than in
the more problematic medium of existence, the earlier portrait of
the knight of faith was marred by an illusory "completeness." But
in what did this "completeness" consist?

We saw in Chapter 5 how his state was described as a kind
of "divine madness" through which "by assuming the burden of
the Paradox" he had broken through to a new conscious world.
The "completeness" of his state consisted in his ability at one
moment in time definitively to break through—to, at one breath,
"assume" the Paradox and, in assuming it, attain *dementia*. But
can the Paradox be so simply and so definitively "assumed"? Is it
really possible within the medium of existence to become mad
this quickly or this irrevocably? It is precisely at this joint of tran-

sition that criticism is directed from the point of view of the *Postscript.*

In *Philosophical Fragments* the Paradox was described as the offense of an eternal being, God, entering into time in the person of Christ. In the *Postscript* it maintains this identity,[8] but now its appropriation becomes a much more tortuous affair. Earlier we had learned to think of the Paradox as an almost magical object— a Medusa's head—which could bring about an immediate shattering of consciousness. But note now how its appropriation by the individual is described.

> With Reason [*Forstanden*] directly opposed to it, the inwardness of faith must lay hold of the Paradox; and precisely this struggle on the part of faith, fighting as the Romans once fought, dazzled by the fierce light of the sun, is inwardness's tension.[9]

Faith now becomes a struggle, not a completed state; the actual "giving up of one's Reason" [10] becomes a life-long exertion "like rolling a burden up a mountain" [11] and not a single act completed at one moment in time. Rather than a state of fulfillment following upon the outcome of a magical event, faith now becomes an unending battle with Reason, "For faith's martyrdom (crucifixion of the Reason) is not a martyrdom of the instant, but precisely the martyrdom of endurance" (*Postscript*, 496). Rooted now in existence, the individual's struggle with his own Reason, his agonized attempt to *believe* against Reason that which *offends* Reason, becomes an exhausting, never-ending combat described in these words.

> And now faith's strife! Is this struggle perhaps a foolish little trick, a mock combat of gallantry, the strife that is more persistent than a 30 years war, because the strife is not merely to acquire but still more hotly to preserve, where every day the heat is as burning as the one day of the battle of Zama! While Reason despairs, faith presses on victoriously in the passion of its inwardness. But when the believer uses all his Reason, every last desperate resource of thought, merely to discover the Paradox's difficulty, then there is indeed no part of his Reason left with which to explain the

Paradox, but for all that there may still be a rich faith-content in inwardness's passion. Sitting quietly in a ship while the weather is calm is not a picture of faith; but when the ship has sprung a leak, enthusiastically to keep the ship afloat by pumping while yet not seeking the harbor: this is the picture. And if the picture involves an impossibility in the long run, that is but the imperfection of the picture; faith persists. While Reason, like a despairing passenger stretches out its arms towards the shore, but in vain, faith works with all its energy in the depths of the soul.[12]

The predicament of the "knight of faith" has now become desperate. "He is half God-forsaken," Johannes remarks, "even when he strives victoriously against Reason in faith's inwardness" (Postscript, 203). Moreover, as we now shall see, this desperation springs directly from his identity as a victim of the "thorn in the flesh."

In an earlier section Johannes has pointed out how his interest in Christianity and its Paradox was founded upon a concern for an "eternal blessedness," and of how such an "infinite interest" is the "conditio sine qua non" of the Christian life. As the Postscript proceeds this "infinite interest" becomes a defining characteristic of both "religiousness A" (the religiosity of resignation) and "religiousness B" (Christianity). With regard to the latter, Johannes writes,

Suppose that Christianity is subjectivity, an inner transformation, an actualization of inwardness [Inderliggjørelsen], and that only two kinds of people can know anything about it: those who with an infinite passionate interest in an eternal blessedness base this their blessedness upon their believing relationship to Christianity, and those who with an opposite passion (but in passion) reject it—the happy and the unhappy lovers (Postscript, 51).

In this way "an infinite passionate interest in an eternal blessedness" is revealed as the sole base on which a believing relationship to Christianity can be established. But the Cerberus which guards the entrance to the last enclosure of Christian inwardness is of course the Paradox—the offense of the God-man. The believer's "blessedness" hinges upon his ability to hold fast this Paradox while all the time his Reason complains its offense. Now it is precisely this tension which constitutes the knight of faith's desperation—his "suffering," if you will. "For it is indeed a suffering, faith's martyrdom even in peaceful times, to have one's soul's blessedness tied to that which Reason despairs over." [13] The knight of faith is infinitely interested in his "soul's blessedness," while this interest is tied precisely to "that which Reason despairs over." In this fatal combination of infinite passion and intellectual offense is found that awful *ambiguity* which is the very essence of the knight's predicament. Estranged from the world, he can have only ambiguous knowledge of the source of this estrangement. Yet it is precisely the ambiguity of this knowledge which furnishes the life blood of faith; it is only when "direct recognition is taken away [that] faith is in its right place" (*Postscript*, 531). This fundamental ambiguity lies at the very heart of the religious life and accounts for the knight's desperation. He must live a life in which constantly "the positive is the index of the negative" (*Postscript*, 387), in which "a revelation is signalized by mystery, blessedness by suffering, faith's certainty by uncertainty, the ease of the paradoxical-religious life by its difficulty, the truth by absurdity" (*Postscript*, 387 footnote). The reference, then, of the phrase "faith's crucifixion of Reason," which occurs so often in the *Postscript*,[14] is not limited to the Paradox. The Paradox becomes the final cross on which human Reason is stretched, but the source as well as the consequences of this crucifixion point beyond it. For the source of Reason's crucifixion lies in that surge towards an "eternal blessedness" whose ultimate end must remain shrouded in mystery, and its consequences are to enable the knight to sustain himself in desperation, to hold out in ambiguity. This ambiguity is the "70,000 fathoms" over which he is stretched—constantly to see blessedness in suffering, revelation in mystery, certainty in uncertainty, and truth in absurdity.

The "knight of faith" like Johannes, like Quidam, like the "subjective thinker," like the "religious individual," and finally like Kierkegaard himself, must suffer the strenuosity of an existence stretched between two worlds. Ultimately, of course, this suffering is only an intensification of that fatal tension which lies at the very heart of consciousness itself. For it is consciousness which sets up the desperate conflict between estrangement and nostalgia. It is consciousness which supplies both the sickness as well as the urge towards cure; both the estrangement, now welcomed by the religious person as a sign of his "maturity," as well as the pressure to overcome it. The suffering of the victim of the "thorn in the flesh" is the suffering of consciousness. Moreover, it is this characteristic agony of consciousness which has become the *sine qua non* of a religious existence. For the religious person has chosen to found his life on ambiguity—ambiguity is the very air he breathes—and ambiguity, we should not forget, is a function of consciousness. In the self-mutilation of consciousness is now to be found the very receptacle of the religious ideal; in the life long crucifixion of reason and in that "dying away from immediacy" so characteristic of consciousness become resignation is found the very heart and substance of the religious life. Stretched between two worlds, it is a life tormented by the "thorn in the flesh."

10

CONCLUSION

With the publication of the *Postscript* in February 1846, Kierke-gaard's pseudonymous authorship was brought to a close.[1] Writing a year later in his journal, Kierkegaard had this to say about the pseudonyms.

> For many years my melancholy [*Tungsind*] has pre-vented me from coming closer to myself in the most pro-found sense. Between my melancholy and myself there lay a whole fantasy-world. It is this which, in part, I have emp-tied out in the pseudonyms (VIII[1] A 27).

The metaphor of "emptying out" [*Udtømmelse*] is used frequently by Kierkegaard in speaking of his pseudonymous authorship.[2] It echoes an earlier judgment which we recall described his author-ship as "the prompting of an irresistible inward impulse," [3] as erupting, so to speak, from the very abscess of his suffering.[4] It is perhaps this intimacy between Kierkegaard and his work—the fact that he was never able to bring much distance between himself and it—which accounts in great measure for its formal incom-pleteness. Many are the questions which the dialectician would wish to pose to Kierkegaard concerning the relationship between the "stages" and between the various pseudonymous authors. Are the "stages" cumulative or successive? Is there any necessary pro-gression between them? Why are there only three? Is the Seducer a fourth stage beyond erotic immediacy yet short of the ethical?

Where are Johannes de Silentio, Johannes Climacus, or Frater
Taciturnus to be placed with respect to the "stages"? These are
only a few of the questions an alert dialectician would pose. They
belong to a list which might be extended much further, and which,
in being extended, would find few answers to its queries. Such a
list, moreover, even if infinitely extended, would bring us no closer
to the vital nerve of Kierkegaard's authorship. For the fact remains
that Kierkegaard is finally uninterested in the formal characteristics
of any dialectic that might be extracted from his authorship. The
doctor inspecting his patient's chart is uninterested in whether the
ebb and flow of fever plots the symmetry of a sine curve, and likewise Kierkegaard's concern lies apart from formality. He is no
verbal architect constructing an edifice of language to encapsulate
the real, but a suffering human being searching desperately for
health. The contours of his work were not laid out in advance,[5]
but sprang naturally from the changing requirements of his quest.
It is health he seeks and not a system.

Yet as soon as we have said this, as soon as we have described
his project as a search for health, we recognize immediately its
quixotic character. For it is a curious kind of health indeed which
Kierkegaard seeks. It is no human health he desires, but a health-
beyond-health, a more-than-health.[6] Human health is inevitably
shadowed by disease; it can grow only in the soil of finitude. But
what Kierkegaard has sought from the very beginning is a health
more appropriate to Gods than to men. It was the health of divin-
ity that he hoped to find by gaining a commanding position above
the antinomies of existence, above the world of order/disorder,
human health/human disease. He sought it first in those *Papirer*
studies which saw him entertaining the possibility of a magical
transformation of life. Later, in the early pseudonymous works,
he pursued his quest in a more systematic and thorough way.
Again and again in these works we saw him investigating the
possibility of a miraculous cure or "breakthrough," and, failing
to break through himself, we saw him return again and again to
imaginative sketches of life as it would be on the "other side."
Judge William's "marriage to life," the Young Man's experience
of "repetition," Johannes de Silentio's imagined "knight of
faith," the "second immediacy" alluded to by Frater Taciturnus:

these are some of the names for the bliss of that ecstatic health which Kierkegaard himself could succeed only in *imagining*. In all these early works the focus of concern lay not in life and its suffering, but rather in life's magical transformation. It is no idle remark to suggest that the renowned "existential" thrust of Kierkegaard's middle works may spring in great measure from the velocity of his earlier flight from existence.

In these middle works Kierkegaard makes the transition from a "poetic" life-view to a "religious" one. The distinction between the two, as we have seen, lies principally in the difference between *escape* and *penetration* as a response to suffering. The poet seeks to *escape* his suffering through fantasy (his course is set away from existence), while the religious man seeks to "penetrate more and more deeply into it." In this way suffering has gained a different valuation depending on whether it is the "poet" or the "religious individual" who confronts it. For the poet, suffering itself has no value; it is the work of art produced out of the suffering which may or may not have value.[7] But for the religious man, suffering itself is valuable, since to him it is a token of that "eternal blessedness" which is the very fount of value. In following the progression from *Either/Or* through the *Postscript* we have witnessed a fundamental change in Kierkegaard's response to existence and its concomitant suffering. While earlier he fled existence in search of a miraculous cure, later he returned to it prepared to embrace its characteristic laceration.

It seems odd to speak of human existence as flawed by a "characteristic laceration," yet it is on the basis of this contention that Kierkegaard's work is most effectively understood. For at the very nerve of his experience there was a single and most private laceration—a solitary, never-absent mutilation of the soul—which informed all of his experience and each of his works.

What was this sickness, this malaise which made Kierkegaard complain on his deathbed that his life was "a great, and to others unknown and incomprehensible suffering"?

It was no less a sickness than *consciousness* itself—that characteristically *human* illness, that disease which made of man (in Nietzsche's words) "the sick animal"—which afflicted Kierkegaard with such a virulent intensity. It was the very fact of being conscious—that fatal splaying of the present moment—which tormented him and made him seek release in an imaginary passage, whole and complete at one moment in time, out of his labyrinth prison into the world which beckoned in the distance. And again later it was this characteristic laceration of consciousness, recognized now in its universal dimensions, which Kierkegaard came to recommend as the very hallmark of a "religious" existence. Called by the Pauline name the "thorn in the flesh," it was this suffering of consciousness—crucifixion of reason on the cross of ambiguity, "dying away from immediacy," urge which never finds consummation—which came to instantiate the religious ideal. As the very vehicle of salvation, what before was to be escaped now is welcomed. Thus it is that the torment which earlier furnished the energy behind Kierkegaard's quest, underwent a transfiguration in becoming the ideal of the religious life. Disvalue was transvalued into value.

In the works following the *Postscript* Kierkegaard continued to stress the religious ideal with ever-increasing severity. Perhaps several citations from the later works and papers will indicate the thrust of this movement as well as the form of his mature religious outlook.

In a work published the following year (1847) and translated into English under the title, *The Gospel of Suffering,* Kierkegaard writes,

> They call themselves *believers* [*Troende*] and mean by that that they are pilgrims, strangers and aliens in the world [*Fremmede og Udlaendinge i Verden*]; moreover, a pilgrim is not so certainly recognized by his staff as the fact that he calls himself a believer in general bears witness to the fact that he is on a journey, for faith means just that: that what I seek is not here, which is precisely the reason I believe it. Faith signifies precisely the deep, strong, blessed unrest which urges on the believer, so that he cannot find rest in this world.[8]

How often in earlier times has not Kierkegaard referred to himself as "a stranger and an alien" [*en Fremmed og Udlaending*],[9] and how often have we not also seen this phrase applied to fictional characters trapped in the "still life" of despair? [10] What better indication of Kierkegaard's changed perspective could we have than his application of this phrase now to the ideal—"the believer"? The estrangement which Kierkegaard knew in his own life, and which in his youth he tried to escape in so many ways, now returns garbed in the glitter of the ideal.

Two years after the publication of the *Postscript*, there appeared a large book of devotional addresses entitled *Christian Discourses*. In a subsection entitled "Joyful Notes in the Strife of Suffering" Kierkegaard etched a long passage which is revelatory of the changed perspective noted above.

> The "once" of suffering is a transition, a passage-way.
>
> Thou must go through it, and though it were to last as long as life, and though it were as hard as a sword which transfixes thy heart, it is yet only a passage-way. It is not true that it is the suffering which goes through thee, it is thou that goest through it—in the eternal understanding of the case entirely unharmed . . .
>
> The "once" of suffering is a passage-way which leaves no trace at all upon the soul, or, still more gloriously, it is a passage-way which purifies the soul by sanctifying it, so that purity remains as the trace left by the passage-way. For as gold is purified in the fire, so is the soul in suffering. . . . So it is with all temporal suffering; in itself impotent, it is not able to take anything; and if the sufferer allows eternity to have a say, it takes away the impure elements, that is, it gives purity.[11]

In this citation the outlines of "the lonely labyrinth" are still visible. Now infinitely extended, it has become the "passage-way" to eternity. Its bereavement—the despair of a life lived out in "that dreadful still life"—has been transmuted into "purification." Instead of being merely a deficient state of consciousness which should be escaped as soon as possible, its very deficiency (its suffering) becomes the cleansing fire which purifies the soul of its "base elements."

But to gain an understanding of the full severity with which Kierkegaard interprets the religious ideal, we must turn from the works of the late 1840's to a consideration of Kierkegaard's final view as expressed a few months before his death in 1855. On July 2 of that year he remarked in his Journal.

July 2

To be a Christian

Of all torments, being a Christian is the most terrible; it is—and that is how it should be—to know hell in this life.

What is a human being most terrified of? Most likely of dying, and most of all of the death-agony, therefore wishing it to be as brief as possible.

But to be a Christian means to be in a state of dying— (you must die off, hate yourself)—and yet, after that you live on, maybe for 40 years, in that state! (We shudder to read about the sufferings a beast undergoes when it is used for vivisection; yet this gives only a glimmering of the pain involved in being a Christian: to be kept alive in a state of death) . . .[12]

And then on September 25, only six weeks before his death, he wrote,

September 25, 1855

Life here below is meant to be Christian

The purpose of life here below is to carry us to the highest degree of *taedium vitae* . . .

Most human beings are so bereft of spirituality, so abandoned by Grace, that the punishment is not applied to them at all. Lost in this life they cling to this life; from being nothing they become nothing; their lives are wasted.

Only those who, brought to this point of *taedium vitae*, are able to hold fast to the thought that God acts from love, so that, in their soul, not even in its innermost recesses, there is left a hidden doubt that God is indeed love: only those are ripe for Eternity.[13]

In passages such as these we are faced with the full severity of Kierkegaard's religious ideal. Here, in its full force, is his mature religious outlook. To be religious, or more precisely, to be a Christian, means to become a walking corpse! One must suffer a "death-agony" which may last 40 years, be kept "alive in a state of death," in order to become a Christian and so be, concomitantly, "ripe for eternity." Here too we catch a final glance of "the lonely labyrinth." Its agonizing death in life (recall now Ahasuerus, the Unhappiest Man, and "the sickness unto death" as a formula for despair) has been transmuted into the very ideal of the Christian-religious form of existence. For it is the suffering of despair now seen in the guise of the "thorn in the flesh"—that suffering where the individual lives like a fish out of water, like a bird imprisoned, like "one who is sick and cannot move because he feels pain everywhere"—it is this suffering which appears now to Kierkegaard as the very substance of a mature religious existence. Thus it is that "the lonely labyrinth" has suffered a metamorphosis in becoming the "thorn in the flesh."

NOTES / INDEX

NOTES

1 Beginnings

1. *E/O*, I, p. 31; Swenson translation altered. In 1837 Kierkegaard observed in his journal: "Philosophy is life's dry nurse; it can stay with us but not give milk" (II A 59).
2. I A 77. For further assertions that this lyrical quality belongs both to philosophy and literature see: II A 739, VIII² B 7, X⁴ A 537, *Dread*, pp. 70–71 footnote.
3. IX B 64. At numerous points Kierkegaard emphasizes how his work was his "education," his "upbringing and development." See X² A 195, X² A 196, X² A 493, and *Point of View*, pp. 73, 75, 137, 151.
4. For further Kierkegaardian assertions of the uniqueness of the individual see I A 126, I A 322, VI A 140, VII¹ A 133, IX A 91, *Sickness*, p. 251 footnote.
5. "While objective thought translates everything into results, and helps all mankind to cheat by copying them off and reciting them by rote, subjective thought puts everything in process and omits the result" (*Postscript*, p. 68; translation slightly altered).
6. "Our language correctly calls emotion [*Affecten*] "Sindslidelse": when we use the word "Affect" we are most likely to think of the convulsive daring which startles us, and thereby forget that it is a kind of suffering" (*Fragments*, p. 61 footnote).
7. Friedrich Nietzsche, *Werke in Drei Bänden*, Herausgegeben von Karl Schlechta (München: Carl Hanser Verlag, 1955), Bd. II, 12; Vorrede (1886) to *Die fröhliche Wissenschaft*.

8. See II A 162; IV A 60, 110; VII¹ A 168; VIII¹ A 27, 177, 205, 250, 641, 645, 650; IX A 65, 67, 208, 451; x¹ A 280, 442, 510, 519; x² A 61, 493; x³ A 92, 489; x⁵ A 89, 105, 146; *Point of View*, pp. 52, 68, 70.
9. Albert Camus, *The Myth of Sisyphus*, trans. by Justin O'Brien (New York: Vintage, 1955), p. 29.

2   Kierkegaard's World

1. Rasmus Nielsen, "Om Søren Kierkegaards mentale Tilstand," *Nordisk Universtets Tidskrift*, 1858, p. 7.
2. Frithiof Brandt, *Den Unge Søren Kierkegaard. En raekke nye bidrag* (København: Levin & Munksgaard, 1929), p. 67.
3. See Alexander Dru, *Journals*, p. xxix and Jean Wahl, *Études Kierkegaardiennes* (Paris: F. Aubier, 1938), p. 48, footnote 3.
4. For example, during the month of August 1847 Kierkegaard had bouillon on 29 out of 31 days—often having it twice in one day! Frithiof Brandt and Else Rammel, *Søren Kierkegaard og Pengene* (København: Levin & Munksgaard, 1935), p. 145. For another observation concerning the sameness of Kierkegaard's meals see Israel Levin's recollections printed in Steen Johansen, *Erindringer om Søren Kierkegaard* (København: Steen Hasselbachs Forlag, 1955), p. 35.
5. For a list of Kierkegaard's drives during the years 1844–47 see Coachman Lassen's receipted bills in *Af Søren Kierkegaards Eftrladte Papirer* (København: Reitzel, 1872), Bind III, pp. 872–73.
6. I have in mind here the famous pencil sketch of Kierkegaard done from memory by W. Marstrand. It is reproduced in Marguerite Grimault, *Kierkegaard par lui-même* (Paris: Editions du Seuil, 1962), p. 146.
7. I am thinking of the little bronze figure by L. Hasselriis preserved in the Frederiksborg Museum. It was the model for the large bronze statue of Kierkegaard which now stands in the courtyard of the Royal Library, Copenhagen. A photograph of a plaster cast for this statue can be found in Walter Lowrie, *Kierkegaard* (New York: Harper Torchbooks, 1962), p. 484.
8. This is not my phrase but Kierkegaard's. In his journal at III A 225 he uses the phrase "still life" to characterize his own life. The whole entry will be quoted later in this chapter.
9. *Dread*, p. 116; translation altered.
10. See for example *Dread*, Chapter IV, Part B, pp. 123–30.

11. This is a central Kierkegaardian metaphor, employed no less than 26 times in *The Concept of Dread* alone! For other works in which the metaphor can be found see *Either/Or, Fear and Trembling, Postscript, Gospel of Suffering,* and *Training in Christianity.*

12. Another characteristically Kierkegaardian metaphor; for examples of its use see *Stages on Life's Way, Postscript, Works of Love,* and *Attack Upon Christendom.*

13. *Repetition,* pp. 74–76. Constantine Constantius complains that "everyone who has thoroughly considered the matter will agree with me that it is never granted to a man in his whole life, even for so much as half an hour, to be absolutely content in all imaginable ways." He then describes the one time when he was closest to pure contentment. Telling us that in this moment of contentment "the whole of existence seemed to be as it were in love with me, and everything vibrated in pre-ordained rapport with my being," he parallels Kierkegaard's own description in the *Papirer* of the moments of continuity.

14. II A 487. Quite a long monograph could be written on Kierkegaard's use of the Hegelian category "bad infinite." For Kierkegaard, this pattern of unceasing succession with no advance is the structure of the atemporal—of the "still life" of despair. See for example *E/O,* II, p. 27 where Judge William uses the phrase "bad infinity of love" to describe the aesthete's sterile flitting from one love affair to another.

 For Hegel's original use of this category see G. W. F. Hegel, *The Science of Logic,* trans. by William Wallace (Oxford: Oxford University Press, 1892), p. 174.

15. VIII¹ A 650. Although not taken from the same 19 April 1848, entry quoted above, this citation is taken from an entry written at about the same time.

16. Hans Brøchner, "Erindringer om Søren Kierkegaard," *Det 19 Aarhundrede,* v (1876–77), 337–74. These recollections are translated in T. H. Croxall, *Glimpses and Impressions of Kierkegaard* (London: James Nisbet & Co., 1959), p. 23.

17. See x³ A 144 and x⁴ A 301 where Kierkegaard complains of these annoyances.

18. Croxall, *op. cit.,* p. 9.

19. Johansen, *op. cit.,* p. 37. There is a certain little mystery concerning Levin's recollection of Kierkegaard's fear of fire. Levin himself dictated these recollections to Premierlojtnant A. Wolff in 1869, and they are preserved in the Kierkegaard Ar-

chives of the Royal Library (D. Pakket 5, Laeg. 31) under the manuscript title, "Hr. Cand. I. Levins Udtalelser om S. Kierkegaard 1858 og 1869." Curiously enough, the last ten lines of the passage which deal with Kierkegaard's fear of fire are not to be found in the manuscript, although these lines were quoted by P. A. Heiberg in his book, *Bidrag til et Psychologisk Billede af Søren Kierkegaard i Barndom og Ungdom* (København: Wroblewski, 1895), p. 66. Faced with this mystery we may choose between two possible explanations: Either (1) Heiberg made up the passage, or (2) he was working from a previous manuscript (or perhaps a private conversation with Premierlojtnant A. Wolff) which is no longer preserved. In light of Heiberg's record of impeccable accuracy I am inclined to opt for the second of the two explanations. It should be mentioned that Johansen also believes the passage in question to be genuine.

20. Albert Camus, *The Myth of Sisyphus*, trans. by Justin O'Brien (New York: Vintage, 1955), p. 5.

21. *Ibid.*, p. 11.

22. Johannes Hohlenberg, *Søren Kierkegaard*, trans. by T. H. Croxall (New York: Pantheon Books, 1954), p. 147.

23. There seems little doubt that the Johannes Climacus described in the unfinished and unpublished essay *Johannes Climacus eller De Omnibus Dubitandum Est* is really Kierkegaard himself. Many of the incidents that Kierkegaard characterizes as having befallen Johannes really happened to him. For example, Johannes describes long imaginary walks he took with his father where the old man would recount with his mind's eye everything they passed. Kierkegaard once told Hans Brøchner that these walks were actual experiences of his childhood. See Georg Brandes, *Søren Kierkegaard: En Kritisk Fremstilling i Grundrids* (København: Glydendal, 1877), p. 10; cf. letter from Søren to Henriette Glahn Kierkegaard, dated 1844, *Breve og Akstykker*, p. 137. It should also be mentioned that Lowrie and Croxall agree in seeing Kierkegaard's sketch of Johannes Climacus as an essay in autobiography. See Walter Lowrie, *A Short Life of Kierkegaard* (Princeton: Princeton University Press, 1942), pp. 45–47, and *Johannes Climacus: De Omnibus Dubitandum Est* (Stanford: Stanford University Press, 1958), pp. 18, 20, 48, 103 footnote 2, 106 footnote 1, 109 footnote 1.

24. Hans Brøchner recalls his many walks with Kierkegaard in the following words. "He was always interesting to accompany, but there was one drawback. His movements were so irregular . . . that you could never walk straight when he was with you. You were successively pushed in towards the houses and cellar holes, and out towards the gutter. And when he gesticulated with his arm and his Spanish cane, walking became still more difficult. You had from time to time to get round the other side of him to keep your place!" (Croxall, op. cit., p. 13). In this regard see also Arthur Abrahams, Minder fra Min Barndom og Tidlige Ungdom (København: 1895), p. 55, where he speaks of Kierkegaard's "uneasy and somewhat skipping gait."

25. All this may be found in Israel Levin's recollections printed in Johansen, op. cit., p. 36.

26. Croxall, op cit., p. 23.

27. Niels Thulstruped., Katalog over Søren Kierkegaards Bibliotek (København: Munksgaard, 1957), pp. 80–82. Omissions in this edition of the auction catalogue have been corrected by H. P. Rohde, "Om Søren Kierkegaard som Bogsamler: Studier i hans Efterladte Papirer og Bøger paa det Kongelige Bibliotek," Fund og Forskning, vii (1961), 79–127; see especially Bilag v, 112–14.

28. Henriette Lund, Erindringer fra Hjemmet (København: Glydendal, 1909), p. 116. For a translation of this episode see Croxall, op. cit., p. 63.

29. Troels-Lund, Et Liv (København: 1924), p. 218. In a similar vein, Julie Sørdring recalls that her father and Kierkegaard used to walk together and that once they gave a poor woman five rigsdaler just to enjoy her surprise. Noted by Croxall, op. cit., p. 12 footnote 3.

30. See ix A 142, ix A 155, ix A 190, Point of View, p. 87.

31. See iii A 17.

32. Croxall, op. cit., p. 15.

33. Ibid., pp. 12–13.

34. Jean-Paul Sartre, Baudelaire, trans. by Martin Turnell (New York: New Directions, 1950), p. 22.

35. Meier Goldschmidt, Livs Erindringer og Resultater, I–II (København: Glydendal, 1877), i, 214–15.

36. Point of View, p. 81. Kierkegaard complains at many points of the pain caused him by his lack of immediacy. See, for ex-

ample, I A 163, I A 164, II A 67, II A 171, II A 172, II A 187, II A 607, II A 807, IX A 92, x⁴ A 39.

37. The autobiographical character Quidam describes himself in this way at *Stages*, pp. 194, 234.

38. *Point of View*, p. 70, "I was always clad in the costume of my deceit, so that I was then as much alone as in the darkness of the night." For further entries where Kierkegaard speaks of his mask-existence, see: I A 161, II A 132, II A 219, II A 417, III A 155, III A 166, IV A 132, VIII¹ A 92, IX A 70, x⁴ A 130, x⁵ A 149.17, XI¹ A 383, *Point of View*, pp. 76, 78, 79.

39. Johansen, *op. cit.*, p. 27.

40. Kierkegaard tells of this at *Point of View*, p. 50.

41. Johansen, *op. cit.*, p. 34.

42. In the following passage Levin gives some idea of the power of Kierkegaard's imagination. "The conception was enough for him, he could poeticize himself into any existence, thus for a week he lived only to feel and think like a miser . . . Once he admitted that he had an enormous desire to commit a real theft, then live with his bad conscience and his fear of being found out. Hence, he unburdened himself in dreams and poetic pictures and with his surprising articulateness and his daemonic fantasy it was surprising the effects he could produce . . .

We talked about Andersen one evening in the Frederiksberg Gardens: 'Andersen has no idea what fairy tales are . .' And then he produced in an instant six or seven fairy tales, so that I became almost uncomfortable. So vivid was his fantasy that it was as if the pictures were before his eyes . . .'" (Johansen, *op. cit.*, p. 34).

43. Denis de Rougemont, "Kierkegaard and Hamlet: Two Danish Princes," *The Anchor Review*, No. 1 (1955), pp. 109–27. See especially pp. 121–27.

44. *Breve og Akstykker*, p. 45; letter to M. H. Hohlenberg, ca. 1838.

45. VIII¹ A 406. For further entries evincing a slowdown and stoppage in lived time see: II A 414, II A 420, III A 51, IV A 221, V A 54, VI A 135.

46. The aesthete in *Either/Or* frequently uses this phrase to communicate a similar feeling of *Weltschmerz*; see, for example, *E/O*, I, p. 29.

47. Letter from Franz Welding to H. P. Barfod, dated Sept. 3, 1869; Johansen, *op cit.*, pp. 11–12.

48. IX A 321. The terms "wanderer" [Vandrer] and "stranger" [Fremmed] are used by Kierkegaard to describe various autobiographical characters appearing in his works. For example: In *Stages* (p. 167) Kierkegaard remarks that "the exception [a term he often applied to himself] is a wanderer, but of a peculiar sort." Another character in the same work is called a "wanderer" and a "stranger" (*Stages*, pp. 260–63). In *Either/Or* Judge William calls his young aesthete friend "a stranger and an alien" (*E/O*, II, 85–86). As will become apparent in the next chapter, the figure of the eternal wanderer, Ahasuerus —the Wandering Jew, exerted a peculiar fascination over Kierkegaard's thoughts in the late 1830's.

49. Camus, *op. cit.*, p. 13.

3 Preparations

1. This work has never been translated into English. The passage in question may be found at *Vaerker*, XIII, 68–69.

2. This passage is drawn from a work published in 1846 entitled *En literaire Anmeldelse* (*A Literary Review*). Although the second half of the essay has been translated under the title *The Present Age*, the first half (containing the cited passage) remains untranslated. See *Vaerker*, VIII, 14.

3. J. N. Mailath, *Magyarischen Sagen: Märchen und Erzählungen* (Stuttgart: 1837). This book is catalogue number 1411 in Thulstrup's edition of *Søren Kierkegaards Bibliotek* (København: Munksgaard, 1957).

4. Thomas Wolfe, *A Stone, A Leaf, A Door: Poems* (New York: 1945), p. 1.

> . . . Remembering speechlessly
> We seek the great forgotten language,
> The lost lane-end into heaven,
> A stone, a leaf, an unfound door.

5. See Knud Jensenius, *Nogle Kierkegaardstudier: 'De Tre Store Ideer'* (København: Nyt Nordisk Forlag, 1932), p. 6.

6. See I C 1–45; II C 1–36, especially 1–10.

7. See I A 11, 12, 14–18, 20.

8. See I A 122, 151, 184, 240, 270, 275, 276, 291, 292; I C 61, 66, 105; II A 70, 123, 165, 188, 491, 598, 683, 732, 733; III A 94.

9. See I A 72, 75, 88, 104, 122, 151, 184, 227, 233, 265, 266, 274, 292, 324, 333; I C 46–49, 51, 52, 54, 58, 59, 61, 66, 96, 100, 102,

104, 106, 107, 109, 110, 112–15; II A 29, 48, 50, 53, 55, 56, 597, 598, 603, 605.

10. See I A 61, 65, 151, 299; I C 60–62, 64, 66, 116–18, 120, 121.
11. See I A 136, 154, 608, 626, 627, 658; II B 2.
12. See I A 154; II A 30, 48, 78–85, 102, 114, 136, 146, 207, 596, 608, 626, 627, 658, 673, 694; III A 49; III B 11, 20.
13. See I C 125, pp. 303–308.
14. A good-sized monograph could be written on the similarities and differences between Kierkegaard's concept of the "life-view" [Livs-Anskuelse] and the phenomenological notion of the "life-world" [Lebenswelt]. Suffice it to say that if modern phenomenologists would agree that there is no single "life-world," but only different "life-worlds," each correlated with a definite "conception of life's significance and of its purpose" (E/O, II, 184), then Kierkegaard would be well pleased with their efforts.

It should be noted that at certain points Kierkegaard uses the term "world-view" [Verdens-Anskuelse] as synonymous with "life-view" [Livs-Anskuelse]. In this regard see Vaerker, III, 244; VI, 423; VII, 57; XIII, 60, 528; XIV, 47.
15. III A 108. See also I A 94–102; II A 786–88, 790.
16. III A 214. See also II A 789, 791, 796, 797, 799.
17. See III B 11.
18. In this regard see Frithiof Brandt, Den Unge Søren Kierkegaard (København: Levin & Munksgaard, 1929), p. 376, and also Jensenius, op. cit., p. 65.
19. See I A 122, 227, 266, 292; I C 58; II A 50, 58, 598.
20. See I C 58, 61, 66; II A 50.
21. See II A 102, 608, 661, 665, 716, 791.
22. Steen Johansen, Erindringer om Søren Kierkegaard (København: Steen Hasselbachs Forlag, 1965), p. 34.
23. Only two years later Kierkegaard reverses the order, putting Don Juan first, Faust second, and Ahasuerus last. See II A 56.
24. For example, see VIII[1] A 645 where Kierkegaard uses the word no less than seven times in describing his mental state.
25. This entry is dated January 2, 1838. During much of the school year 1837–38 Kierkegaard taught Latin to the next to highest class at the Borgerdydskole.
26. Jensenius, op. cit., p. 36.
27. II A 127. The same idea is mentioned at II A 599.
28. This was the name Michael Pedersen Kierkegaard was known

by in his later years. Even Søren Kierkegaard's elder brother, Peter, uses this name in referring to the father in a letter dated 1877. See *Journals*, p. 570.

29. Croxall, *Glimpses and Impressions of Kierkegaard* (London: James Nisbet & Co., 1959), p. 10.

30. *Repetition*, p. 13; translation altered.

31. P. A. Heiberg, *Søren Kierkegaards Religiøse Udvikling* (København: Glydendal, 1925), p. 17.

32. Two months before his death, Kierkegaard remembered his youth in these words. "Oh, in the days of youth it is of all torments the most frightful, the most intense, not to be like others, never to live a single day without being painfully reminded that one is not like others, never to be able to run with the herd, which is the delight and the joy of youth, never to be able to give oneself out expansively, always, so soon as one would make the venture, to be reminded of the fetters, the isolating peculiarity which, isolating to the border of despair, separates one from everything which is called human life and merriment and joy" (*Attack*, pp. 285–86).

33. Hjalmar Helweg, *Søren Kierkegaard: En Psychatrisk-Psychologisk Studie* (København: Hagerup, 1933), p. 49.

34. In contemplating his own engagement, Quidam remarks, "What are all gloomy thoughts but a cobweb, and what is melancholy but a mist which flies before this reality, a sickness which is healed by the sight of this health, this health which indeed is mine since it is hers who is my life and future" (*Stages*, p. 201).

35. *Stages*, p. 240. The extent to which this part of *Stages* is autobiographical might be gauged by the letter the fictitious Quidam sends to his beloved; word for word it is the same letter Kierkegaard sent Regine, breaking off their engagement!

36. *Stages*, pp. 242–43. See also *Stages*, pp. 345, 347, 354; v B 102.4. At ix Λ 451 Kierkegaard remarks that if he had married Regine, then "I would never have become myself."

37. During the last months of the engagement Kierkegaard had started drafts for the essay, "Aesthetic Validity of Marriage." Ultimately this essay became the first of Judge William's letters to his "young friend" published in the second volume of *Either/Or*. See Walter Lowrie, *Kierkegaard* (New York: Harper Torchbooks, 1962), p. 209; Johannes Hohlenberg,

Søren Kierkegaard, trans. by T. H. Croxall (New York: Pantheon Books, 1954), p. 110; *E/O,* I, xvi.

38. In *Repetition* Kierkegaard attempts just such a novel in the first person. Characteristically enough, before the novel is half over he has introduced another life-view in the form of letters from Constantine Constantius' "young man," and the novel is built on the contrast between these views.

39. This was a comic farce entitled, *Striden mellem den gamle og den nye Saebekielder* (II B 1–21). It is not a very good play, but one typically Kierkegaardian line should be saved for posterity. At II B 16 one of the characters, Hr. Hastvaerksen, exclaims, "Philosophy me here and philosophy me there. It is not philosophy that matters. It is practical questions, life-questions —in short, life."

40. Martin Thust, "Das Marionettentheater Søren Kierkegaards," *Zeitwende,* I, No. 1 (1925), 18–38.

41. *Postscript,* unpaginated—corresponds to page 551. I have altered somewhat the translation; see *Vaerker,* VII, unpaginated —corresponds to page 545.

42. Letter to Emil Boisen, Oct. 31, 1841; *Breve og Akstykker,* p. 71.

43. Letter to Emil Boisen, Dec. 14, 1841; *Breve og Akstykker,* p. 81.

44. Alexander Dru, Introduction to *Journals,* p. xliii. Dru is not the only critic who has remarked on the unity of the group of pseudonymous writings published during the years 1843–46. See in this regard Walter Lowrie, *Kierkegaard* (New York: Harper Torchbooks, 1962), pp. 286, 290 and Johannes Hohlenberg, *Den Ensommes Vej* (København: Hagerup, 1948), pp. 14–15. As Hohlenberg points out, Kierkegaard's pseudonymous authorship really comes to a close with the publication of the *Postscript* in 1846. His use of the pseudonym "Anti-Climacus" for the books *The Sickness unto Death* and *Training in Christianity* sprang from modesty—he recognized that he himself did not live up to the ideal of the Christian life presented in these works. They are not truly pseudonymous in the same sense as the earlier works, and hence may be omitted from a study of Kierkegaard's pseudonymous authorship.

The same, however, cannot be said for a slight volume entitled, *Prefaces [Forord]* by "Nicholas Notabene." Published on the same day as *The Concept of Dread* (17 June 1844) there is no doubt of its pseudonymity. But there is some doubt as to its interest or importance. Literally a book made up only of prefaces, it is an exercise in wit on Kierkegaard's part. It is unlikely that he wished us to give it more importance than the single sentence which he himself gave to it in the *Postscript* under the chapter heading, "A Glance at a Contemporary Effort in Danish Literature." Owing to its unimportance it has been omitted from our investigation.

4 Either/Or

1. See among other reviews the following. Meier Goldschmidt, *Corsaren*, No. 129 (March 10, 1843), pp. 1–3; Anonymous, *For Lit. og Kritik*, 1 (1843), 377–405; Anonymous, *Faedrelandet*, Feb. 20, 1843. It should be noted that on February 27th Kierkegaard mischievously published a short column in *Faedrelandet* entitled, "Who is the author of *Either/Or?*"
2. J. L. Heiberg, [Review article on *Either/Or*], *Intelligensblade*, II (1843), 289.
3. *Ibid.*, p. 291.
4. These are listed in *Papirer*, III, 321–23.
5. *E/O*, I, p. 21. The source for this diapsalm can be found in the *Papirer* at II A 435, entry for 21 May 1839.
6. *E/O*, I, 20–21. The source for this diapsalm can be found at II A 637. It was written on a loose sheet of paper during the year 1837.
7. *E/O*, I, 21. The source for this diapsalm can be found at II A 421, entry for 12 May 1839.
8. *E/O*, I, 40–41. A similar entry can be found in Kierkegaard's journal at I A 169, entry for 10 June 1836.
9. In a footnote to the English translation of *Either/Or* (*E/O*, I, 450), Professor Eduard Geismar is quoted as giving this equivalent for the Greek word coined by Kierkegaard.
10. *Begrebet Angest* (København: Reitzel, 1844).
11. *Dread*, p. 38; translation altered.
12. Kierkegaard applies this phrase to the fictitious Quidam of *Stages on Life's Way* (See *Stages*, p. 303). It seems to me to characterize vividly at least one aspect of the experience of dread. See also II A 127 and II A 191. At x^2 A 384 Kierkegaard remarks that "dread is really nothing but impatience."
13. *E/O*, II, 199. See also *E/O*, II, 11, 13, 203, 208.
14. All these ploys are suggested in *E/O*, I, 287–95.

15. *Stages*, p. 30. In the first section of *Stages on Life's Way* (from which this citation is drawn), Kierkegaard amplifies many of the ideas only suggested in *Either/Or*. In the *Postscript* (p. 253) he points out how in a certain sense *Stages on Life's Way* is a "repetition" of *Either/Or*.

16. All these citations are from the diapsalm quoted in Section One of this chapter.

17. See *E/O*, I, 242, 252, 257, 412; *E/O*, II, 7, 38, 39, 43, 44, 96, 128, 144, 148.

18. In one of the diapsalmata A remarks, "I can describe hope so vividly that every hoping individual will acknowledge my description; and yet it is a deception, for while I picture hope, I think of memory" (*E/O*, I, 35).

19. At *E/O*, II, 135 the Judge remarks, "But for an aesthetic representation there always is required a concentration in the moment, and the richer this concentration is, the greater is the aesthetic effect. Now it is only by this concentration that the happy, the indescribable moment, the moment of infinite significance, in short, *the* Moment, acquires its true value." In this regard see also *Stages*, 147; *E/O*, II, 22 and 190.

20. *E/O*, II, 85f. Lowrie translates the Danish *Udlaending* as "pilgrim"; I choose "alien."

21. *E/O*, I, 24. The substance of this diapsalm can be found in a letter to M. H. Hohlenberg, ca. 1838. See *Breve og Akstykker*, p. 45.

5 *Repetition, Fear and Trembling*

1. See *Point of View*, p. 12f.

2. See *Edifying Discourses*, I, 5, 59; II, 5; III, 5, 69; IV, 5.

3. *Postscript*, p. 229; translation slightly altered.

4. The first discourse of the third group is directed to this theme; see *Edifying Discourses*, II, 1–26.

5. At IV B 59 Kierkegaard himself associates the name "Eremita" with the hermetic and the lonely.

6. Kierkegaard made the following notation in his personal copy of *Either/Or*. ". . . The first part continually comes to grief upon time; which is why the second part first and foremost established its worth by showing in the first essay that the aesthetic resolves itself in time, and in the second essay, that to be able to become, to acquire history, is the significance of the temporal and the finite" (IV A 213).

7. Kierkegaard applies this designation to Constantine's state of

mind in his discussion of *Repetition* in the *Papirer*. See IV B 117.

8. *Repetition*, p. 158. See also page 154 where Constantine speaks of "the young man whom I have brought into being. . . ."

9. It is perhaps a measure of Kierkegaard's art that he succeeds in reduplicating the tension and austerity of Job's conflict with God in his description of the Young Man's struggles with himself. Just as in the Book of Job all human categories and explanations are eschewed in order that God might appear out of the whirlwind bearing the mighty imperative that man should not question but worship, so the Young Man suspends all human categories and explanations to prepare himself for the thunderstorm of "repetition." We should note too that both Job and the Young Man ultimately *are* satisfied by this breakthrough from beyond which offers *no* explanation.

10. J. L. Heiberg, *Urania: Aarbog for 1844* (København: 1843), pp. 97–102.

11. IV B 110–24, 258–312.

12. IV B 117, 283–84; translated by Lowrie in Translator's Introduction to *Repetition*, p. xxi.

13. IV B 117, 285; translated by Lowrie in Translator's Introduction to *Repetition*, p. xxii.

14. See *Repetition*, pp. 91, 94.

15. (1) IV B 111, 270; (2) IV B 117, 284; (3) IV B 117, 287; (4) IV B 117, 308.

16. IV A 148. The motto is drawn from Seneca, *De tranquillitate animi*, XVII, 10.

17. Johannes de Silentio applies this name to the state of mind of his hero, Abraham (*Trembling*, p. 30). With equal justice it might be applied to the Young Man's experience of repetition.

18. See Walter Lowrie, *Kierkegaard* (New York: Harper Torchbooks, 1962), p. 254f.

19. Scc, for example, G. W. F. Hegel, *The Phenomenology of Mind*, trans. by J. B. Baillie, 2nd ed. revised (London: George Allen & Unwin Ltd., 1949), p. 511f.

20. *Trembling*, p. 125; translation slightly altered.

21. Johannes Climacus writes in the *Postscript*, "Out of love for mankind . . . , and moved by a genuine interest in those who make everything easy, I conceived it as my task to create difficulties everywhere" (*Postscript*, p. 166).

22. "The man who has performed the cloister-movement has only

one movement more to make, that is, the movement of the absurd" (*Trembling*, p. 156).

23. *Trembling*, p. 72. Lowrie translates *Udlaending* as "foreigner." Earlier (*E/O*, II, 85f) he has translated *Udlaending* as "pilgrim." I have chosen to uniformly translate the phrase *en Fremmed og Udlaending* as " a stranger and an alien."

24. *Trembling*, p. 20. Here once again Lowrie varies his usage, translating *Fremmed* as "sojourner." I subsititute "stranger" for "sojourner" in the first sentence of this quotation.

25. *Trembling*, p. 115; translation slightly altered.

26. Looking back on the work of the past years in 1848, Kierkegaard wrote in his journal, "As poet and thinker I have represented all things in the medium of fantasy, myself living in resignation" (VIII[1] A 650).

6   Philosophical Fragments

1. "Such a dread I got of Christianity, and yet felt myself so strangely drawn towards it . . ." (IX A 210).

2. This paragraph is a recapitulation of Kierkegaard's discussion on pages 11-16 of *Philosophical Fragments*.

3. This formula is repeated over and over again in *Fragments*; see pp. 16, 18, 20, 21, 22, 24, 25, 34, 37.

4. If we care to look closer at this derivation we shall discover that certain unannounced assumptions also play a part in the argument. The omnipotence of God is one that quickly comes to mind, and others could be adduced.

5. "It is well-known that Christianity is the only historical phenomenon which in spite of the historical, nay precisely by means of the historical, has intended itself to be for the single individual the point of departure for his eternal consciousness, has intended to interest him otherwise than merely historically, has intended to base his eternal happiness on his relationship to something historical" (*Fragments*, p. 137).

6. Cf. David Swenson's footnote to his translation of *Fragments*, pp. 222-23.

7. Kierkegaard himself calls attention to this double meaning in observing, "Yet it [the entry of God into time in Christ] is an historical fact, and only for the apprehension of Faith. Faith is here taken first in the direct and ordinary sense [belief], as the relationship of the mind to the historical; but secondly also in the eminent sense, the sense in which the word can

be used only once, i.e. many times, but only in one relationship" (*Fragments*, p. 108).

8. "So much then is clear, that the organ for the historical must have a structure analogous with the historical itself. . . . Now belief has precisely the required character; for in the certainty of belief [Danish: *Troen*] there is always present a negated uncertainty, in every way corresponding to the uncertainty of coming into existence" (*Fragments*, pp. 100–101).

9. In this regard see Paul Holmer, "Kierkegaard and Logic," *Kierkegaardiana II* (København: Munksgaard, 1957), 25–42.

10. The full citation reads, "But between God and his works there is an absolute relationship; God is not a name but a concept. Is this perhaps the reason why his *essentia involvit existiam?*" (*Fragments*, p. 51). In this regard see also the *Postscript* where Kierkegaard writes, "God is a highest conception, not to be explained in terms of other things, but explainable only by explaining more and more profoundly the conception itself" (*Postscript*, p. 197).

11. I am indebted to Professor Douglas Berggren for this simile.

12. "Faith does not have to do with essence, but with being [historical existence], and the assumption that the God is determines him eternally and not historically. The historical fact for a contemporary is that the God has *come into existence*; for a member of a later generation the historical fact is that the God has been present through *having come into existence*. Herein precisely lies the contradiction. No one can become immediately contemporary with this historical fact, as has been shown in the preceding; it is the object of Faith" (*Fragments*, pp. 108–9).

13. *Fragments*, p. 72. See also p. 64 where Kierkegaard again asserts the identity of "the Paradox" and "the Moment."

14. "But in that case is not Faith as paradoxical as the Paradox? Precisely so; how else could it have the Paradox for its object, and be happy in its relation to the Paradox? Faith is itself a miracle." (*Fragments*, p. 81).

15. Nicholas of Cusa, *De visione dei*, ix, 11; cited by Joseph Campbell, *The Hero with a Thousand Faces* (New York: Meridian Books, 1956), p. 89.

16. *Postscript*, p. 501. I have altered the Lowrie translation, changing "understanding" to "Reason" and thus assuring uniformity with the translation of *Forstanden* in the *Fragments*. See also

x² A 349 where Kierkegaard speaks of "Reason's crucifixion."

17. In the *Papirer* Kierkegaard speaks of "the sufferings of inwardness involved in becoming a Christian: parting with one's understanding and being crucified on the cross of the Paradox" (IX A 414).

18. *Fragments*, p. 46. Later on in the *Postscript* he amplifies his earlier discussion. "If the thinker with a resolving *posse* comes upon an *esse* that he cannot resolve, he must say: this is something I cannot think. He thus suspends his thinking with respect to it; and if he nevertheless persists in trying to establish a relationship to this reality as a reality, he does not do so by way of thought, but paradoxically" (*Postscript*, p. 285).

19. Kierkegaard offers this formula of the essence of Christian belief. "If the contemporary generation had left nothing behind them but these words: 'We have believed that in such and such a year the God appeared among us in the humble figure of a servant, that he lived and taught in our community, and finally died.' it would be more than enough. The contemporary generation would have done all that was necessary; for this little advertisement, this *nota bene* on a page of universal history, would be sufficient to afford an occasion for a successor" (*Fragments*, p. 130).

7   The Concept of Dread

1. See v B 39, 42. It should be remembered that in the published version of *Fragments* "S. Kierkegaard" appears on the title page not as *author*, but as *editor*.

2. What we do learn about Johannes Climacus, we learn in the Preface to *Fragments*. Like Victor Eremita, Constantine Constantius, and Johannes de Silentio, he too would seem to be a spectator of life, not a participant. He writes, "To have an opinion is both too much and too little for my uses. To have an opinion presupposes a sense of ease and security in life, such as is implied in having a wife and children; it is a privilege not to be enjoyed by one who must keep himself in readiness day and night, or is without assured means to support. Such is my situation in the realm of spirit" (*Fragments*, p. 6).

3. See *Dread*, p. 5.

4. *Dread*, p. 1. In this regard it should be noted that an early draft of the title-page of *Fragments* characterizes the focus of the investigation as "a dogmatic-philosophical problem" (v B 39).

5. See *Postscript*, p. 241.
6. This was the way Kierkegaard spelled the term in the middle of the 19th century. Modern Danish drops the "e," spelling the word like its Germanic ancestor.
7. IV A 107. See also V A 71, an entry from the same year in which *Dread* was published (1844), where Kierkegaard remarks, "At the present time I suffer much from the dumb nausea of thoughts. There is a dread over me, I cannot say what it is that I cannot understand. Just as Nebuchadnezzar, I must pray not only for an explanation of the dream but also that someone will tell me what it was I dreamed." For further entries where Kierkegaard complains of his personal experience of dread see II A 18, II A 32, II A 584, VIII¹ A 363, x² A 493. For a further description of what Kierkegaard calls his "severe education, the education from inborn dread to faith" (x² A 493), see Hjalmar Helweg, *Søren Kierkegaard: En Psychiatrisk-Psychologisk. Studie* (København: Hagerup, 1933), pp. 65–143.
8. *Dread*, p. 145; translation altered. The cited passage is drawn from J. G. Hamann, *Hamann's Schriften*, Herausgegeben von Fr. Roth (Berlin: 1821), Bd. VI, 194.
9. III A 235. Kierkegaard concludes his citation with the words "this holy hypochondria" found in the sixth line of the passage later cited in *Dread*.
10. In a four page section in *The Concept of Dread* entitled "Objective Dread" Kierkegaard qualifies this view with the assertion that animals and plants can feel a kind of dread which is best described in the Biblical phrase (Romans VIII: 19) "the anxious longing of creation." Because this section is so brief it would seem that this was no more than a momentary lapse into Hegelian poppycock. See *Dread*, pp. 50–54.
11. *Dread*, pp. 37–38; translation altered.
12. *Dread*, p. 38; translation altered.
13. *Dread*, pp. 39–40. The phrase "even less can it grasp hold of itself" was omitted without indication in Lowrie's translation. See *Vaerker*, IV, 315.
14. In his Translator's Preface to *Dread* Lowrie writes, "Having now translated in whole or in part twenty-three of SK's books, I have the impression that this is the most tormenting of them all. It seems to me also that this book shows the greatest unevenness of style. Sudden transitions of style are everywhere observable in SK's works, and it is likely they reflect the changes

of mood in a man who was characterized by blended 'mania' and depression; here the situation is not exactly that, here there are no purple passages, no sublime heights attained, the poet is not in evidence; but he does dive to great depths, and then for long stretches move pedestrianly" (*Dread*, p. ix).

15. *Dread*, p. 38; cited above this chapter, Section II.

16. *Dread*, p. 86. See also *Dread*, p. 69, where Kierkegaard observes that "it holds good that the object of dread is a nothing."

17. *Dread*, p. 113. Lowrie translates *det Daemoniske* by the phrase "the demoniacal," and *det Indesluttede* or *Indesluttetheden* by two phrases: (1) "close reserve," and (2) "the shut-up." In this and the following passages I uniformly translated *det Daemoniske* or its derivatives as "the daemonic," and *Indesluttetheden* or its derivatives as "confinement" or "the confined" —all this after a suggestion by Professor George Kimball Plochmann.

18. *Dread*, p. 110; translation altered.

19. *Dread*, pp. 115–16.

20. "Like the daemonic, the sudden is dread of the good. The good [*det Gode*] in this context means continuity, for the first expression of salvation is continuity" (*Dread*, p. 116; translation altered).

21. *Dread*, pp. 118–19; translation altered.

22. Rudolph Friedmann, *Kierkegaard* (New York: New Directions, 1949), p. 24.

8 Stages on Life's Way

1. See IV A 60; VI A 119; VII[1] A 126; VIII[1] A 43, 161, 177, 205; X[5] A 89.

2. In a journal entry from early 1846 Kierkegaard describes in the past tense a call he made to his doctor to determine whether (in his own words) "the discord between the psychical and the physical could be resolved so that I might realize the universal" (VII[1] A 126). The precise date of this visit is unknown, but it seems likely that it was made sometime during the preceding year (1845).

3. See *Fortale* to *Papirer*, v, ix–x.

4. See *Postscript*, p. 253.

5. IV A 107. In a note written in his personal copy of *Either/Or* Kierkegaard remarks that even before *Either/Or* had been published he was already at work on a "story" entitled "Un-

happy Love." The editors of the *Papirer* believe that this story was an early draft for *Guilty?/Not Guilty?* If their hypothesis is correct, Kierkegaard must have begun work on *Guilty?/Not Guilty?* at least as early as 1842; see IV A 215 and *Fortale to Papirer*, v, x.

6. The extent to which *Guilty?/Not Guilty?* is an autobiographical account may be gauged by the identity of the letter the fictitious Quidam sends to his fiancée: word for word it is the same letter Kierkegaard sent Regine, breaking off their engagement! See x^5 A 149, where Kierkegaard himself comments on this odd fact. To gain a further comprehension of the autobiographical character of *Guilty?/Not Guilty?* the reader is invited to compare Quidam's diary with Kierkegaard's own story of his engagement, written down on August 24, 1849, and recorded in Volume x^5 of the *Papirer* under the heading, "My relation to 'her.' "

7. *Stages*, p. 425; translation slightly altered.

8. *Stages*, p. 388; translation altered.

9. Frater Taciturnus remarks with regard to Quidam, "I cannot conceive whence he gets the new and higher passion which is religiousness. Might it be the ethical which by its negative pressure helps him past the metaphysical (for that is where my place is) into the religious? I do not know" (*Stages*, pp. 394–95). For other statements of Frater Taciturnus concerning his relation to Quidam see also pp. 399, 402, and 418.

10. *Stages*, p. 435. For other comments concerning this "second immediacy" see *Stages*, p. 364 and *Papirer*, viii^1 A 649–50.

11. Frater Taciturnus begins his commentary with the admission that he has really "conjured up" the fictitious Quidam and his diary. See *Stages*, p. 363.

12. The Frater applied this phrase to Quidam's diary in remarking, "Fortunately my hero does not exist outside my thought-experiment. He cannot be exposed to ridicule in real life" (*Stages*, p. 367).

13. See IV A 217, viii^1 A 650; IX B 64; x^1 A 250, 510; x^3 A 489; x^4 A 560; *Point of View*, pp. 18, 83, 86, 131–32, 142–44, 155.

9 *Concluding Unscientific Postscript*

1. The full title of the *Postscript* is *Concluding Unscientific Postscript to the Philosophical Fragments*. The format of the original editions stresses the incongruity in size between the two:

the 164 pages of the *Fragments* measure only 4½ in. by 6½ in., while the 480 pages of the *Postscript* measure 6½ in. by 8½ in.

2. H. P. Barfod, and H. Gottsched, eds., *Af Søren Kierkegaards efterladte Papirer* (København: Reitzel, 1869–81), Bind VIII, p. 595. Boisen's notes are translated by Alexander Dru in *Journals*, pp. 548–53.

3. x^4 A 560. For other mention of the "thorn in the flesh" see VIII^1 A 119, IX A 119, x^1 A 643, x^2 A 20.

4. See above Chapter 2, Section III.

5. *Postscript*, p. 19. In this and all future citations I translate the Danish *en ewig Salighed* as "an eternal blessedness," as opposed to Lowrie, who translates it as "an eternal happiness." In Danish the word *Salighed* carries an unambiguous religious sense of "blessedness" or "blissfulness" which is lost in the more common term "happiness." The common word for "happiness" in Danish is *Lykke*.

6. The following rather obtuse passage is the best definition of "subjectivity" [*Subjectivitet*] that we have. "The development or transformation of the individual's subjectivity, its infinite concentration in itself over against the conception of an eternal blessedness, that highest good of the infinite—this constitutes the developed potentiality of the primary potentiality which subjectivity as such presents" (*Postscript*, p. 116).

7. "Religiousness A must first be present in the individual before there can be any question of becoming aware of the dialectic of B" (*Postscript*, p. 494).

8. "That God has existed in human form, has been born, grown up, and so forth, is surely the paradox *sensu strictissima*, the Absolute Paradox" (*Postscript*, p. 194).

9. *Postscript*, p. 201. The Danish term *Forstanden* is translated by Lowrie as "understanding," while earlier, in *Philosophical Fragments*, it has been translated as "Reason." In order to assure uniformity with the earlier translation (cited often in Chapter 4) *Forstanden* will be translated as "Reason" in this and all future citations. I have slightly altered Lowrie's translation of this passage to bring it into closer conformity with the original text.

10. This phrase is used several times at *Postscript*, pp. 501–2.

11. See *Postscript*, p. 502.

12. *Postscript*, pp. 201–2 extended footnote. I have slightly altered Lowrie's translation of this passage.

13. *Postscript*, p. 259. I have slightly altered Lowrie's translation of this passage.
14. See, for example, *Postscript*, pp. 496, 501, 531.

10 Conclusion

1. See Chapter 3, footnote 44, for a discussion of why the two books by Anti-Climacus are not pseudonymous in the same sense as the earlier works.
2. See, for example, *Point of View*, pp. 18, 73, 86.
3. *Point of View*, p. 7; see Chapter 1 of this study.
4. IX A 217; see Chapter 1 of this study.
5. Nowhere in the *Papirer* entries prior to 1847–48 are we given any indication that Kierkegaard ever had in mind a comprehensive plan for his pseudonymous works. In the posthumously published *Point of View for My Work as an Author* (written during the summer of 1848) he claims that his whole pseudonymous authorship was a complicated deception designed to convert the Danish people to the Christianity of the New Testament. Given our intimate knowledge of Kierkegaard's interior life during the period 1835–46 this is a perfectly ridiculous claim and most critics have rejected it. Niels Thulstrup, for example, writes that "Kierkegaard's later explanations are an expression partly of his self-understanding at the different times when these explanations were written, and partly of how he at these times desired to be understood by his reader" (*Fragments*, Commentary, p. 147). In a recent study, *Meddelelsens Dialektik* (København: Munksgaard, 1962), Lars Bejerholm argues that "Kierkegaard himself is well aware of the fact that his [later] explanation of the function of his pseudonymous writings has nothing to do with the reasons which actually caused him to use pseudonyms in 1843–46" (p. 316). For a persuasive explanation of why Kierkegaard in 1848 formulated a patently false explanation of his authorship, see Bejerholm's book pp. 292–322.
6. For this insight I am indebted to my friend Carleton Dallery.
7. This point is made superbly by the first diapsalm in *Either/Or*. "What is a poet? An unhappy man who in his heart harbors a deep anguish, but whose lips are so fashioned that the moans and cries which pass over them are transformed into ravishing music. His fate is like that of the unfortunate victims whom the tyrant Phalaris imprisoned in a brazen bull, and slowly

tortured over a steady fire; their cries could not reach the tyrant's ears so as to strike terror into his heart; when they
reached his ears they sounded like sweet music" (E/O, I, 19).

8. *Gospel of Suffering*, pp. 5–6. It should be noted that *The Gospel of Suffering* [*Lidelsernes Evangelium*] was published originally not as an independent work, but as Part III of *Edifying
Discourses in Various Spirits* (1847).

9. See above Chapter 2, Section IX.

10. See above Chapter 4, Section VII; Chapter 5, Section V; Chapter 8, Section III.

11. *Christian Discourses*, pp. 107–8.

12. XI² A 422; translated in Gerda M. Andersen, *The Diary of
Søren Kierkegaard*, (New York: Philosophical Library, 1960),
pp. 200–201.

13. XI² A 439; translated in Andersen, *Diary*, pp. 201–2.